ECONOMY AND DEMOGRAPHIC PROFILE OF URBAN RAJASTHAN (EIGHTEENTH-NINETEENTH CENTURIES)

The study is chiefly based on archival sources of different regions of Rajasthan. Different aspects of economy and human settlement are explored with the support of statistical details, charts and maps. I believe that this trend of division of periods and pattern of presentation will attract researchers in the future.

PROFESSOR G.S.L. DEVRA
Former Vice Chancellor, Kota University

Based on original sources, Dr. Jibraeil's book *Economy and Demographic Profile of Urban Rajasthan (Eighteenth-Nineteenth Centuries)* reflects on demography in general and growth of Urban Centres in particular. The book will be of a great help to the researchers who are working on various trade routes, commodities as well as agricultural production in Rajasthan and other link states.

PROFESSOR SUNITA ZAIDI
Former Rhodes Fellow, Oxford,
Department of History and Culture,
Jamia Millia Islamia, New Delhi

The volume deals with the inter-relations between agricultural production, agrarian trade, markets, towns and population of urban Rajasthan in the eighteenth-nineteenth centuries.

The factors for the growth of the agrarian markets are discussed in the light of the archival sources like *arhsattas, toji-do-varkhi-baje-talke, sava bahis* and *khas-rukka-parwana bahis*, of Amber (Jaipur), Hadauti (Kota), Bikaner and Marwar (Jodhpur) respectively. For this work since direct data on population count before 1881 is elusive the author has used house-count as well as different kinds of taxes (*kholari, jhumpari* and *dhuan*) while calculating the population of different urban centres. The question that how some of these markets gradually earned the status of towns is shown through available evidence.

This study also displays that how the higher receipts from *sair-jihat* (non-agrarian taxes) in various areas of Rajasthan, worked in the evolution of agrarian markets into *qasbas*.

This volume is essential reading for scholars of Agrarian History of Rajasthan in the colonial period.

Jibraeil is Assistant Professor at the Centre of Advanced Study, Department of History, Aligarh Muslim University, Aligarh.

Economy and Demographic Profile of Urban Rajasthan (Eighteenth-Nineteenth Centuries)

JIBRAEIL

Routledge
Taylor & Francis Group
LONDON AND NEW YORK

First published 2018
by Routledge
4 Park Square, Milton Park, Abingdon, Oxon OX14 4RN
605 Third Avenue, New York, NY 10017

First issued in paperback 2023

Routledge is an imprint of the Taylor & Francis Group, an informa business

Publisher's Note
The publisher has gone to great lengths to ensure the quality of this reprint but points out that some imperfections in the original copies may be apparent.

Print edition not for sale in South Asia (India, Sri Lanka, Nepal, Bangladesh, Afghanistan, Pakistan or Bhutan)

British Library Cataloguing in Publication Data
A catalogue record for this book is available from the British Library

Library of Congress Cataloging in Publication Data
A catalog record for this book has been requested

ISBN: 978-1-03-265341-9 (pbk)
ISBN: 978-1-138-59820-1 (hbk)
ISBN: 978-0-429-48649-4 (ebk)

DOI: 10.4324/9780429486494

Typeset in Agaramond 11/13
by Kohli Print, Delhi 110 051

MANOHAR

To the memory of my parents

Janab Haji Hasan Raza and
Mrs Kitab-un-Nisha

Contents

Illustrations

MAPS

GRAPHS

FIGURES

Tables

Abbreviations

Ain	*Ain-i-Akbari*
IESHR	*Indian Economic and Social History Review*
IHR	*Indian Historical Review*
EI	*Epigraphia Indica*
JRIHR	*Journal of Rajasthan Institute of Historical Research*
Khyat	Muhnot Nainsi, *Khyat*
PIHC	*Proceedings of Indian History Congress*
PRHC	*Proceedings of Rajasthan History Congress*
PUPHC	*Proceedings of Uttar Pradesh History Congress*
RAS	Royal Asiatic Society
RSA	Rajasthan State Archives
RORI	Rajasthan Oriental Research Institute
Tod	James Tod, *Annals and Antiquities of Rajasthan*
VS	Vikram Samvat

Acknowledgements

This book is a revised version of this author's doctoral thesis awarded at the Aligarh Muslim University. In the course of revision some new evidence has been examined which were even commented by the two experts of the thesis; one from Canada and second from India. One whole chapter on trading centres of Marwar (Pali and Nagaur) has been added. The present revised work was undertaken on the advice of my teacher and supervisor Prof. B.L. Bhadani and a few other scholars who have worked on Rajasthani sources, such as Prof. Dilbagh Singh and Prof. G.S.L. Devra, who suggested revising the thesis in the light of some other relevant archival records and with new additions because this is such a rare work, particularly on urban centres and population for the whole of Rajasthan.

To begin with, therefore, first I wish to express my deep sense of gratitude to Prof. B.L. Bhadani (Retired Professor, Coordinator and Chairperson, Centre of Advanced Study, Department of History, Aligarh Muslim University) for his keen interest and valuable suggestions during the entire period of the completion of this book. I am especially thankful to him for helping me for interpretation of important data-based documents.

I, lack words to express my debt of gratitude to such a great scholar of Rajasthan as Late Prof. S.P. Gupta who always provided his valuable time to discuss issues, related to my work such as dialects, tabulations and nature of documents during my research. In this context I am also grateful to Prof. Dilbagh Singh (Retired Professor, Head, Centre of Historical Studies, Jawaharlal Nehru University, New Delhi), Mr. Punam Chandra Joiya (Research Officer) and Mr. Mangtu Ram (In-charge of Kota records), Rajasthan State Archives, Bikaner.

I am greatly indebted to my esteemed well-wishers, particularly Prof. Ali Athar, Centre of Advanced Study, Department of History,

Aligarh Muslim University), Prof. Abdul Matin (Department of Sociology, Aligarh Muslim University), Prof. Yaqub Ali Khan and Dr S. Bashir Hasan (Centre of Advanced Study, Department of History, Aligarh Muslim University), Mr Tahsinur Rahman Warsi (Associate Professor, Department of Architecture, Aligarh Muslim University), Prof. Jigar Mohammad (Department of History, University of Jammu & Kashmir), Prof. Ayub Ali Khan (Kakatia University, Warrangal), Prof. Inayat Ali Zaidi and Prof. Sunita Zaidi (Department of History and Culture, Jamia Millia Islamia University, New Delhi), Prof. S.P. Vyas and Prof. K.L. Mathur (J.N.V. University, Jodhpur), Dr Firdos Anwar (Associate Professor, Department of History, Kirori Mal College, University of Delhi), Prof. Nishat Manzar and Prof. R.P. Bahuguna (Department of History and Culture, Jamia Millia Islamia University, New Delhi), Dr Nasim Ahmad (General Physician, Aligarh), Dr Mayank Kumar (Associate Professor, Department of History, Satyawati College, University of Delhi), Dr Mukesh Kumar Singh (Associate Professor, Department of History, Shivaji College, University of Delhi), all of whom encouraged me to revise and publish my thesis in the form of a book. Equally, I am grateful to my other colleagues, well-wishers and friends in Aligarh Muslim University, Jamia Millia Islamia University, University of Delhi, Jawaharlal Nehru University and University of Rajasthan, from whom I received constant encouragement during the preparation of this book.

Mr. Faiz Habib deserves special mention for his keen interest and his ability in the preparation of maps for my book. He is not only an expert in cartography but a very good human being too. Moreover his father, scholar extraordinaire Prof. Irfan Habib also helped me in understanding the minute details of Inch maps. My eternal gratitude to both of them. Another of my friend Mr. Shams Imran supported me at the time of correction of this work and checking of data and graphs. I have no words to appreciate and thank him for his immense support. My student Ms S. Sumbul Arif, helped me in the setting of the bibliography, and has compared the figures of the tables of the book.

I would like to thanks the staff bearers of Rajasthan State Archives, Bikaner for providing facilities and generous access to me for my book. I should also acknowledge my gratefulness to the staff of Maulana Azad Library, Aligarh Muslim University, Rajasthan Oriental Research Institute, Jodhpur, National Archives, New Delhi and Research Library of Centre of Advanced Study, Department of History, Aligarh Muslim University. All of them extended their wholehearted cooperation and allowed me to use their precious collections. My special thanks to the people of Bikaner, particularly who provided me all the facilities during my numerous visits to the place.

It is not possible for me to express due regards to my respected parents Janab Haji Hasan Raza Sahab and Mrs. Kitab-un-Nisha, my brothers, Mohd Israfeel, Mohd. Israeel and other close relations, whose love, affection and supplications have given me immense help in all ups and downs of my life and their full support and goodwill has been a source of abiding inspiration throughout my life.

I express my gratitude to Ramesh Jain of Manohar Publishers & Distributors, New Delhi for publishing the book and bringing it out in time. I am equally grateful to Siddharth Chowdhury for seeing the volume to the press.

Finally, at this moment, how can I forget the sacrifices of my wife Priyanka Singh F. Naaz and my sons Zaid and Saim. Their firm support sustained me during my frequent and long visits to Rajasthan to collect data.

Aligarh Muslim University JIBRAEIL

CHAPTER 1

Nature of Rajasthani Sources on Urban History

The archival, non-archival, numismatical, inscriptions and archaeological data form the backbone of the historical research for all the periods. Rajasthan is extremely rich in all the five categories of sources. The state archive at Bikaner possesses enormous material both in Persian as well as in Rajasthani. Besides this, the region is also rich in private collections possessed by many business families, *jagirdars* and revenue officials. The bardic literature (such as the *khyat* and *baat*) is enormous which provide very relevant information.

This vast archival material was first utilized by Syed Nurul Hasan and Satish Chandra.[1] The information on agricultural production, food grain prices and rural society was tapped in two subsequent studies on Amber region by S.P. Gupta and Dilbagh Singh.[2] Similarly, the material on Jodhpur (Marwar), Kota and Bikaner was studied by G.D. Sharma, B.L. Bhadani, Masanori Sato, Madhu Tandon Sethia and G.S.L. Devra respectively.[3] These studies provided a new insight into the agrarian economy of seventeenth to nineteenth centuries. They had studied the structure and stratification of the village and urban society and traced the changes taking place in agricultural production, non-agricultural taxes, revenue demand and prices.

The archival sources provide valuable data on the *qasbas* and cities. The information on them is related to number of houses of different categories of people, taxes, markets, trade and commerce. The information contained in the sources throws ample light on the status, growth and development of towns and cities.

Our study of the urban centres and their population is based primarily on the archival sources such as *arhsattas, yaddastis, chithis, dastur-ul-amals, amal-dasturs, arzdashts, nirkh-bazars, takhminas, khasras, toji-do-varkhi-baje-talke, taqsims, sava-bahis, zakat bahis, kagad bahis, rukka parwana bahis*, etc.[4] These records are compiled in the form of *tojis, do-varkhis, natthi, bahis*, etc., which are available for Jaipur, Kota, Bundi, Jodhpur, Shekhawati and Bikaner.

A few points may, however, be made here regarding the use of these documents. They are in Rajasthani and are dated as Vikram Samvat (VS) though some early documents often used the *hijri* and the *fasli* years.[5] Persian terms are used profusely in the Rajasthani style. The influence of Persian on Medieval Rajasthan is enormous which demonstrates the synthesis in language and culture in medieval Rajasthan.[6]

Our documentary evidence is rich and varied in nature. It may be classified as follows:

(a) Documents giving information of various *qasbas*/villages and their details about area under crops, tax on individuals, etc.
(b) Documents providing accounts of incomes and expenditure at the *qasba*/village and *pargana* level.
(c) Agricultural production in *kharif* and *rabi*, land tax, peasants, their number of houses, ploughs and amount of tax collection, and sometimes the names of the traders.
(d) Non-agricultural taxes under different heads such as *sair-jihat, kholari, jamadari*, etc.
(e) *Dhuan* (house-tax) and *jagat* (transit) taxes and the names of individual peasants with their castes.

JAIPUR STATE RECORDS

The Jaipur revenue records are in loose sheets or *farads*, locally known as *toji* and written in local *dhundhari* dialect. The main categories of documents are *arhsatta mujmali, arhsatta bhoomi, arhsatta ek-harfi muwazana, jama-bandi, dastur-ul-amal, yaddashti, chithis, arzdasht, nirkh-bazars, takhmina, khasras*, etc., which are utilized in author's study.

The *arhsatta mujmils* are ledgers of receipts and disbursement maintained *pargana*-wise. They furnished revenue information to the *diwan's* office related to the *pargana.* This includes number of *qasbas*/villages, villages in *jagir, inam, bhoomi* and *khalsa,* the total assessment for the *pargana,* income, expenditure, *baqi,* etc.[7] The *arhsatta bhoomi zamindari* contains detailed lists of the items of taxes under various heads of the *bhoomi* and *zamindari* areas.[8] The *muwazana* records were compiled in the early nineteenth century on the basis of information given in the various categories of records such as *arhsatta, awarija, jamabandi, khasra, dastur-ul-amal* and *chithis.*[9] They furnished information on *qasbas* and villages in the *pargana.* The *pargana* level *jamabandi* records were prepared with the help of the *chaudharis* and the *qanungos.* The documents are very useful in ascertaining the magnitude of land revenue (*mal*) under *batai* and the incidence of *jihat* taxes in a *pargana.* The *dastur-ul-amal* and *amal-dastur* are a body of rules and regulations for the guidance of revenue officials.[10] The *yaddashtis* (memoranda) were compiled by hereditary village officials (*patels* and *patwaris*) and state functionaries. They offer us the number of ploughs and bullocks held by each peasant in a *qasba*/village and also the extent of cultivation in a *pargana* comprising villages and *qasbas.*[11] The *chithis* (letters) were written by the *diwan* of Jaipur state to the administrative officials of the *parganas* such as the *amils, amins* and *faujdars.* The *arzdashts* were written by the *amil,* the *faujdar* and other officials of Jaipur to their ruler. The *nirkhbazar* were prepared by the *panch mahajan* (association of merchants) of the *qasba.* They recorded the daily market prices of each commodity prevalent in the market.[12] *Takhmina* and *khasra* documents were compiled by the *patel* and the *patwari* of the village. Among the above-mentioned documents, the *arhsattas* are the most important documents which helped us in reconstructing the organization and composition of the urban centres. Their evidence on agricultural and non-agricultural taxes under the heads *mal-o-jihat,*[13] *sair-jihat*[14] and *siwai jamabandis*[15] is of extreme importance. Remaining series of documents provided supplementary information related to the topic.

The data contained under the *sair-jihat* are of extreme importance for the study of the non-agricultural sector which essentially indicates the size of the urban sector. The *sair-jihat* consists of various customary fees or taxes collected from the residents of a *qasba*/village, such as transit duties, house taxes, taxes on animals, etc. It also includes certain impositions, allowances or remunerations payable to certain local officials and grain merchants.[16] The *arhsattas* of the different *qasbas* of eighteenth-nineteenth century provide detailed breakup of the *sair-jihat.* S.P. Gupta counted the items of taxation (both agricultural and non-agricultural) from various documents, whose total reaches up to 88.[17] While author's counting for urban areas come to 25.[18] For instance, *jhunpari, chhaili, kagadsyahi, khutchaka, kharachsahengi, bhetdasraha, tapdari, oonaghori, charai, chitradatal, rajbatai, chaknijranai, iqtalai, lata-kharach, suganbhet, hisabanau, gharipala moth-mata, kasoorzabti, tasmatseri*, etc.[19] With the help of these data, we can estimate the composition of a *qasba* and estimate the number of persons residing in a particular town or city.

Evidence about *jhunpri* (house tax) is of extreme importance. This tax was paid by the residents of villages and towns. This implies the counting of houses of a locality which can be used to estimate the population. By comparing the data of the two periods the growth and development of the *qasbas* could also be traced.

DOCUMENTS OF THE STATES OF KOTA AND BUNDI

The records of Kota and Bundi are in Hadauti dialect, strikingly akin to the Gujarati script, and provide information about the revenue administration of south-eastern Rajasthan.[20] A huge collection of these records is available at Rajasthan State Archives, Bikaner, and at Kota. These records are arranged in *bhandar* and *basta* chronologically. The nomenclature and contents of these documents testify the efforts of the Kota chiefs to model the administration of their state on the pattern of the Mughal administration. The categories of documents are known as *do-varkhi-parchazat, kota-mal-hasil, talik bahis, jamabandis taqsims, khasra*, etc. *Toji taqsim* covers the period between VS 1711/AD 1654 and VS 1900/AD 1843 and *toji-do-varkhi-baje-talke* between VS 1703/AD 1646 and

VS 1928/AD 1871 respectively.[21] These documents are extremely useful for the study of the urban centres of Kota state. Thus a variety of documents appears to have been prepared according to the Mughal standards from seventeenth century onwards.[22] Not only this, but hundreds of adaptations of Mughal administrative terms can be seen in various documents.[23]

The *talik bahis* carry letters written by the *diwan* to the various officials at the *pargana/mauza* and *qasba* level carrying instructions on a variety of subjects.[24] *Jamabandis* provide us with a detailed account of revenue assessed and realized from a village in a *pargana* from a single harvest or both.

The most important documents related to urban areas are *baje-talke* in the form of *toji-do-varkhi* and *toji-taqsim* which are in profusion. These papers are signed by the *qanungos* and other officers.[25] *Taqsim* contains records of the number of *tappas/qasbas* and villages in a *pargana*. They provide information about the newly-cultivated land along with the revenue realized from it and the classification of land under *khalsa, jagir, nalaiq* (unfit for cultivation), *doli* (religious grants), *sasari, chakari* (service grants), *inami* and *baki bigha*.[26] The assessed revenue (*rekh*) is also recorded in these documents.[27] The information contained in these documents is useful for urban studies.

Another category of documents called *toji-do-varkhi* (*do-varkhi-parchajat, do-varkhi-jamakharch* and *do-varkhi mal-jihat*) provides details regarding the rate of assessment, the mode of payment, and the classification of land, villages and *qasbas*. They offer miscellaneous information on a variety of subjects.[28]

All the documents offer evidence about the non-agricultural production, merchants and markets. An effort has been made to analyse the data contained in these documents on the composition of the artisan population in the *qasbas* and their wages employed in the state *karkhanas*. They also throw light on the merchants and markets and the relationship between the state and the merchants in the region. The study of the role of merchants in the rural/urban areas is of extreme value.[29]

The *baje-talke-do-varkhi* documents pertaining to the collection of various *birads* in the *qasbas* reflect the composition of the *mahajans*, Brahmins, artisans and menial population living there and their economic and social status. These documents have been utilized to examine the relationship of merchants with the state and the growth of urban centres and trade network in the region.[30] They also record the name of the castes (Brahmin, Banias, menial castes, etc.) with their landholdings and houses in *qasbas* for different years of the eighteenth-nineteenth century in Kota. Besides these, other records such as *baje-talke, arhsattas, talik-bahis, kagzat barads, mafiyat jagir,* etc., too are important for revenue administration and agrarian aspect of urban centres.

In Bundi most of the revenue records are similar to those of Kota. But some of them are different and more informative like *muwazana* records, locally called *tahsil* records of *kotwali chotra.*[31] The best kept records of Bundi state are that of the *tahsil* records. They contain the history of *khalsa* and *jagir* village/*qasbas* of the eighteenth century.[32] Other varieties of records such as *patta talik* and *taqsim parganawar* are useful for the study of urban centres.

RECORDS OF THE STATES OF JODHPUR AND BIKANER

The Jodhpur and Bikaner records are in local Marwari dialect. They contain information on revenue, agricultural, non-agricultural taxes, professional taxes in urban areas and on trade and commerce from seventeenth century onwards. The major documents of Jodhpur state include *hukumat bahi, qanungo bahi, jamabandi bahi, jamabandi-qabuliyat bahi, hawala bahi, sanad parwana bahi, khasrukka parwana bahi, patta bahi, haqeeqat khata bahi, kharita bahi*, etc.

The *hukumat bahis* and *qanungo bahis* of Marwar are useful for the study of land revenue administration.[33] The *jamabandi bahis* give details about income and expenditure. They record the land revenue assessment, rate of demand and magnitude of land revenue demand.[34] Other important records are *sanad parwana bahi, khasrukka parwana bahi* and *patta bahi.* In *sanad parwana bahi*, the copies of the *parwanas* sent by the ruler of Jodhpur to the village officials are preserved. They provide information on different type of taxes and cesses, rate of land revenue (*bhog*) demand and various methods of revenue assessment such as *batai* and *zabti*. Besides, the duties and functions of the *pargana* officials are mentioned in these *bahis*.[35] The *khas-rukka parwana bahis* contain the *rukkas* sent by the Jodhpur rulers to the *jagirdars* or *pattayats*. They provide information about those villages / *qasbas* which are granted in *sasan* to the Brahmins and Charans. These grants were given to them in the form of land which was free from all obligations. The grant holders were entitled to collect land revenue and other cesses in their territories.[36]

The records of Bikaner are also in *bahis* which are available under different designations such as: *hasil bahis, jagat* (*zakat*) *bahis, kamthana bahis, sawa bahis, kagad bahis, zamin-ri-kagdo-ri-bahis, chittha-wa-kooch-mukam-ri bahis, habob bahis, lekha bahis, jama kharach bahis, vivah bahis, patta bahis, khata bahis* and *parwana bahis*.

The *hasil* and *kagad bahis* provide information about the mode of assessment and collection, the categories of peasants, the relations between the tenant and the landlord in the *khalsa* areas during the eighteenth-nineteenth century. They contain data on *bhog, dhuan* (house-tax), *deshprath* (tax on settled persons at village), *mukata* (lump sum) and *malba* (the name of original tax which the Jat community imposed upon them). The total number of taxes comes to about 50.[37]

The *jagat bahis* contain valuable evidence on the commodities of commercial importance and trade routes in the region. The State of Bikaner occupied a significant position in northern India as a commercial centre both on account of its various *mandis* and trade routes. It served as an important link between the commercial centres situated at Delhi, Bhiwani, Nagaur, Phalodi, Pali, Sindh, Multan and Ahmadabad. Some of the important places of the state which were on the known trade routes were Nohar, Bhatner (now known as Hanumangarh), and Anupgarh. On this route, Pugal and Lunkaransar were two other commercial centres. The trade route between Bikaner and Bhatinda passed through Lunkaransar, Mahajan and Bhatner, etc.[38] Information about these routes is available in the *jagat* (*zakat*) *bahis*.

The Bikaner state had an administrative set-up for the collection of the commercial taxes (*jagat*). Its headquarters at Bikaner were called *shri mandi* and its branches were called *mandis*. These *mandis* were located on trade routes and generally developed into commercial towns like; Lunkaransar, Anupgarh, Reni, Rajgarh, Nohar, Bidasar, Mahajan, Pugal, Rajaldesar, Ratangarh, Churu and Bhadra. To assist these *mandis,* there were *bahari chowkis* or *baharli chowkis* (out checkposts) near the village or towns located on the trade routes. The in-charge of such *jagat* (*zakat*) *chowkis* was called the *bhulawariya,* who used to collect the transit tax (*jagat*/*zakat*) and send it to the headquarters. In order to strengthen the *zakat* administration, *zakat chowkis* were established by the state at various entry points where traders were supposed to pay *jagat* and get a transit permit for their merchandize. After that they were free to sell their goods and move them out of the state. These *zakat chowkis* were supervised by a *Naib Girdawar* or a *Daroga* of the state.

The *jama kharch* and the *sava bahis* provide the information about the income and expenditure of the state. The main sources of state income were *bhog* (*mal*), *dhuan bhanch, jagat/zakat, peshkash, jhunparifarohi, nazrana, zurmana,* etc. New sources of income were added in the nineteenth century which was court and registry fees, *talbana,* income from interest and bills of payments, cash collections, house rents, etc.

The *sava bahi* of Bikaner are useful for the study of urban areas and for the estimation of population of different castes of eighteenth-nineteenth century.[39] The information of *dhuan* tax is helpful for the estimation of population of a *qasba.* The *bahi* records the number of houses inhabited by members of various castes or groups with total collection from the *dhuan* (house) tax.[40] The caste-wise figures of the number of houses enable us to work out the composition of various groups and professionals such as: Banias, Gujars, Jats, Lilgars, Manihars, Darzis, Khatis, Chhinpas, Rajputs, Rangrez, Kumbhars, Brahmins, Chands, Jogis, Kalals, etc.[41]

Beside these archival records, private records of business family of Churu, *khyat* and *bat* literatures in Rajasthani and Hindi are also utilized to supplement the evidence on the population. Administration and census reports of different periods were employed for the comparison. With their help we were able to trace the changes, if any, in the population of pre-census and census period. The data on caste-censuses of 1931 provide extremely useful information for the comparison of the caste composition of the towns of pre-census period. Through this study, we attempted to indicate the castes which disappeared from the urban areas.

The other useful *bahis* related to Bikaner state are *lekha bahis, kamthana bahis, parwana bahis,* and *habob bahis*, which provide information about artisans, towns and taxes.

The records of various states were utilized mainly for the estimation of the population of the towns. In addition, we have also attempted to extract data on the markets and market taxes which may roughly indicate the size of the town and ratio of urban-rural population.

For Mewar and Jaisalmer we could not get adequate archival data but we have utilized the information contained in Tod's *Annals and Antiquities of Rajasthan* (Three Volumes) and other sources of pre-census period.

NOTES

1. S. Nurul Hasan, S.P. Gupta and K.N. Hasan, 'The Pattern of Agricultural Production in the Territories of Amber', *PIHC*, Mysore, 1966, pp. 244-64; S. Nurul Hasan and S.P. Gupta, 'Prices of Food Grains in the Territories of Amber', *PIHC*, Patiala, 1967, pp. 345-67; Satish Chandra, 'Some Aspects of Indian Village Society in Northern India During the 18th Century', *IHR*, 1974, pp. 51-64.
2. S.P. Gupta, *The Agrarian System of Eastern-Rajasthan (c.1600-c.1750)*, Manohar, New Delhi, 1986; Dilbagh Singh, *State, Landlords and Peasants: Rajasthan in the 18th Century*, Manohar, New Delhi, 1990.
3. B.L. Bhadani, *Peasants, Artisans and Entrepreneurs: Economy of Marwar in the 17th Century*, Rawat Publication, Jaipur, 1999; Masanori Sato and B.L. Bhadani, *Economy and Polity of Rajasthan: Study of Kota and Marwar (17th-19th Centuries)*, Publication Scheme, Jaipur, 1997; Madhu Tandon Sethia, *Rajput Polity: Warriors, Peasants and Merchants (1700-1800)*, Rawat Publication, Jaipur, 2003; G.D. Sharma, *Administrative System of the Rajput*, Rajesh Publications, New Delhi, 1979; G.S.L. Devra, *Rajasthan Ki Prashashnik Vyavastha* (*1564-1818* AD), Dharati Prakashan, Bikaner, 1981.

4. *Arhasatta parganawar* VS 1664/AD 1607 to VS 1862/AD 1805; *Yaddashti parganawar, Chithis parganawar, Toji-do-varkhi parganawar/tappa, Toji Taqsim parganawar/tappa, Sava bahis qasba*-wise, RSA, Bikaner.
5. Gupta, op. cit., p. XIII (Introduction).
6. Ibid.
7. Different years of *Arhasatta Mujmil.*
8. *Arhasatta bhoomi* and *Zamindari.*
9. Dilbagh Singh, op. cit., p. 6
10. Ibid.
11. Ibid.
12. Ibid., p. 7.
13. The *Malo-jihat* comprises revenue realized through *zabti* (*zabti* proper) and *qarar-ijara* (fixed farmed out revenue). The meaning is explained by S.P. Gupta in his well-known book *Agrarian System*, op. cit., pp. 145-53; Irfan Habib, *The Agrarian System of Mughal India*, 2nd revd. edn., Oxford University Press, New Delhi, 1999, pp. 283-84.
14. Habib, ibid., pp. 110-300. Also explained in the context of Rajasthan by Gupta, op. cit., p. 156.
15. Literally *Siwai jamabandi* means revenue realized in addition to *jamabandi.*
16. Gupta, op. cit., p. 150.
17. Ibid.
18. *Arhasatta parganawar*, op. cit.
19. Part of *Sair jihat* in the *qasbas* in the different years of *Arhasatta.*
20. Girija Shankar Sharma, *Sources on Social and Economic History of Rajasthan (17th-20th Centuries)*, Vikash Prakashan, Bikaner, 2005, p. 46.
21. *Toji-Taqsim*, VS 1711/AD 1654 to VS 1900/AD 1843 and *Toji-do-varkhi*, VS 1703/AD 1646 to VS 1928/AD 1871, RSA, Bikaner.
22. Sethia, op. cit., p. 14.
23. Ibid.
24. R.K. Saxena, *Peasant and the State*, Panchsheel Prakashan, Jaipur, 1999, p. 3.
25. *Taqsim*, VS 1711/AD 1654 to VS 1900/AD 1843, op. cit., cf. Saxena, *Peasant and the State*, op. cit., p. 4.
26. *Taqsim parganawar*, VS 1711/AD 1654 to VS 1900/AD 1843.
27. Ibid.
28. *Toji-do-varkhi*, op. cit., cf. Saxena, op. cit., p. 3.
29. Sethia, op. cit., pp. 13-14.
30. *Toji-do-varkhi*, op. cit., cf. Sethia, op. cit., p. 15.
31. *Muwazana* records of different years of Bundi State preserved in the RSA, Bikaner.

32. Ibid.
33. *Jalorhukumat-ri-bahi* and *qanungoh bahis.* Cf. Girija Shankar Sharma, op. cit.
34. *Jamabandi-ri-bahis* of different *parganas*, RSA, Bikaner.
35. *Sanad parwana bahis* VS 1844/AD 1787 to VS 1884/AD 1827, RSA, Bikaner.
36. *Khas-rukka parwana bahis,* VS 1722/AD 1665 to VS 1856/AD 1799, Jodhpur, RSA, Bikaner.
37. Different *Bahis* (*hasil bahis, kagad bahis and sava bahis*) of Bikaner State. Its details are available in *List of Bikaner Bahis* (for 17th-19th centuries), part I, RSA, Bikaner, pp. I-XIII.
38. Information on trade routes is available in the *zakat/jagat bahis* of Bikaner, RSA, Bikaner.
39. See, *Sava bahis* of different *qasbas* especially *qasba* Churu, RSA, Bikaner.
40. *Sawa bahis* of *qasba* Churu, RSA, Bikaner.
41. Ibid.

CHAPTER 2

Geography of Rajasthan

James Tod, was the pioneer in employing the term 'Rajasthan' for the title of his celebrated book.[1] But at the administrative level, the term appears to have been derived from Rajputana. The nomenclature was given by the British to all the Rajput principalities.[2] In Medieval times the terms 'Rajasthan' or *Raythan* were employed to indicate the headquarters of the royal seat[3] of the Rajput rulers. Rajasthan, situated in the north-western part of India between 23°3'N and 30°12'N latitudes and 69°30'E and 78°17'E longitudes covers an areas of about 342,274 sq. km.[4] It is bound on the east by Uttar Pradesh, on the south by Gujarat, on the west by Pakistan and on the north by Punjab and north-east by Haryana[5] (see Map 2.1: An Outline Map of Rajasthan). In the sixteenth century the province was called *suba* Ajmer which was bound by the Mughal provinces of Delhi in the north, that of Agra in the east, Malwa in the south-east, Gujarat in the south and Multan and Sind in the west.[6] The *suba* comprised the principalities of Mewar (Udaipur), Marwar (Jodhpur), Amber (Jaipur), Bikaner, Sirohi, Jaisalmer, Kota and Bundi.[7] These semi-autonomous states were parts of the *suba*.[8] Besides, there were certain areas which were formerly parts of other *subas* but latter on incorporated into Rajasthan such as Gagraon (*suba* Malwa), Bayana, Hindaun, Dholpur, Alwar, Tijara and Todabhim of *suba* Agra.[9]

Geographically, Rajasthan is divided into different parts, such as plains and hilly region. The plains lie between 24°30' and 30°12'N and 69°15' and 76°45'E, including the *Marushthali* (eastern portion of the *Thar*) and the adjoining Bagar (steppe land) to the west of the Aravallis extending over the western districts of Rajasthan, namely; Jaisalmer, Barmer, Jodhpur, Jalor, Pali and Nagaur, along with the northern and eastern portions comprised

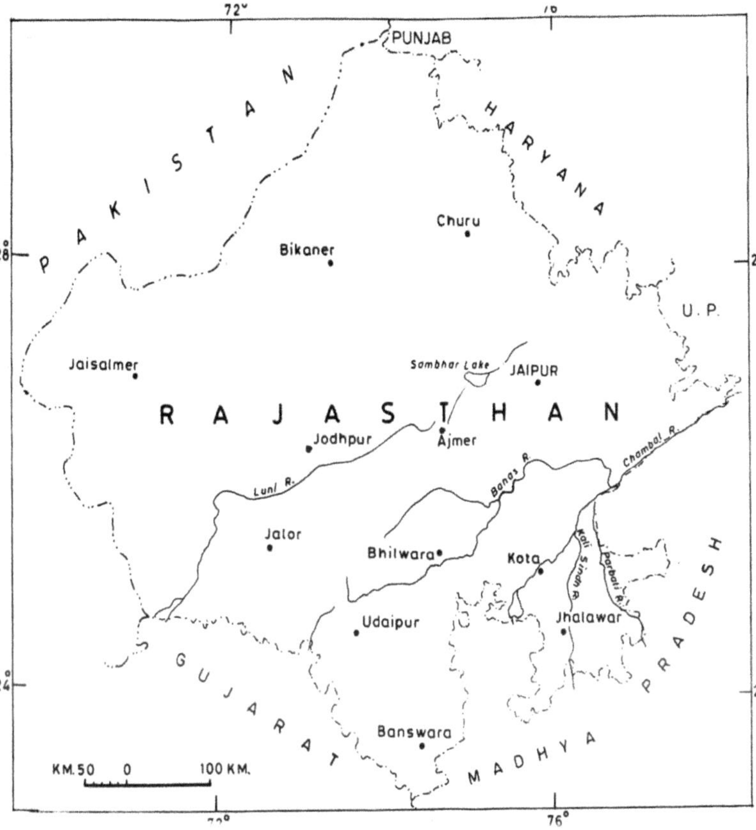

Map 2.1: An Outline Map of Rajasthan

of Bikaner, Ganganagar, Sikar, Jhunjhunu and Churu districts. It covers an area of 196,747 sq. km.[10] The Aravali ranges[11] form the chief topographical feature in Rajasthan, extending from Champaner in Gujarat in a north-easterly direction up to near Delhi, covering 692 km.[12] It divides the province into two natural divisions, viz., the north-west and south-east of the Aravali, about three-fifth of Rajasthan lies north-west of this line, and comprises mainly desert and semi-desert. Its extent is about 60,000 sq. miles and covers the former states of Jaisalmer, Bikaner, major portions of Jodhpur and a part of Jaipur.[13] It is dry, ill-watered and less productive, so far as agriculture is concerned. The south-eastern region is formed by the modern districts of Banswara, Dungarpur, Udaipur, Bhilwara, Bundi, Kota and Jhalawar.[14] This region is more hilly, comparatively well-watered and consequently more wooded and rich in agriculture.[15] The western and southern part of the Aravali is drained by rivers and their tributaries. The major river Luni rises in the Aravali range and flows in the south-west direction. It is finally lost in the Rann of Kutch. It has several tributaries mostly rising in the Aravali hills, with neither the main nor any of its tributaries being perennial. Nainsi describes at length the area through which various rivers run and also mentions the streams that join the Luni.[16] The junction of the two rivers, Gilari (Guhiya) and Sukri, at Sojhat support a small fertile tract.[17]

The western part of Rajasthan, particularly Jaisalmer, Bikaner and Barmer is marked by sand dunes. This part is well punctuated by exposed rock surface.[18] The rainfall is 10 cm per year and transport is difficult. These features of physiography, climate and aridity have made this area inhospitable.[19]

The soils of the Rajasthan plain are generally characterized as sandy containing 90 to 95 per cent sand and 5 to 7 per cent clay.[20] Red desert soil covers Nagaur, Jodhpur, Pali, Jalor, parts of Churu and Jhunjhunu districts.[21] A yellowish brown sandy soil extends over Nagaur and Pali districts.[22]

Other types of soil, i.e. red sandy, clay loam, red sandy loam and loam (alluvial types) soils are limited in their extent and less important for the location of settlement.[23] However, the loam (alluvial type) is significant for cultivation as well as for large and prosperous rural settlements in the areas of Neem-ka-thana and Khetri.[24] In the sandy region the cover is very thin and only a few small trees can be observed here and there. Large parts of the area are covered with scrubs which are thorny and have a stunted growth.[25]

The western arid and semi-arid part of the state is important for its livestock production. This industry provides subsidiary occupations to the desert inhabitants, particularly the nomadic tribes who depend for their livelihood on their livestock.[26]

URBAN GROWTH

Towns and cities in Rajasthan started to grow in the early medieval period. The majority of the towns sprang up in and around forts, religious edifices and markets.[27] Besides these, the royal seats of the rulers developed into cities and trade centres. Many townships also emerged on the trade routes.[28] These towns and cities attracted a large number of craftsmen and other employment seekers which enlarged their population.[29] The commercial policy of the Rajput rulers played an important role in augmenting the population of the urban centres.[30] The newly-emerged commercial towns became prominent.[31]

The towns are generally known as *qasbas* or urban centres in contrast to the *shahars* or imperial cities. As both these units shared common urban features such as a fixed market, a concentration of non-agricultural population (merchants, bankers, traders, artisans, military garrison and nearby forts) and perhaps though not invariably, local political elites.[32] The basis for the classification of an urban centre as a *qasba* or a *shahar* in the Mughal period derived primarily from the extent of their administrative jurisdiction.[33] The administrative hierarchy as defined in the *Ain-i-Akbari* consisted of the successive grouping of territorial units from the primary unit of the village to the *tappa* (a large village or sometimes a *qasba*) followed by the *pargana*, *sarkar* and *suba*.[34] The administrative centres of large units, such as the *sarkar* and *suba* were ordinarily termed as *shahar*, while their constituent units, the *pargana* and the *tappa*, were termed *qasba*.[35]

This is not always correct. Sometimes the *pargana* headquarter could develop into a city and *tappa* might remain as a village. So the development of the *pargana* headquarters and *tappa* into *qasba* or city entirely depended on their location. As in the case of Jodhpur and Jaipur, both were *pargana* headquarters. But the former grew into a city while the latter remained a *qasba*.

The evidence about the expansion of towns and cities is definite for the seventeenth century. Large number of towns and cities developed in different Rajput principalities. This implies the concentration of a large number of people there. According to one estimate about Marwar, the urban population to that of the total was between 15 and 17 per cent in the second half of the seventeenth century. This demonstrates the expansion of the urban sector. Our sources such as the *arhsattas, taqsims, sawa bahis, toji-do-varkhi baje-talke,* etc. confirm this phenomenon in other areas too. The information on the urban centres for different localities is enormous. The *arhasattas* record more than a hundred *qasbas* in the Kachhwaha territory alone.[36] More or less the same number of towns are found in Kota.[37] In Bikaner it comes to about more than 25.[38] For Jodhpur we could find more than 30 *qasbas.*[39] For Jaisalmer this figure comes to 24,[40] while for Mewar we could not find more than 18 *qasbas*[41] presumably because of deficiency in our documents (see Table 2.1 and Graph 2.1). The expansion of the urban centres certainly opened up the employment opportunities for people of different professions. Gradually, with the passage of time, artisans from different parts, from within the province and outside of it, were attracted there and towns developed into big cities and became entrepôt.

The role of the settlement pattern is extremely important for the growth of the urban centres. The settlement is influenced by multiple factors such as environmental, availability of water, trade routes, religious and pilgrim centres and seat of royalty.

TABLE 2.1: NUMBER OF TOWNS IN DIFFERENT PRINCIPALITIES IN THE PRE-CENSUS PERIOD

Name of the State	Number of Towns Eighteenth-Nineteenth Centuries
Jaipur	110
Kota	78
Bikaner	27
Jodhpur	32
Jaisalmer	24
Mewar	18
Total	289

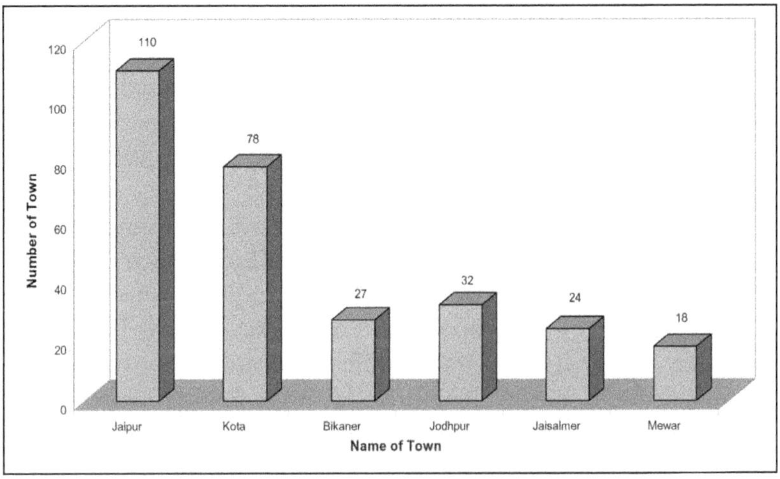

Graph 2.1: A Comparison of the Number of Towns in Different Principalities in the Pre-Census Period

It has been plausibly postulated that at least for Rajasthan, five main types of urban centres can be identified.[42] One, production centres (agricultural towns); two, commercial centres (route towns); three, administrative centres; four, pilgrimage centres and lastly fifth, market towns.

(a) Agricultural towns developed as collecting and distributing centres for the agriculture and livestock products of the region. The majority of these towns were generally confined to the wetter eastern areas with fairly established economies. For example Bilara, Pipar, Merta, Jaitaran and Sojhat, etc., were important agricultural towns in the Luni basin, and Chirawa, Ramgarh and Losal, etc., in Shekhawati area in the north-eastern region.[43]

(b) Route towns developed along the main routes, i.e. from north India to south-west India along with Aravallis, and Indus to Ganga Valley. Rajgarh, Churu, Ratangarh, Kuchaman and Pali were important halting and trade centres for the *carvans* on the Delhi-Ahmadabad route. Nohar, Hanumangarh, and Suratgarh along the northern-route from Indus to Ganga Valley, and Pali, Bhinmal, Balotra, and Barmer on southern route connecting the central India with lower Indus Valley. The dry tracts between these routes were left untouched by the medieval routes. These centres were important for exchange of local products and handicrafts with products of other regions of India.[44]

(c) Administrative centres were developed into towns in the states of Jodhpur, Bikaner, and Jaipur, e.g. Jodhpur, Pokaran, Merta, Phalodi, Nagaur, Barmer and Jalor in Jodhpur State. Bikaner, Sujangargh, Shardarshahar and Shri Dungargarh in Bikaner State. Sikar, Khetri, Jhunjhunu in Jaipur State. These were fortified settlements, therefore, important defense centres meant to protect the people confined in their jurisdiction.[45]

(d) Religious and pilgrim centres were also developed into towns and cities of Rajasthan,[46] i.e. Ajmer, Nagaur, Ladnun, Gagraun, Kapasan, etc.

(e) The trade routes linking villages, *qasbas* and cities and market can be traced with reasonable accuracy. Export of grain from the surplus to deficit areas appears to have been a regular feature in the seventeenth-century Marwar[47] and in the eighteenth-century Jaipur and other states.[48] Grain from the villages of each *pargana* was generally directed towards the city headquarters[49] to feed its population. It appears that some *pargana* and *tappa* headquarters had developed into townships essentially as grain marts and were thus dependent for grain supply on local rather than long distance trade *qanungo bahi* contains the information on grain trade between the rural areas of Jalor and the capital city of Jodhpur, Siwana and Sanchor.[50]

Many factors also played a significant role in the enlargement of urban population. Prominent among them were opportunities of employment and commerce. The demand for crafts attracted artisans in large numbers to settle down at these places.

The second reason for settling was the high-walled residence and fort of the rulers (locally known as *garh*) surrounded by the quarters of a large group of professional warriors. Such centres or *garhs* had many advantages, they furnished some degree of protection during a time when internecine wars was a scourge, and they afforded security to a greater degree than was possible in a village. Thus, most of the towns in this region originated as strategic, political and social centres of small semi-independent territories.[51] Artisans and traders gravitated to these centres and in a number of instances a centre became so specialized in some features of trade, commerce or manufacture as to acquire considerable fame in course of time.[52] The old capital towns of Tonote (Jaisalmer), Mandor (Jodhpur), Bagor (Bikaner), Jalor, Nagor, etc., originated as administrative centres of regional importance to which other functions were appended later on.[53] The names ending in *garh* express the intrinsic strategic importance of the site and nature of military or political origin of towns, such as Suratgarh, Ratangarh, Rajgarh, Lachmangarh. Other names also with such endings as *ner, pur, shahar, nagar*, etc. (all meaning settlement or towns) and the names of the founders mostly speak for their political or administrative origin, although in later times some of them were located for economic advantages as market towns.[54] Some of them capital cities,[55] while assuming different names from time to time under the ruling dynasties.[56] Some of them became famous after the names of tribes and republics.[57] For instance Bikaner was founded by Rao Bika (1489), Jodhpur by Rao Jodha (1459), Sardarshahar by Maharaja Sardar Singh.[58] Some names ending with *mer* (meaning rock area), show the unique physical characteristics of the sites. Jaisalmer for example is situated on a rocky basement.[59]

URBAN PRODUCTIONS

During eighteenth-nineteenth century, both food as well as cash crops raised wheat, gram, rice, *bajra* (millet), *jowar*, barley; pulses, like *moong, moth, urd*; oil seeds like *til* (sesamum), *sarso* (mustard); and cash crops namely, cotton, opium, sugar cane and indigo.[60]

Looking at the geographical condition, the different regions produced different crops. In the State of Jaipur, there were two major crop seasons, viz. *kharif* (*syalu*) and *rabi* (*unhalu*) as in most other part of the states and the country. The important *jinsi* crops of the *kharif* season were *bajra, jowar*; pulses like *moth, urd* and *moong*[61]; while *chola*, sugar-cane, cotton and *makka* (maize) were the crops also occupying the larger areas in the region. The other significant crops were *til*, vegetables, indigo, tobacco,[62] etc. The main *rabi* crops were wheat, gram, *sarso*, *gojaro* and barley produced in the area.[63] The other known crops in the region were *guwar*, *saal*, *mandavo*, carrot, sweet-potato (*shakarkandi*) and opium (*dodi*).[64]

Kota lying in the green belt of Rajasthan was agriculturally an important district. There were also two main crop seasons, *kharif* and *rabi*. The *kharif* crops included; *jowar*, maize, paddy, *moong*, *urd* and *til*. Important crops of the *rabi* season were wheat, barley, gram and linseed.[65] In this series an important source known as *toji-do-varkhi-baje-talke* provides information about production in *qasba* Sangod.[66] In this *qasba*, the main crops (*kharif* and *rabi* both) were *jowar*, *moong*, cotton, *chola*, maize, *shakarkand* (sweet potato), *kosumbo* (opium), *tambakhu* (tobacco), *sunn* and *neel* (indigo) produced.[67]

NOTES

1. James Tod, *Annals and Antiquities of Rajasthan*, vols. I, II and III, Humphrey Milford, Oxford University Press, London, 1920.
2. Ibid., vol. I, p.1.
3. Munhta Nainsi, *Khyat*, ed. Badri Prasad Sakariya, vol. I, 1960.
4. V.C. Mishra, *Geography of Rajasthan*, National Book Trust, New Delhi, 1967, p. 1, also *Census of India*, vol. I, part II-A, p. 84.
5. K.C. Jain, *Ancient Cities and Towns of Rajasthan*, Motilal Banarsidass, Delhi, 1972, pp. 19-20.
6. B.L. Gupta, *Trade and Commerce in Rajasthan During the 18th Century*, Jaipur Publishing House, Jaipur, 1987, p. 1.
7. Ibid.
8. Ibid.
9. Ibid.
10. R.L. Singh, *India: A Regional Geography*, National Geographical Society of India, rpt., Varanasi, 1987, pp. 49-50. Author corrected the location of the districts.
11. According to geologists, it is the oldest mountain chain of India, Jain, *Ancient Cities and Towns of Rajasthan*, op. cit., pp. 19-20.

12. Jain, *Ancient Cities and Towns of Rajasthan*, op. cit., pp.19-20, cf. Mishra, *Geography of Rajasthan*, op. cit., p. 4.
13. Mishra, pp. 19-20.
14. Ibid.
15. Ibid.
16. Bhadani, *Peasants, Artisans and Entrepreneurs*, op. cit., p. 5, cf. Nainsi, *Marwar-ra-pargana-ri-Vigat,* ed. Narain Singh Bhati, vol. II, 1969, pp. 281-2.
17. Ibid.
18. Ibid., p. 1.
19. Ibid., p. 3.
20. Singh, *India: A Regional Geography*, op. cit., p. 57.
21. Ibid.
22. Ibid.
23. R.C. Sharma, *Settlement Geography of the Indian Desert*, Kumar Brothers, New Delhi, 1972, p. 29.
24. Ibid.
25. Singh, *India: A Regional Geography*, op. cit., p. 57.
26. Ibid.
27. Jain, *Ancient Cities and Towns of Rajasthan,* op. cit., pp. 69-70.
28. Ibid.
29. Ibid.
30. Ibid.
31. Ibid., p. 71.
32. Madhavi Bajekal, 'Agricultural Production and the Peasant Economy of Eastern Rajasthan in the 18th Century' (cyclostyle). This article was provided by Prof. B.L. Bhadani, AMU, Aligarh.
33. Ibid.
34. Ibid.
35. Ibid.
36. *Arhsattas* of different years of Jaipur region, RSA, Bikaner.
37. *Taqsims* ofdifferent years of Kota region, RSA, Bikaner.
38. *Sava Bahis* of different years of Bikaner, RSA, Bikaner.
39. *Report Mardum Sumari Raj Marwar*, 1891-2, part 3 (2 vols.), part I, 1895, part II, 1896, Jodhpur. Also see Tod, op. cit.
40. Tod, op. cit., p. 1245.
41. Ibid., p. 585.
42. *The Cambridge Economic History of India*, ed. Tapan Raychaudhuri and Irfan Habib, vol. I, *c. 1200-c. 1750,* Cambridge University Press, London; Orient Longman, Delhi, 1982, p. 435.

43. Sharma, *Settlement Geography of the Indian Desert*, op. cit., p. 87. Cf. *Arhsatta qasba* Ramgarh, Khatu and Shahpur for the eighteenth century.
44. Sharma, *Settlement Geography of the Indian Desert*, op. cit., p. 86.
45. Ibid., p. 87.
46. The religious and pilgrimage centres were Ajmer (centre of *Chishtiya Silsila*), Nagaur (centre of *Suhrawardiya* and *Chishtiya Silsila* both), Khatu, Jhunjhunu, and Singhana, etc.
47. Bhadani, *Peasants. Artisans and Entrepreneur*, op. cit., p. 298.
48. *Arhsattas* of Shekhawati region especially for *qasba* Ramgarh, Khatu, Shahpur and Khandela. And *arhsatta qasba* Sanganer, VS 1773/AD 1716, VS 1790/AD 1733. *Toji-do-varkhi-baje-talke, qasba* Sangod, VS 1798/AD 1741.
49. Grain as revenue payment from the villages of *pargana* Phalodi was carted to its *qasba*. Cf. *Hasal-pargana-ri-bahi*, VS 1746/AD 1689, Bikaner *bahi's, hasal bahis*, no. 3, ff. 30-4. For Jalor see, *Qanungo bahi*, VS 1720/AD 1663, MS no. 79, *Kanmal Ram Lal Mehta Collection*, RSA, Jodhpur, now housed at Bikanar. For details see, Bhadani, *Peasants, Artisans and Entrepreneurs*, op. cit., pp. 298-307.
50. See *qanungo bahi*, VS 1720/AD 1663., RSA, Bikaner.
51. Singh, *India: A Regional Geography*, op. cit., pp. 66-7.
52. Ibid., p. 67.
53. Ibid.
54. Ibid.
55. Jain, *Ancient Cities and Towns of Rajasthan*, op. cit., p. 69.
56. Ibid.
57. Ibid.
58. Singh, *India: A Regional Geography*, op. cit., pp. 66-7.
59. Ibid.
60. Gupta, *Agrarian System of Eastern Rajasthan*, op. cit.; Dilbagh Singh, *The State, Landlords and Peasants*, op. cit.
61. *Arhsattas* of different years for the State of Jaipur, RSA, Bikaner.
62. Ibid.
63. Ibid.
64. Ibid.
65. *Toji-do-varkhi-baje-talke* documents of different years for the state of Kota, RSA, Bikaner.
66. Ibid., *qasba* Sangod, VS 1798/AD 1741.
67. Ibid.

CHAPTER 3

Urban Centres of Rajasthan

The study of towns and cities of Rajasthan and their population in the eighteenth-nineteenth centuries is quite fascinating, though the information available is not very extensive and is scattered, particularly for the eighteenth century. An attempt has been made to piece together the data on the large number of *qasbas* and urban centres in different areas of Rajasthan. We have included in our study almost all the towns or townships and cities of eighteenth century for which the terms *qasba*, *shahar* and *nagar* are employed in our documents.

There is no direct evidence about the size of a town which enables us to know about its population. Documents available give a record record of the estimated income which is technically called either *rekh*[1] or *jama* which composed of both agricultural and non-agricultural taxes. Besides this, we get data on total collection, i.e. *hasil*[2] and *jagat*[3] (*zakat* in Persian, transit duty). They can provide us a rough index to know the size of the population of a few towns.

It has been mentioned earlier in Chapter 2, that there were a large number of towns and cities in different Rajput principalities of Rajasthan, which is evident from the documents of the eighteenth-nineteenth century. We get information about 290 towns scattered all over the western and eastern region of Rajasthan.[4] Of these, Jaipur contains 111 *qasbas*[5] followed by Kota (78),[6] Jodhpur (32),[7] Bikaner (27),[8] Jaisalmer (24)[9] and Mewar (18).[10] We have plotted most of the *qasbas* on Maps (see end of chapter), but a few of them could not be located.[11] In the following Tables (Tables 3.1, 3.2, 3.3, 3.4, 3.5 and 3.6), *qasbas* of different regions are listed (also see Maps 3.1, 3.2, 3.3, 3.4, 3.5 and 3.6 at the end of this chapter). The estimated income (*jama* or *rekh*) of available urban centres along with the year is mentioned in it. Alongside the population of 1891 is also recorded.

TABLE 3.1: *QASBAS* IN JAIPUR STATE

Name of the Town	Year	Assessment *jama* (Rs.)	Population 1891
Qasba Alsisar	VS 1781/AD 1724	–	–
Qasba Malsisar	VS 1796/AD 1739	–	–
Qasba Chirawa	VS 1813/AD 1756	–	6,701
Qasba Jhunjhunu	VS 1807/AD 1750	–	12,262
Qasba Singhana	VS 1822/AD 1765	–	5,901
Qasba Baswa	VS 1807/AD 1750	4,510	6,117
Qasba Nawalgarh	VS 1813/AD 1756	–	12,567
Qasba Bharkol	VS 1796/AD 1739	–	–
Qasba Harsan	VS 1822/AD 1765	2,607	–
Qasba Narnaul	VS 1821/AD 1764	3,191	–
Qasba Khetri	VS 1790/AD 1733	–	8,418
Qasba Sikar	VS 1770/AD 1713	–	19,897
Qasba Khandela	VS 1864/AD 1807	1,370	10,067
Qasba Gaonri	VS 1770/AD 1713	–	–
Qasba Nimkathana	VS 1770/AD 1713		5,733
Qasba Kotputli	VS 1826/AD 1769	1,201	7,589
Qasba Pragpur	VS 1812/AD 1755	1,051	–
Qasba Kanwat	VS 1813/AD 1756	1,566	–
Qasba Shri Madhopur	VS 1813/AD 1756	–	6,130
Qasba Khatu	VS 1781/AD 1724	1,848	–
Qasba Mau	VS 1790/AD 1733	–	–
Qasba Ramgarh	VS 1816/AD 1759	3,074	–
Qasba Ringas	VS 1828/AD 1771	–	–
Qasba Amarsar	VS 1813/AD 1756	–	–
Qasba Bhabra	VS 1790/AD 1733	2,852	–
Qasba Bairat	VS 1815/AD 1758	5,843	5,748
Qasba Shahpura	VS 1813/AD 1756	–	4,590
Qasba Manoharpura	VS 1811/AD 1754	–	4,644
Qasba Chandwaji	VS 1780/AD 1723	760	–
Qasba Ajabgarh	VS 1808/AD 1751	6,508	–
Qasba Jaitpur	VS 1798/AD 1741	1,838	–
Qasba Jobner	VS 1800/AD 1743	701	–
Qasba Kalakh	VS 1862/AD 1805	2,025	–
Qasba Amber	VS 1827/AD 1770	2,313	–

contd.

TABLE 3.1 contd.

Name of the Town	Year	Assessment *jama* (Rs.)	Population 1891
Qasba Jamwa Ramgarh	VS 1811/AD 1754	–	–
Qasba Nainwa	VS 1790/AD 1733	–	–
Qasba Jaipur	VS 1828/AD 1771	79,058	1,65,408
Qasba Sanganer	VS 1772/AD 1715	54,104	–
Qasba Jhak	VS 1808/AD 1751	659	–
Qasba Rehlana	VS 1811/AD 1754	–	–
Qasba Danta Ramgarh	VS 1811/AD 1754	–	–
Qasba Chaksu/Chatsu	VS 1771/AD 1714	4,038	7,870
Qasba Phagi	VS 1808/AD 1751	1,216	–
Qasba Lalsot	VS 1810/AD 1753	6,694	8,163
Qasba Nawai	VS 1779/AD 1722	–	5,832
Qasba Malpura	VS 1827/AD 1770	2,651	8,345
Qasba Tonk	VS 1818/AD 1761	7,613	45,944
Qasba Malarna	VS 1807/AD 1750	–	–
Qasba Toda Rai Singh	VS 1815/AD 1758	3,947	5,649
Qasba Swai Madhopur	VS 1811/AD 1754	–	13,972
Qasba Khandahar	VS 1820/AD 1763	2,015	–
Qasba Rewari	VS 1790/AD 1733	–	–
Qasba Hasanpur	VS 1820/AD 1763	–	–
Qasba Jalalpur	VS 1796/AD 1739	–	–
Qasba Tijara	VS 1790/AD 1733	–	7,049
Qasba Mandawar	VS 1820/AD 1763	1,853	4,942
Qasba Rampur	VS 1811/AD 1754	6,307	–
Qasba Pahari	VS 1811/AD 1754	–	–
Qasba Alwar	VS 1783/AD 1726	–	51,427
Qasba Mahwa	VS 1790/AD 1733	–	–
Qasba Thana Ghazi	VS 1808/AD 1751	5,952	–
Qasba Maujpur	VS 1790/AD 1733	–	–
Qasba Kathumar	VS 1773/AD 1716	–	–
Qasba Punkhar	VS 1796/AD 1739	–	–
Qasba Reni/Rini	VS 1807/AD 1750	3,068	–
Qasba Khoh/Khohri	VS 1808/AD 1751	2,641	–
Qasba Narayana	VS 1811/AD 1754	2,049	–
Qasba Dausa	VS 1821/AD 1764	1,051	8,416
Qasba Todabhim	VS 1820/AD 1763	2,565	7,053
Qasba Sakarai	VS 1790/AD 1733	–	–
Qasba Gijgarh	VS 1821/AD 1764	2,502	–
Qasba Hijndaun	VS 1829/AD 1772	8,125	12,996
Qasba Chalkalyan	VS 1790/AD 1733	–	–

contd.

TABLE 3.1 contd.

Name of the Town	Year	Assessment *jama* (Rs.)	Population 1891
Qasba Dadri	VS 1790/AD 1733	–	–
Qasba Rastega	VS 1827/AD 1770	–	–
Qasba Kot	VS 1830/AD 1773	–	–
Qasba Veer Janandpuro	VS 1865/AD 1808	1,594	–
Qasba Antela	VS 1798/AD 1741	5,289	–
Qasba Vahrojara	VS 1820/AD 1763	1,181	–
Qasba Chhaihara	VS 1821/AD 1764	–	–
Qasba Bhangarh	VS 1808/AD 1751	1,154	–
Qasba Jovener	VS 1801/AD 1744	1,136	–
Qasba Varaichi	VS 1801/AD 1744	–	–
Qasba Kotla	VS 1770/AD 1713	–	–
Qasba Kuwavo	VS 1768/AD 1711	500	–
Qasba Paparda	VS 1768/AD 1711	–	–
Qasba Ujerpur	VS 1807/AD 1750	4,195	–
Qasba Kama	VS 1825/AD 1768	6,130	–
Qasba Chhani	VS 1791/AD 1734	895	–
Qasba Nansreja	VS 1857/AD 1800	–	–
Qasba Thanawaboli	VS 1813/AD 1756	–	–
Qasba Pindayan	VS 1822/AD 1765	2,530	–
Qasba Patari	VS 1817/AD 1760	8,981	–
Qasba Pawat	VS 1809/AD 1752	4,263	–
Qasba Banawara	VS 1770/AD 1713	–	–
Qasba Bhagotgarh	VS 1811/AD 1754	10,004	–
Qasba Bhinaya	VS 1813/AD 1756	–	–
Qasba Masooda	VS 1811/AD 1754	–	–
Qasba Bhadalav	VS 1807/AD 1750	–	–
Qasba Bhundora	VS 1813/AD 1756	–	–
Qasba Bhunsawar	VS 1811/AD 1754	–	–
Qasba Lawari	VS 1811/AD 1754	–	–
Qasba Lalgarh	VS 1841/AD 1784	2,668	–
Qasba Bahatri	VS 1813/AD 1756	–	–
Qasba Sacheri	VS 1829/AD 1772	2,554	–
Qasba Siroj/Sironj	VS 1789/AD 1732	6,429	11,737
Qasba Hastera	VS 1779/AD 1722	3,965	–
Qasba Maujabad	VS 1827/ AD 1770	2,740	–
Qasba Baspur	VS 1813/AD 1756	–	–
Qasba Rawas	VS 1770/AD 1713	–	–
Qasba Udeyee	VS 1819/AD 1762	–	–

TABLE 3.2: *QASBAS* IN KOTA STATE

Name of the Town	Year	Assessment *rekh* (Rs.)	Population 1891
Qasba Ganeshganj	VS 1849/AD 1792	7,000	–
Qasba Kotra	VS 1881/AD 1824	800	–
Qasba Barod	VS 1849/AD 1792	7,000	–
Qasba Mau	VS 1843/AD 1786	1,500	–
Qasba Siswali	VS 1843/AD 1786	6,682	–
Qasba Mandawar	VS 1843/AD 1786	1,900	–
Qasba Mangrol	VS 1843/AD 1786	12,000	5,714
Qasba Ramgarh	VS 1881/AD 1824	2,800	–
Qasba Digodh	VS 1813/AD 1756	–	–
Qasba Kota	VS 1813/AD 1756	–	38,624
Qasba Kethune	VS 1849/AD 1792	1,135	–
Qasba Ranpura	VS 1813/AD 1756	-	–
Qasba Anta	VS 1831/AD 1774	5,017	–
Qasba Rajgarh	VS 1843/AD 1786	3,766	–
Qasba Arandkhera	VS 1813/AD 1756	–	–
Qasba Koela	VS 1849/AD 1792	5,000	–
Qasba Baran	VS 1849/AD 1792	6,000	7,067
Qasba Khandela	VS 1830/AD 1773	5,000	–
Qasba Jetpur	VS 1843/AD 1786	1,300	–
Qasba Khuri	VS 1843/AD 1786	–	–
Qasba Rahlai	VS 1849/AD 1792	6,500	–
Qasba Atru	VS 1843/AD 1786	–	–
Qasba Aton	VS 1843/AD 1786	–	–
Qasba Sangod	VS 1843/AD 1786	10,200	5,046
Qasba Jolpa/Jolava	VS 1843/AD 1786	3,000	–
Qasba Kanwas	VS 1881/AD 1824	6,100	–
Qasba Kotri	VS 1843/AD 1786	–	–
Qasba Chechat	VS 1843/AD 1786	8,000	–
Qasba Panwar	VS 1829/AD 1772	1,975	–
Qasba Kaithuni	VS 1887/AD 1830	4,000	–
Qasba Khanpur	VS 1843/AD 1786	–	–
Qasba Shergarh	VS 1843/AD 1786	–	–
Qasba Kunjor	VS 1849/AD 1792	9,000	–
Qasba Harigarh	VS 1881/AD 1824	5,800	–
Qasba Golana	VS 1843/AD 1786	10,000	–
Qasba Chhipa Broad	VS 1887/AD 1730	2,000	–
Qasba Gagraon	VS 1887/AD 1730	800	–
Qasba Richwa	VS 1828/AD 1771	3,000	–
Qasba Aklera	VS 1849/AD 1792	3,500	–

contd.

TABLE 3.2 contd.

Name of the Town	Year	Assessment *rekh* (Rs.)	Population 1891
Qasba Raipur	VS 1843/AD 1786	500	–
Qasba Ratlai	VS 1843/AD 1786	–	–
Qasba Delanpur	VS 1881/AD 1824	1,450	–
Qasba Sarda	VS 1843/AD 1786	–	–
Qasba Ghatoli	VS 1843/AD 1786	4,000	–
Qasba Bhalta	VS 1881/AD 1824	2,500	–
Qasba Sarra	VS 1843/AD 1786	–	–
Qasba Manohar Thana	VS 1843/AD 1786	–	–
Qasba Kakurji	VS 1828/AD 1771	2,000	–
Qasba Sarhara	VS 1843/AD 1786	–	–
Qasba Vikaeeji	VS 1843/AD 1786	2,100	–
Qasba Mohi	VS 1843/AD 1786	–	–
Qasba Javarnagar	VS 1829/AD 1772	17,000	–
Qasba Dhulot	VS 1829/AD 1772	10,000	–
Qasba Vasthuni	VS 1829/AD 1772	2,500	–
Qasba Vanigo	VS 1843/AD 1786	–	–
Qasba Umedgarh	VS 1830/AD 1773	4,000	–
Qasba Bhori	VS 1830/AD 1773	20,000	–
Qasba Khatakheri	VS 1843/AD 1786	700	–
Qasba Javar	VS 1849/AD 1792	1,308	–
Qasba Avo	VS 1843/AD 1786	12,000	–
Qasba Atavo	VS 1843/AD 1786	12,000	–
Qasba Narsanggarh	VS 1843/AD 1786	3,000	–
Qasba Vosadaro	VS 1849/AD 1792	5,559	–
Qasba Madhkargarh	VS 1881/AD 1824	2,400	–
Qasba Sakhet	VS 1887/AD 1730	2,000	–
Qasba Arhara	VS 1843/AD 1786	–	–
Qasba Varsano	VS 1881/AD 1824	1,000	–
Qasba Karvargarh	VS 1849/AD 1792	1,000	–
Qasba Urmal	VS 1849/AD 1792	1,600	–
Qasba Khairabad	VS 1843/AD 1786	–	–
Qasba Achhet	VS 1849/AD 1792	2,000	–
Qasba Kasidhji	VS 1849/AD 1792	5,000	–
Qasba Lunra	VS 1849/AD 1792	8,000	–
Qasba Nandgaon	VS 1849/AD 1792	2,000	–
Qasba Bharla	VS 1881/AD 1824	4,000	–
Qasba Bulwara	VS 1843/AD 1786	–	–
Qasba Makangarh	VS 1881/AD 1824	600	–
Qasba Rampura	VS 1887/AD 1730	500	–

TABLE 3.3: *QASBAS* IN BIKANER STATE

Name of the Town	Year	Assessment (Rs.)	Population 1891
Qasba Hanumangarh	VS 1911/AD 1854	31,093	1,367
Qasba Tibi	VS 1921/AD 1864	64,824	–
Qasba Sardargarh	VS 1921/AD 1864	15,258	–
Qasba Suratgarh	VS 1921/AD 1864	24,468	2,659
Qasba Anupgarh	VS 1912/AD 1855	6,743	–
Qasba Nohar	VS 1881/AD 1824	23,657	5,655
Qasba Bhadra	VS 1881/AD 1824	68,402	3,256
Qasba Reni	VS 1882/AD 1825	–	–
Qasba Rajgarh	VS 1871/AD 1814	25,263	4,677
Qasba Churu	VS 1882/AD 1825	17,376	14,014
Qasba Bhinasar	VS 1931/AD 1874	10,225	–
Qasba Ratangarh	VS 1911/AD 1854	13,586	10,536
Qasba Ratannagar	VS 1921/AD 1864	9,442	–
Qasba Rajaldesar	VS 1882/AD 1825	1,947	4,397
Qasba Chhapar	VS 1921/AD 1864	4580	–
Qasba Sujangarh	VS 1931/AD 1874	23,113	9,781
Qasba Surpura	VS 1951/AD 1894	–	–
Qasba Shri Dungargarh	VS 1951/AD 1894	–	2,469
Qasba Lunkaransar	VS 1931/AD 1874	4,301	–
Qasba Sardarshahar	VS 1921/AD 1864	18,999	9,196
Qasba Bikaner (Sadar)	AD 1820	–	56,252
Qasba Bahaduran	AD 1820	–	–
Qasba Mahajan	AD 1820	–	–
Qasba Jethpur	AD 1820	–	–
Qasba Bidasar	AD 1820	–	–
Qasba Deshnokh'	AD 1820	–	–
Qasba Senthal	AD 1820	–	–

TABLE 3.4: *QASBAS* IN JODHPUR STATE

Name of the Town	Year	Assessment *rekh* (Rs.)	Population 1891
Qasba Shiv	1820s	–	901
Qasba Newa	1820s	–	–
Qasba Phalodi	1820s	–	10,497
Qasba Nagaur	1820s	–	17,191
Qasba Didwana	1820s	–	11,376
Qasba Maroth	1820s	–	–
Qasba Parbatsar	1820s	–	–
Qasba Merta	1820s	–	7,142
Qasba Jaitaran	1820s	–	4,801
Qasba Bilara	1820s	–	11,384
Qasba Jodhpur	1820s	–	61,759
Qasba Sojhat	1820s	–	12,624
Qasba Pali	1820s	4,100	17,153
Qasba Sankra	1820s	–	–
Qasba Desuri	1820s	–	–
Qasba Bali	1820s	–	5,354
Qasba Shergarh	1820s	–	–
Qasba Pachpadra	1820s	–	5,125
Qasba Balotra	1820s	–	5,435
Qasba Siwana	1820s	–	–
Qasba Jalor	1820s	–	9,657
Qasba Jaswantpura	1820s	–	–
Qasba Sanchor	1820s	6,000	2,635
Qasba Barmer	1820s	–	5,610
Qasba Pipar	1820s	9,150	8,153
Qasba Bhinmal	1820s	–	–
Qasba Indawar	1820s	12,000	1,063
Qasba Nandla	1820s	–	310
Qasba Machola	1820s	–	–
Qasba Bhadrajan	1820s	2,500	1,837
Qasba Morsin	1820s	5,000	2,500
Qasba Bharunda	1820s	3,000	1,584
Qasba Kotra	1820s	–	1,279

TABLE 3.5: *QASBAS* IN JAISALMER STATE

Name of the Town	Year	Assessment *rekh* (Rs.)	Population 1891
Qasba Jaisalmer	AD 1815	–	10,500
Qasba Bekampur	AD 1815	–	–
Qasba Sirara	AD 1815	–	–
Qasba Nachna	AD 1815	–	–
Qasba Katori	AD 1815	–	–
Qasba Kaba	AD 1815	–	–
Qasba Kuldaro	AD 1815	–	–
Qasba Satla	AD 1815	–	–
Qasba Jinjiniali	AD 1815	–	–
Qasba Devi Kot	AD 1815	–	–
Qasba Bhap	AD 1815	–	–
Qasba Balana	AD 1815	–	–
Qasba Saliasa	AD 1815	–	–
Qasba Baru	AD 1815	–	–
Qasba Chan	AD 1815	–	–
Qasba Loharki	AD 1815	–	–
Qasba Naontala	AD 1815	–	–
Qasba Lahti/Lohawat	AD 1815	–	–
Qasba Dangari	AD 1815	–	–
Qasba Bijorai	AD 1815	–	–
Qasba Mandai/Mundawa	AD 1815	–	–
Qasba Ramgarh	AD 1815	–	–
Qasba Birsalpur	AD 1815	–	–
Qasba Girjasar	AD 1815	–	–

TABLE 3.6: *QASBAS* IN MEWAR STATE

Name of the Town	Year	Assessment *rekh* (Rs.)	Population 1891
Qasba Udaipur	AD 1822	–	46,693
Qasba Banera	AD 1822	–	5,760
Qasba Begun	AD 1822	–	5,882
Qasba Bhilwara	AD 1822	–	10,343
Qasba Bhindar	AD 1822	–	6,790
Qasba Choti Sadri	AD 1822	–	5,368
Qasba Chittorgarh	AD 1822	–	–
Qasba Deogarh	AD 1822	–	7,400
Qasba Jahajpur	AD 1822	–	5,106
Qasba Kapasin	AD 1822	–	–
Qasba Khairwara	AD 1822	–	648
Qasba Kotra	AD 1822	–	–
Qasba Nathdwara	AD 1822	–	9,331
Qasba Pur	AD 1822	–	6,800
Qasba Salumbar	AD 1822	–	6,029
Qasba Magra	AD 1822	–	–
Qasba Mandal Garh	AD 1822	–	–
Qasba Rajnagar	AD 1822	–	–

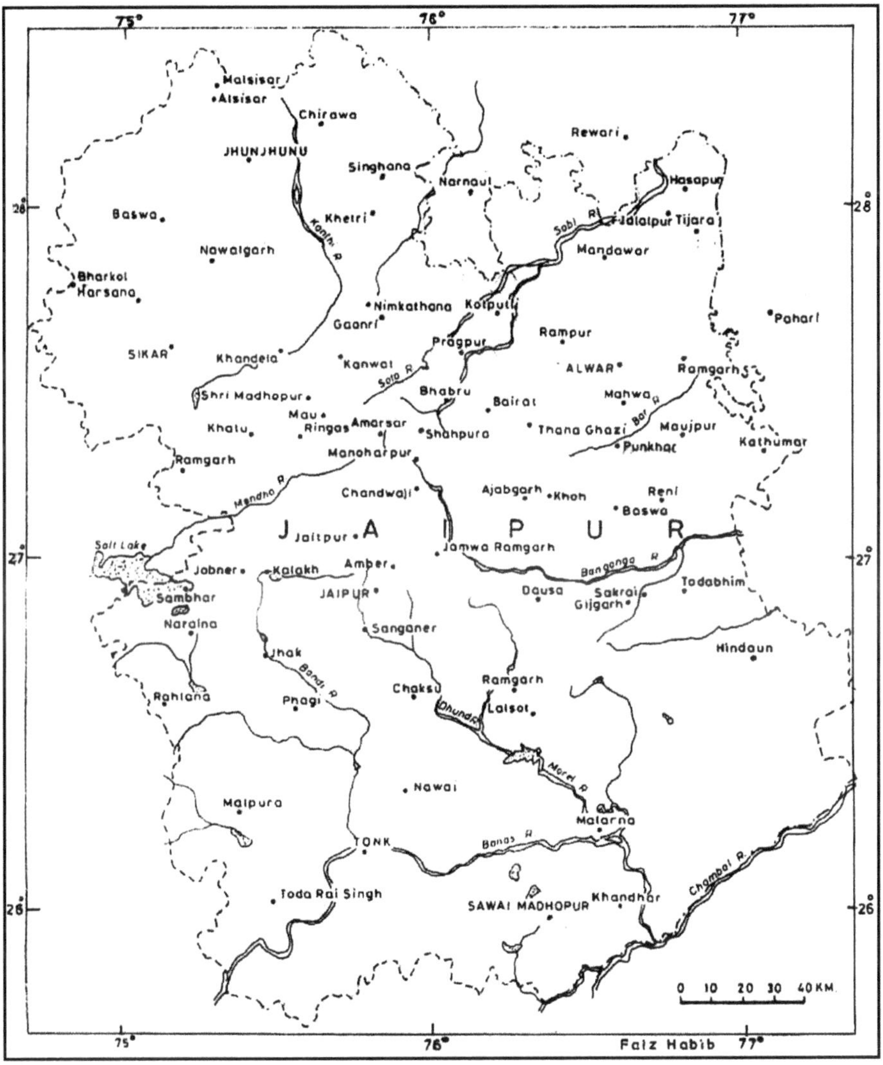

Map 3.1: *Qasbas* in Jaipur State (Eighteenth-Nineteenth Centuries)

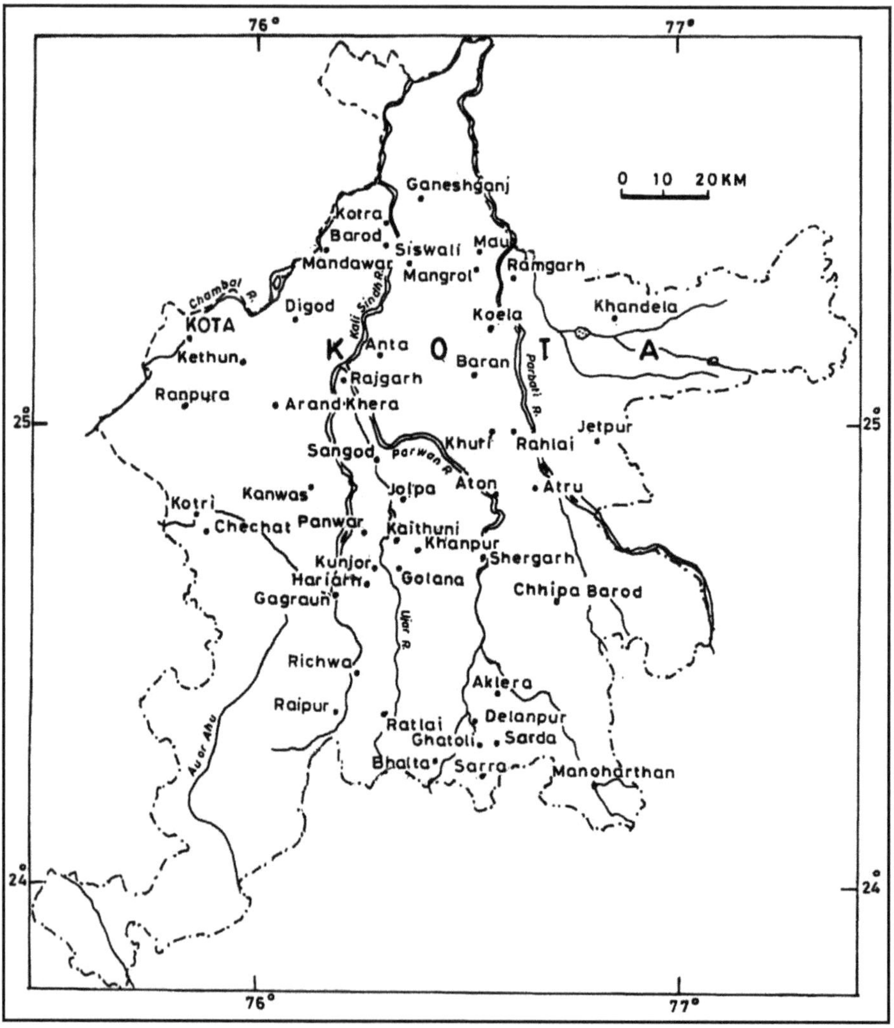

Map 3.2: *Qasbas* in Kota State (Eighteenth-Nineteenth Centuries)

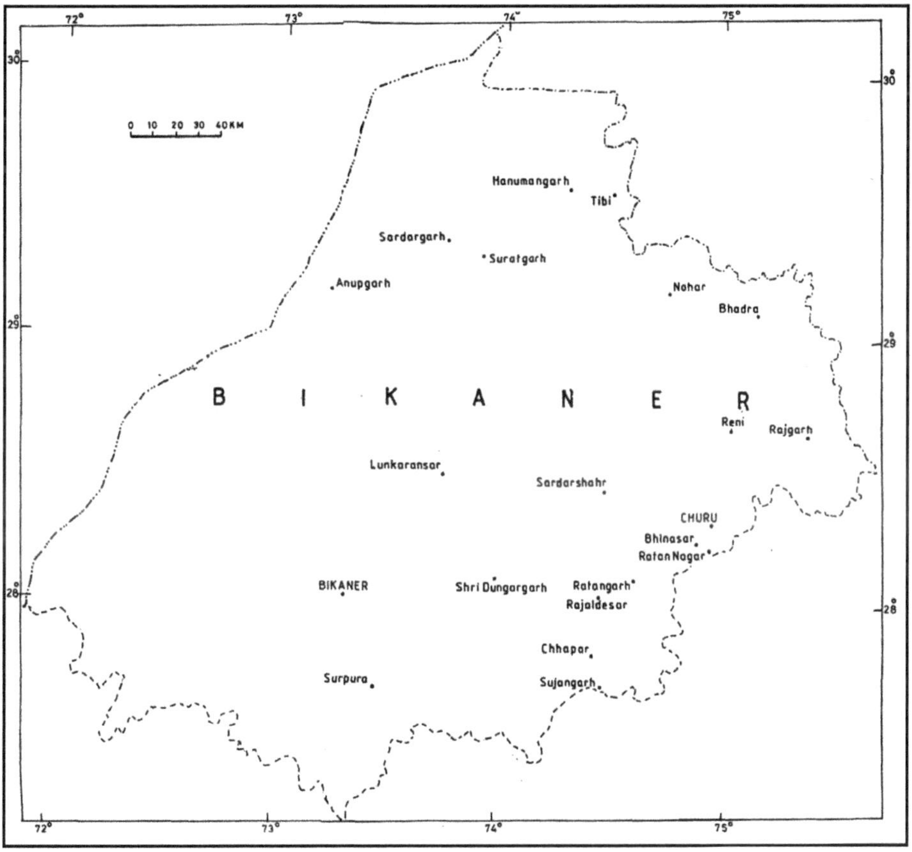

Map 3.3: *Qasbas* in Bikaner State (Eighteenth-Nineteenth Centuries)

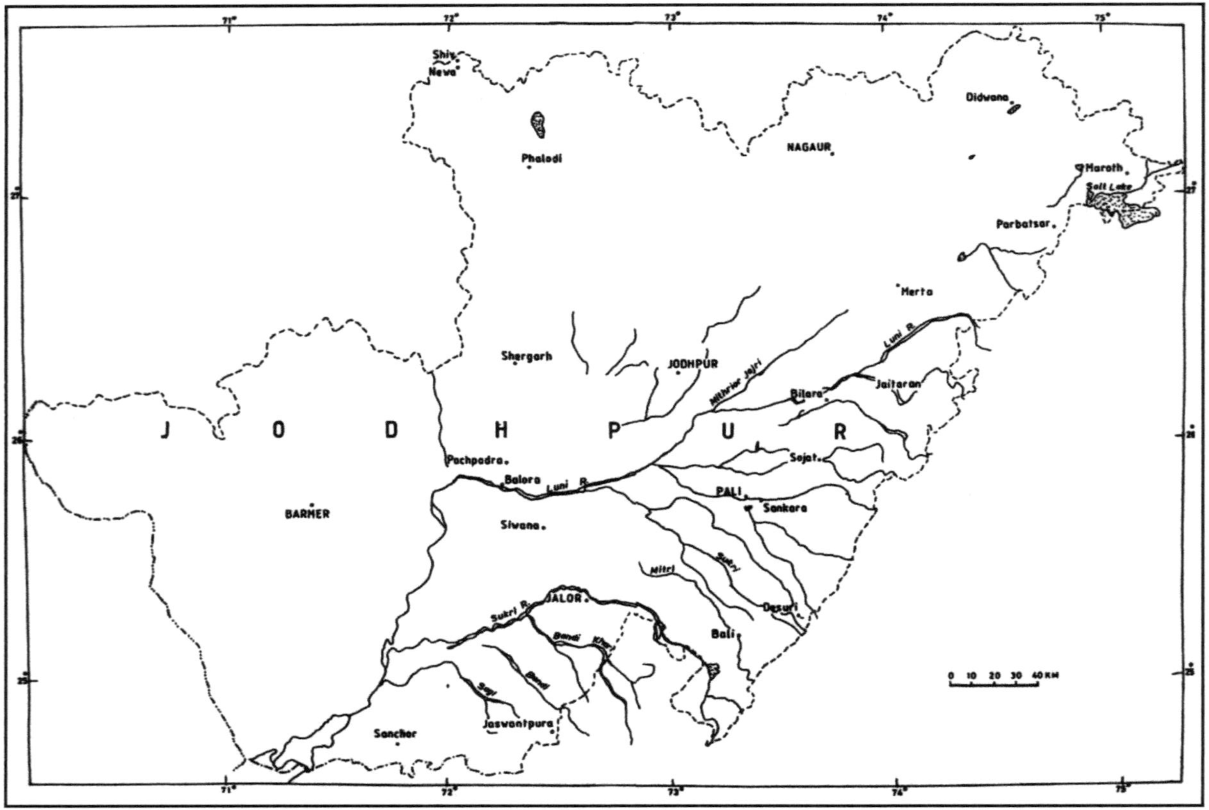

Map 3.4: *Qasbas* in Jodhpur State (Eighteenth-Nineteenth Centuries)

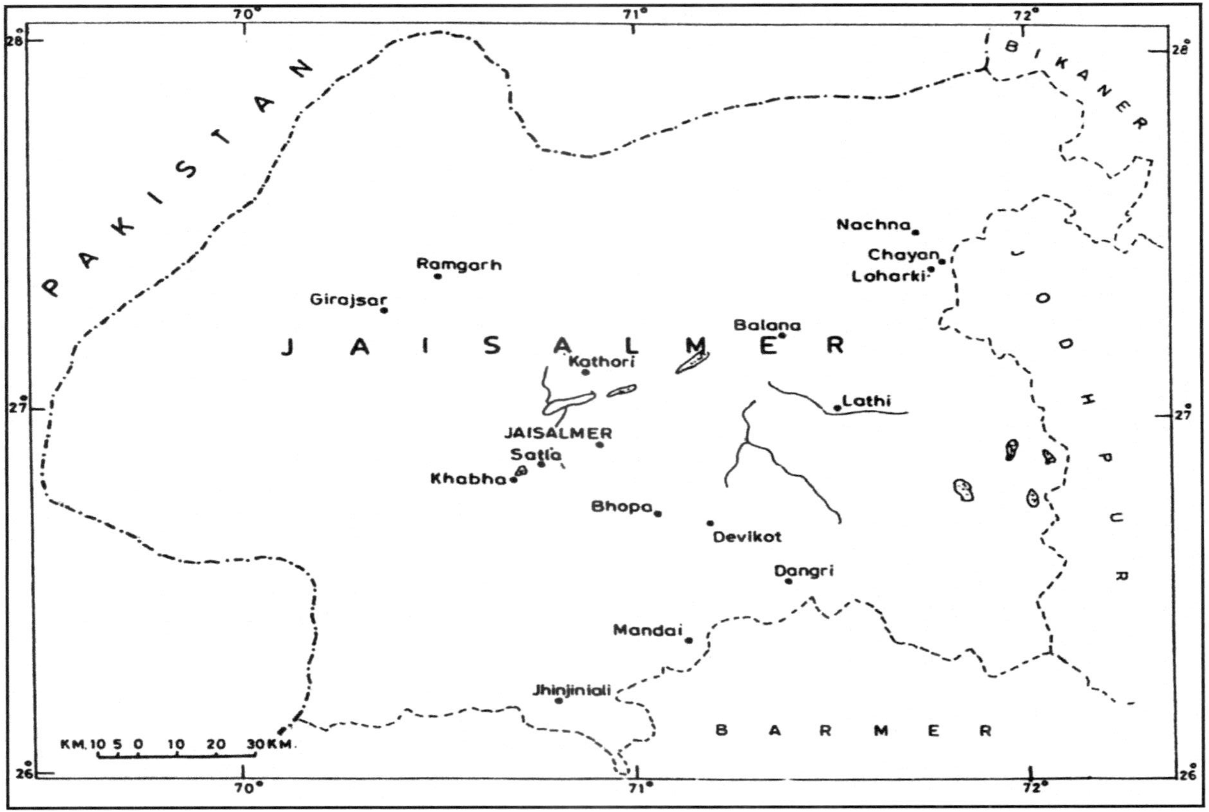

Map 3.5: *Qasbas* in Jaisalmer State (Eighteenth-Nineteenth Centuries)

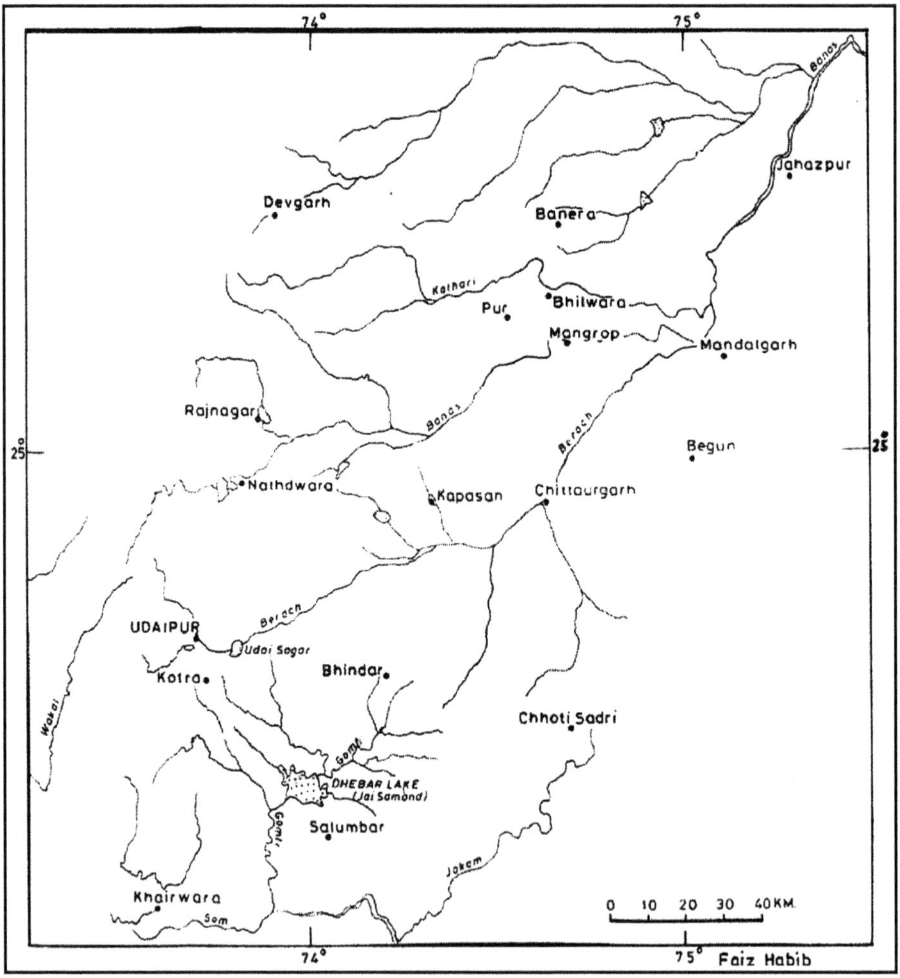

Map 3.6: *Qasbas* in Mewar State (Eighteenth-Nineteenth Centuries)

NOTES

1. *Toji Taqsims* of different years of Kota State, RSA, Bikaner.
2. *Arhsattas* of different years of Jaipur State, RSA, Bikaner.
3. *Sava bahis* of different years for *qasbas* of Bikaner State, RSA, Bikaner.
4. The Rajasthani sources such as *arhsattas, taqsims, toji-do-varkhi-baje-talke, sava bahis* and *Annals and Antiquities of Rajasthan* (3 vols.).
5. *Arhsattas* of different years of Jaipur State.
6. *Toji taqsims* of different years of Kota State.
7. Different years of documents of Jodhpur state and *Mardum-sumari-raj-Marwar*, vol. II, Jodhpur, 1892.
8. *Sava bahis* of different years for *qasbas* of Bikaner State.
9. James Tod, *Annals and Antiquities of Rajasthan*, Humphrey Milford, Oxford University Press, London, 1920.
10. Ibid.
11. See the maps of the *qasbas* of Jaipur, Kota, Jodhpur, Bikaner, Jaisalmer and Mewar States given in this chapter.

CHAPTER 4

Growth of Urban Centres and Pattern of Agricultural Production in the Shekhawati Region

The territory of Kyamkhanis conquered by Rao Shekha (founder of the Shekhawat clan) which was later on expanded under his descendants came to be known as Shekhawati.[1] The first reference of Shekhawati comes from an *Arzdasht* of *Maghvadi* 9, VS 1766/AD 1709 available in the Rajasthan State Archives, Bikaner.[2] Thereafter, this designation was employed by Col. W.N. Gardner in VS 1860/AD 1803[3] and Mountstuart Elphinstone in VS 1865/AD 1808. By the time of James Tod the territory under the Shekhawats had earned a political sanctity which is attested by a separate section on Shekhawati in his book.[4]

The Shekhawati area is located in the north-east of Rajasthan and is on the north-west of Jaipur.[5] Before Independence it was bound on the north by the states of Bikaner, on the west by Jodhpur, on the south by Jaipur and on the east by Patiala. Now it is bound on the north-west by Churu, on the south by Nagaur, on the south-west by Jaipur, on the south-east by Alwar and on the east by Haryana.

The region of Shekhawati was the hereditary territory of the Shekhawats; therefore, the documents pertaining to the area remained in the private archives of the *thikanedars*. Unfortunately, we do not have access to them. Later in the eighteenth century some portions of these *parganas* were assigned to the Kachhwaha rulers by the Mughals. Therefore, the records of this period are available in the Rajasthan State Archives, Bikaner. Important among them are the *arhsattas* and *chitthis*. The *arhsattas* are a mine of information under different heads such as total amount of *syalu* (*kharif*)[6] and *unhalu* (*rabi*)[7] income from *malo-jihat*[8] and *sair-jihat*[9] in both the harvests. In addition, they also offer us the *zabti*[10] area under each crop and the revenue realization in kind under crop sharing (*batai-jinsi*).[11]

An attempt has been made in this chapter to study the growth of urban centres and pattern of agricultural production in the Shekhawati region.[12] An effort has also been made to establish the relationship between the agricultural production and the emergence of *qasbas* in this region.

According to Elphinstone, 'the Shekhawati itself is a sandy plain, scattered with rocky hills, ill-watered and badly cultivated; yet it contains several large towns'.[13] This statement requires to be examined in the light of the documents. For this we have information for earlier periods contained in the *arhsattas* of different *parganas* including *qasbas* such as Amarsar, Khatu, Manoharpur, Shahpur, Ramgarh, Reengas, Shrimadhopur, Sikarai and Khandela (see Map 4.1).

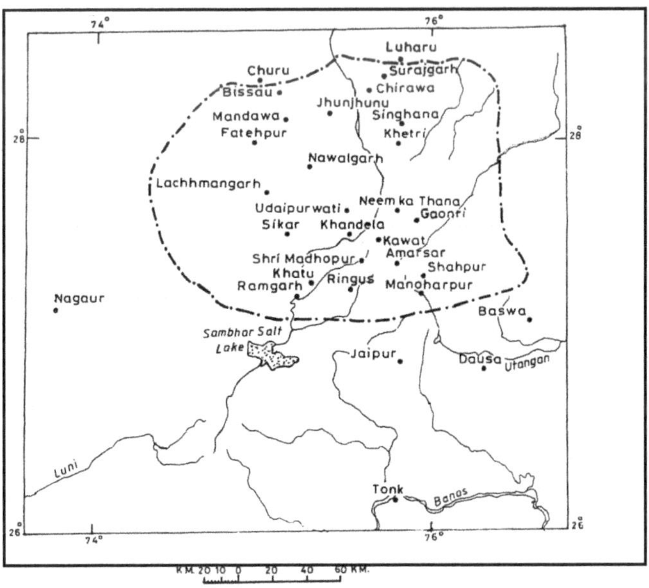

Map 4.1: *Qasbas* of Shekhawati
(Eighteenth-Nineteenth Centuries)

The *arhsattas* provide valuable information under different heads such as:

(a) Amount of revenue realization under the *kharif* and the *rabi* harvests.
(b) Area under crops, cash revenue rates (*zabti*) and the total collection from each crop in money.
(c) The total collection of revenue in grain under the *batai-jinsi* system; its sale price and the monetary value of it.

URBAN PRODUCTIONS

The study of the crop pattern of eleven *qasbas* in the southern portion of the Shekhawati region is studied in this chapter. The sampled towns are Amarsar, Khatu, Manoharpur, Shahpur, Gaori, Kawat, Ramgarh, Reengas, Shrimadhopur, Sikarai and Khandela. The map of the Shekhawati region (information for seven *qasbas*) representing the crops of various kinds in the southern part may be helpful for a clear understanding about the crop pattern.[14] The total number of crops produced in *kharif* and *rabi* comes to approximately 20. Out of these, about four belong to *rabi* and the rest to *kharif*. In *kharif*, *bajra*, *jowar*, *gunwar*, *til*, *chola*, *moth* and *moong* were the most important crops assessed under the *batai-jinsi* while *makka* (maize); *vani* (cotton), *torai* (a vegetable), *mandavo*, *shakarkand* (sweet potato), *varh* (sugar cane), *dodi* (opium) and vegetables were raised and taxed under the *zabti* crops.[15]

Table 4.1 has been prepared on the basis of the information available about the food crops and 'cash crops' of various *qasbas* (also see Map 4.2), which shows that in *qasba* Khatu *bajra*, *moth*, *moong*, *gunwar*, *chola*, *makka*, *mandavojau* and *gehoon* were the main food crops while *vani* (cotton), *varh* (sugar cane), *dodi* (opium), *gajar* (carrot), and *sabzi* (vegetables) were the cash crops.

In *qasba* Shahpur *bajra*, *moth*, *moong*, *til*, *chola*, *makka*, *jau*, *gehoon* (wheat) and *chana* (gram) were the food crops while *vani*, *varh*, *dodi*, *gajar*, *sabzi*, and *shakarkand* were the cash crops. In *qasba* Kawat *bajra*, *moth*, *moong*, *til*, *gunwar*, *chola*, *makka*, *mandavo*, *jau* and *gehoon* were the food crops while *vani*, *sabzi*, *saal* and *tambakhoo*

TABLE 4.1: CROPS IN THE *QASBAS* OF SHEKHAWATI REGION

Year	*Qasba*	Crops in the *Qasbas* of Shekhawati Region								
		Bajra	*Moth*	*Moong*	*Til*	*Gunwar*	*Chola*	*Makka*	*Vani*	*Dodi*
VS 1816/ AD 1759	Khatu	A*	A	A	N.A. **	A	A	A	A	N.A
VS 1793/ AD 1736	Shahpur	A	A	A	N.A.	N.A.	N.A.	N.A.	N.A.	N.A
VS 1794/ AD 1737	Shahpur (I)	A	A	A	A	A	A	A	A	N.A
VS 1794/ AD 1737	Shahpur	N.A.	N.A.	N.A.	A	A	N.A.	N.A.	A	A
VS 1813/ AD 1756	Kaawat	A	A	A	A	A	A	A	A	N.A
VS 1821/ AD 1764	Kaawat	A	A	A	A	A	A	A	A	N.A
VS 1816/ AD 1759	Ramgarh	A	A	A	A	A	N.A.	A	A	N.A
VS 1820/ AD 1763	Ramgarh	A	A	A	N.A.	A	N.A.	A	A	N.A
VS 1827/ AD 1770	Kaawat	A	N.A.	N.A.	N.A.	N.A.	A	A	N.A.	N.A
VS 1844/ AD 1787	Sikrai	N.A.	N.A.	N.A.	N.A.	N.A.	N.A.	N.A	N.A	N.A
VS 1864/ AD 1807	Khandela	A	A	A	A	N.A.	N.A.	A	N.A	N.A

Notes: *'A' denotes available, **N.A. denotes not available, and (a)** also denotes available.

contd.

TABLE 4.1 contd.

Year	*Qasba*	Crops in the *Qasbas* of Shekhawati Region								
		Mandao	*Gaajar*	*Shakarkand*	*Seen*	*Jau/Gojai*	*Gehoon*	*Chana*	*Varh*	*Tambakhoo*
VS 1816/ AD 1759	Khatu	A1	N.A.	N.A.	N.A.	N.A.	N.A.	N.A.	N.A.	N.A
VS 1793/ AD 1736	Shahpur	N.A.	A	N.A.	N.A.	A	A	N.A.	N.A.	N.A
VS 1794/ AD 1737	Shahpur (I)	N.A.	A	A	A	N.A.	N.A.	N.A.	N.A.	N.A
VS 1794/ AD 1737	Shahpur	N.A.	A	N.A.	N.A.	A	A	A	A	N.A.
VS 1813/ AD 1756	Kaawat	A	N.A.	N.A.	N.A. saal (a)**	A	A	N.A.	N.A.	N.A
VS 1821/ AD 1764	Kaawat	A	N.A.	N.A.	N.A. saal (a)**	A	A	N.A.	N.A.	N.A
VS 1816/ AD 1759	Ramgarh	N.A.	N.A.	N.A.	N.A.	A	A	N.A.	N.A.	N.A
VS 1820/ AD 1763	Ramgarh	A	N.A.	N.A.	N.A.	A	A	N.A.	N.A.	N.A
VS 1827/ AD 1770	Kaawat	N.A.	N.A.	N.A.	N.A.	N.A.	N.A.	N.A.	N.A.	A
VS 1844/ AD 1787	Sikrai	N.A.	N.A.	N.A.	A	A	A	N.A	N.A	A
VS 1864/ AD 1807	Khandela	N.A.	A	N.A.	N.A.	A	N.A.	N.A.	N.A	N.A

Map 4.2: Shekhawati Crops Produce
(Eighteenth-Nineteenth Centuries)

were the cash crops. In *qasba* Ramgarh *bajra, moth, moong, til, gunwar, makka, mandavo, jau* and *gehoon* were the food crops while *vani, gajar* and *sabzi* were the cash crops. In *qasba* Sikarai *jau* and *gehoon* were the main food crops while *sabzi* and *tambakhoo* were the cash crops. In *qasba* Khandela *bajra, moth, moong, til, makka* and *jau* were the main food crops while vegetables were the main cash crop.[16] *Gehoon* (wheat), *chana* (gram) and *jau* (barley) were important *rabi* crops assessed according to the division of crops, i.e. *batai-jinsi.*

The revenue records have entry of the total amount collected under *kharif* and *rabi.* The break up is given under the head *malo-*

jihat and *sair-jihat.* The *malo-jihat* comprises revenue realized from *zabti*, *qarar-ijara*[17] (fixed revenue), *batai-jinsi* (crop sharing) and *jihat. Mal* seems to represent the original tax (land revenue) and *jihat* the cesses collected to meet the expenses incurred in connection with the assessment and collection of *mal.*[18]

A study of the cesses grouped under *sair-jihat* shows that they were imposed as either customary fees or as taxes from the residents of a village, such as transit duties, house-tax, tax on animals, etc. The *sair-jihat* also included certain impositions, allowances or remunerations payable to certain local officials and grain merchants, etc.[19] We have collected the data and depicted in two tables (Tables 4.2 and 4.3).

Tables 4.2 and 4.3 show first, that the state income derived from *rabi,* was higher than the *kharif,* in almost all the *qasbas,* and second that the state income was mainly from *malo-jihat,*[20] which ranged between 65.27 and 98.93 per cent in *kharif,* and between 86.76 and 99.76 per cent in *rabi.* The income from *sair-jihat* was subordinate to it but not insignificant ranging from 1.06 to 34.73 per cent in *kharif* and between 0.24 and 13.26 per cent in *rabi.*[21]

The wide gap between the minimum and maximum income creates confusion, which could be dispelled by thorough analysis of the data of an individual *pargana.* Some important and pertinent points emerge from the analysis of these data. The income from *sair-jihat* in *qasba* Khatu under *rabi* comes to 13.26 per cent in AD 1724 and 12.97 per cent in AD 1759, and under *kharif* it is 13.26 per cent in AD 1724, and 30.17 per cent in AD 1759.[22] There is also interesting information about the same *pargana* where the ratio of *sair-jihat* under *kharif* comes to 34.73 per cent in AD 1760.[23] Similarly the proceeds from *sair-jihat* under *kharif* were over 30 per cent in the *qasba* Ramgarh in two years in VS 1821/AD 1764 and VS 1824/AD 1767. The income from the *rabi* crop is either negligible or not available.[24] The higher receipt from *sair-jihat* shows increase in the non-agrarian taxes. It may be inferred that these areas were developing the agrarian marts and earned the status of a *qasba.* Even here, we can say that the enormous availability of *malo-jihat* shows that most of the *qasbas* either had vast agricultural base or could be designated as semi-urban centres.

TABLE 4.2: STATE INCOME FROM *SYALU* (*KHARIF*)

Year	*Qasba*	Total amount of *kharif* in rupees	Amount of *Mal-o-Jihat* in rupees	(B) as *% of* (A)	Amount *Sair-Jihat* in rupees	(C) as % of (A)
		(A)	(B)	(%)	(C)	(%)
VS 1768/AD 1711	Amarsar	N.A.	N.A.	N.A.	N.A.	N.A.
VS 1769/AD 1712	Amarsar	N.A.	N.A.	N.A.	N.A.	N.A.
VS 1780/AD 1723	Khatu	N.A.	N.A.	N.A.	N.A.	N.A.
VS 1781/AD 1724	Khatu	924.00*	801.00	86.76	123.00	13.26
VS 1816/AD 1759	Khatu	948.00	662.00	69.83	286.00	30.17
VS 1820/AD 1763	Khatu	508.00	375.00	73.81	133.00	26.19
VS 1821/AD 1764	Khatu	N.A.	N.A.	N.A.	N.A.	N.A.
VS 1793/AD 1736	Manoharpur	N.A.	N.A.	N.A.	N.A.	N.A.
VS 1793/AD 1736	Shahpur	2706.00	2453.00	90.65	253.00	9.35
VS 1794/AD 1737(I)	Shahpur	3698.00	3414.00	92.32	284.00	7.68
VS 1794/AD 1737(II)	Shahpur	3701.00	3500.00	94.56	201.00	5.43
VS 1813/AD 1756	Gaori	N.A.	N.A.	N.A.	N.A.	N.A.
VS 1821/AD 1764	Gaori	N.A.	N.A.	N.A.	N.A.	N.A.
VS 1813/AD 1756	Kaawat	658.00	651.00	98.93	7.00	1.06
VS 1818/AD 1761	Kaawat	N.A.	N.A.	N.A.	N.A.	N.A.
VS 1821/AD 1764	Kaawat	340.00	292.00	85.88	48.00	14.11
VS 1816/AD 1759	Ramgarh	1131.00	1048.00	92.66	83.00	7.34
VS 1817/AD 1760	Ramgarh	740.00	667.00	90.14	73.00	9.86
VS 816/AD 1759	Khatu	550.00	359.00	65.27	191.00	34.73

contd.

TABLE 4.2 contd.

Year	*Qasba*	Total amount of *kharif* in rupees	Amount of *Mal-o-Jihat* in rupees	(B) as *% of* (A)	Amount *Sair-Jihat* in rupees	(C) as % of (A)
		(A)	(B)	(%)	(C)	(%)
VS 1820/AD 1763	Ramgarh	297.00	242.00	81.48	55.00	18.52
VS 1821/AD 1764	Ramgarh	209.00	146.00	69.85	63.00	30.15
VS 1824/AD 1767	Ramgarh	243.00	170.00	69.95	73.00	30.05
VS 1828/AD 1771	Ramgarh	258.00	N.A.	N.A.	N.A.	N.A.
VS 1828/AD 1771	Khatu	15.00	N.A.	N.A.	N.A.	N.A.
VS 1828/AD 1771	Reengus	70.00	N.A.	N.A.	N.A.	N.A.
VS 1824/AD 1767	Shrimadhopur	N.A.	N.A.	N.A.	N.A.	N.A.
VS 1824/AD 1767	Kaawat	N.A.	N.A.	N.A.	N.A.	N.A.
VS 1826/AD 1769	Kaawat	152.00	145.00	95.39	7.00	4.60
VS 1827/AD 1770	Shrimadhopur	N.A.	N.A.	N.A.	N.A.	N.A.
VS 1827AD 1770	Kaawat	157.00	137.00	87.26	20.00	12.74
VS 1827/AD 1770	Gaori	N.A.	N.A.	N.A.	N.A.	N.A.
VS 1844/AD 1787	Sikrai	N.A.	N.A.	N.A.	N.A.	N.A.
VS 1846/AD 1789	Sikrai	N.A.	N.A.	N.A.	N.A.	N.A.
VS 1864/AD 1807	Khandela	791.00	740.00	93.55	51.00	6.45

Note: *More than eight *annas* (*aath anna*) is converted into round figure one rupee while less than eight *annas* is converted into 0 rupee.

TABLE 4.3: STATE INCOME FROM *UNHALU* (*RABI*)

Year	*Qasba*	Total amount of *rabi* in rupees	Amount of *Mal-o-Jihat* in rupees	(B) as *% of* (A)	Amount *Sair-Jihat* in rupees	(C) as % of (A)
		(A)	(B)	(%)	(C)	(%)
VS 1768/AD 1711	Amarsar	N.A.	N.A.	N.A.	N.A.	N.A.
VS 1769/AD 1712	Amarsar	N.A	N.A.	N.A.	N.A.	N.A.
VS 1780/AD 1723	Khatu	3770.00	3618.00	95.96	152.00	4.03
VS 1781/AD 1724	Khatu	924.00	801.00	86.76	123.00	13.26
VS 1816/AD 1759	Khatu	2602.00	2265.00	87.02	337.00	12.97
VS 1820/AD 1763	Khatu	N.A.	N.A.	N.A.	N.A.	N.A.
VS 1821/AD 1764	Khatu	N.A.	N.A.	N.A.	N.A.	N.A.
VS 1793/AD 1736	Manoharpur	N.A.	N.A.	N.A.	N.A.	N.A.
VS 1793/AD 1736	Shahpur	4163.00	4153.00	99.76	10.00	0.24
VS 1794/AD 1737 (I)	Shahpur	4183.00	4169.00	99.67	14.00	0.33
VS 1794/AD 1737 (II)	Shahpur	4207.00	4193.00	99.67	14.00	0.33
VS 1813/AD 1756	Gaori	N.A.	N.A.	N.A.	N.A.	N.A.
VS 1821/AD 1764	Gaori	660.00	640.00	96.96	20.00	3.03
VS 1813/AD 1756	Kaawat	908.00	901.00	99.22	7.00	0.77
VS 1818/AD 1761	Kaawat	574.00	567.00	98.78	7.00	1.21
VS 1821/AD 1764	Kaawat	1000.00	930.00	93.00	7.06	7.00
VS 1816/AD 1759	Ramgarh	1943.00	1917.00	98.66	26.00	1.34
VS 1817/AD 1760	Ramgarh	801.00	775.00	96.75	26.00	3.25

contd.

TABLE 4.3 contd.

Year	*Qasba*	Total amount of *rabi* in rupees	Amount of *Mal-o-Jihat* in rupees	(B) as *% of* (A)	Amount *Sair-Jihat* in rupees	(C) as % of (A)
		(A)	(B)	(%)	(C)	(%)
VS 1818/AD 1761	Khatu	1469.00	1337.00	91.01	132.00	8.99
VS 1820/AD 1763	Ramgarh	2276.00	2259.00	99.25	17.00	0.75
VS 1821/AD 1764	Ramgarh	1441.00	1346.00	93.00	96.00	6.60
VS 1824/AD 1767	Ramgarh	N.A.	N.A.	N.A.	N.A.	N.A.
VS 1828/AD 1771	Ramgarh	250.00	N.A.	N.A.	N.A.	N.A.
VS 1828/AD 1771	Khatu	18.00	N.A.	N.A.	N.A.	N.A.
VS 1828/AD 1771	Reengus	100.00	N.A.	N.A.	N.A.	N.A.
VS 1824/AD 1767	Shrimadhopur	N.A.	N.A.	N.A.	N.A.	N.A.
VS 1824/AD 1767	Kaawat	166.00	159.00	95.79	7.00	4.21
VS 1824/AD 1767	Kaawat	N.A.	N.A.	N.A.	N.A.	N.A.
VS 1827/AD 1770	Shrimadhopur	N.A.	N.A.	N.A.	N.A.	N.A.
VS 1827/AD 1770	Kaawat	N.A.	N.A.	N.A.	N.A.	N.A.
VS 1827/AD 1770	Gaori	N.A.	N.A.	N.A.	N.A.	N.A.
VS 1844/AD 1787	Sikrai	N.A.	1995.69	N.A.	N.A.	N.A.
VS 1846/AD 1789	Sikrai	1672.00	1623.00	97.06	48.00	2.87
VS 1864/AD 1807	Khandela	579.00	560.00	96.71	19.00	3.29

Tables 4.4 and 4.5 have been compiled from the data contained in the revenue records on the state's share from individual crops under both *kharif* and *rabi* and the area under each crop in different *qasba* headquarters.

TABLE 4.4: QUANTITY AND AMOUNT UNDER *BATAI JINSI* (*KHARIF* & *RABI*)

Year/ *Qasba*	*Batai Jinsi-Syalu (Kharif)*			*Batai Jinsi-Unhalu (Rabi)*		
	Crops	Quantity (*mann*)	Amount in rupees	Crops	Quantity (*mann*)	Amount in rupees
VS 1816/	*Bajra*	350.23	355.00			
AD 1759	*Moth*	148.07	150.00			
(Khatu)	*Moong*	14.26	19.00			
	Gunwar	4.36	5.00			
VS 1793/	*Bajra*	275.12	344.00	*Jau*	2,563.36	2,868.50
AD 1736	*Moth*	2.36	4.00	*Gehoon*	8,25.26	1,269.50
(Shahpur)	*Moong*	14.39	25.00			
VS 1794/	*Bajra*	130.38	163.00			
AD 1737	*Makka*	1,141.16	1,288.00			
(Shahpur I)	*Cotton*	450.14	613.00			
	Moth	334.10	412.00			
	Moong	13.23	23.00			
	Chola	29.10	33.00			
	Gunwar	108.03	82.00			
	Til	0.03	00.15			
vs 1794/	*Gunwar*	108.30	83.00	*Jau*	4,297.26	3,157.00
ad 1737	*Til*	0.30	0.53	*Gehoon*	737.36	949.00
(Shahpur II)				*Chana*	8.14	14.00
vs 1813/	*Bajra*	62.11	188.00	*Jau*	233.08	455.00
ad 1756	*Moth*	26.38	89.80	*Gehoon*	94.38	271.29
(Kaawat)	*Chola*	52.18	161.28	*Gojai*	52.22	131.37
	Makka	8.32	28.19			
	Gunwar	5.25	9.00			
	Til	0.32	3.50			
	Saal	1.12	2.50			
VS 1821/	*Bajra*	46.30	37.14	*Jau*	745.34	382.50
AD 1764	*Moth*	228.37	157.87	*Gehoon*	143.37	99.25
(Kaawat)	*Makka*	14.00	9.33	*Gojai*	164.21	109.82
	Saal	67.21	65.82			

contd.

TABLE 4.4 contd.

Year/ *Qasba*	*Batai Jinsi-Syalu (Kharif)*			*Batai Jinsi-Unhalu (Rabi)*		
	Crops	Quantity (*mann*)	Amount in rupees	Crops	Quantity (*mann*)	Amount in rupees
	Til	0.3	0.56			
	Gunwar	0.16	0.48			
VS 1816/	*Bajra*	563.35	644.00	*Jau*	1,532.14	1,545.00
AD 1759	*Moth*	311.75	344.00	*Gehoon*	269.29	363.00
(Ramgarh)	*Moong*	20.9	25.00			
	Gunwar	16.33	12.00			
VS 1820/	*Bajra*	73.00	72.00	*Jau*	2,316.30	18.00
AD 1763	*Moth*	90.30	86.00	*Gehoon*	370.26	424.00
(Ramgarh)	*Moong*	27.20	30.00			
	Gunwar	2.37	2.00			
VS 1824/	N.A.	N.A.	N.A.	*Jau*	152.37	440.75
AD 1767				*Gojai*	103.30	334.75
(Kaawat)						
VS 1827/	*Bajra*	146.36	59.00			
AD 1770	*Chola*	129.00	41.50			
(Kaawat)						
VS 1844/	N.A.	N.A.	N.A.	*Jau*	1413.25	604.39
AD 1787				–	19.09	10.87
(Sikrai)				–	70.36	47.75
VS 1864/	*Bajra*	720.13	558.00	*Jau*	330.35	301.00
AD 1807	*Moth*	46.10	47.00	*Gehoon*	108.15	155.00
(Khandela)	*Moong*	37.20	42.00			
	Til	27.15	4.00			

Table 4.4 shows *bajra* and *moth* were produced in almost all the *qasbas* and the major state share came from these crops in *kharif*, while *jau* (barley) and *gehoon* form the major source of income in *rabi*. Interestingly, the peasants of almost all the *qasbas* produced *jau* extensively. It was used for different purposes as mentioned below:

(a) It was the staple food of the poorer classes in many parts of the country.[25]
(b) Seeds, malts, etc., of barley were used for medicinal and chemical purposes also.[26]

TABLE 4.5: *ZABTI* (*SYALU AND UNHALU*)

Year/ *Qasba*	Crops	Area in *bigha* and *biswa*	Amount in rupees	Remarks
VS 1816/	*Makka* (maize)	51.07	67.85	
AD 1759	*Mandavo*	5.10	9.18	
(Khatu)	*Chola*	1.10	1.12	
	Torai (veg)	2.01	4.50	
	Vani (cotton)	0.17	1.06	
	Carrot	3.07	6.87	
VS 1793/ AD 1736 (Shahpur)	Vegetables	79.31	157.00	Vegetables also available in *Unhalu* as area/ *bigha* = 5.10 and amount in Rs. 10.50
VS 1794/ AD 1737	*Varh* (sugar cane)	110.16	706.57	
(Shahpur I)	Vegetables	84.10	190.50	
	Shakarkand (sweet potato)	00.07	1.60	
	Seen	00.12	1.32	
	Dodi (opium)	1.00	2.00	
VS 1794/ AD 1737	*Vani* (cotton)	110.16	83.00	
(Shahpur II)	Vegetables	84.13	0.53	
	Carrot	191.19	142.00	
VS 1813/ AD 1756	*Gaajar* (carrot)	6.13	37.12	
(Kaawat)	*makka*	60.14	85.16	
	pyaaz (veg) (onion)	3.11	198.25	
VS 1821/	Carrot	2.24	162.25	
AD 1764	*Kaadapop*	1.24	137.25	
(Kaawat)	*Shakarkand*	0.10	2.24	
VS 1816/	*Makka*	3.00	2.93	
AD 1759	Cotton	13.07	12.75	
(Ramgarh)	*Torai* (veg)	4.00	0.25	
	Carrot	4.04	10.62	
VS 1820/	*Makka*	9.12	9.59	
AD 1763	*Mandavo*	16.21	18.87	
(Ramgarh)	*Vani*	9.14	9.71	
	Carrot	2.23	4.75	

contd.

TABLE 4.5 contd.

Year	Crops	Area in *bigha* and *biswa*	Amount in rupees	Remarks
VS 1827/	*Makka*	13.16	32.50	
AD 1770	*Torai*	0.08	1.75	
(Kaawat)				
VS 1844/	Wheat	217.22	974.43	This is an
AD 1787	*Jau*	32.14	129.81	information of
(Sikrai)	Vegetables	2.21	8.75	*unhalu*
	Tamakhoo (tobacco)	2.24	34.00	
VS 1864/	*Makka*	73.11	176.50	
AD 1807	Vegetables	6.00	18.75	
(Khandela)				

(c) Barley attracted considerable attention owing to its cheapness and value as fodder. The straw of even ripe barley is a fairly good fodder when cut up as *bhussa* (straw/husk) but is inferior to that of wheat.[27]

(d) The grain is much employed in parts of India and is being used for many domestic, industrial and other purposes.[28]

CASH CROPS

Vani, tambakhoo, shakarkand, varh, dodi including *saal* and *sabzi* were cash crops and most preferred by the peasants of Shekhawati. The areas under each crop is shown in Table 4.5, which shows *vani, varh, tambakhoo* and *sabzi* cultivation as cash crop in most of the *qasbas*. Table 4.1 also shows that *tambakhoo, varh, dodi, shakarkand, saal, seen* (a type of fodder) and *gaajar* were produced in some of the *qasbas*.[29] In Shahpur about 38 per cent of the total land recorded was under sugar cane in the year VS 1794/AD 1737,[30] while cotton acquired more than 40 per cent land in Ramgarh in VS 1816/AD 1759 adding VS 1820/AD 1763,[31] opium contributed few percentages in Shahpur. Table 4.1 also shows that tobacco was produced in the towns of Kawat and Sikarai in the years AD 1767 and 1787 respectively.[32] Vegetable cultivation covered almost all the *qasbas* and covered a sizeable portion of land. While *shakarkand* in Shahpur, *seen* in Shahpur and Sikarai, *saal* in Kawat and Sikarai, *gaajar* was produced in the towns of Khatu, Shahpur and Ramgarh.[33]

Makka (maize) was the main crop produced in *qasba* Ramgarh in VS 1816/AD 1759 and VS 1820/AD 1763,[34] while *mandavo* in *qasba* Khatu in VS 1816/AD 1759.[35]

The dominance of cotton, sugar cane, opium, tobacco, rice course, sweet potato, carrot and vegetables demonstrate the preference of peasants for cash crops.

The above work is based on a close scrutiny of the data contained in the *arhsattas*, which indicates that the *pargana* headquarters were primarily emerging as agrarian open markets. Subsequently these were acquiring the status of *qasbas.*

NOTES

1. James Tod, *Annals* and *Antiquities* of *Rajasthan*, vol. III, Humphrey Milford, Oxford University Press, London, 1920, pp. 1378-9.
2. Jaipur *Arzdasht*, VS 1762-75/AD 1705-18, p. 59 also see Raghunath Singh Kali Pahari, *Shekhwati Pradesh Ka Rajnitik Itihas Shekhwati Pradesh Ka Rajnitik Itihas*, Tha. Mallusingh Smriti Granthagar, Jhunjhunu, 1998, p. 1.
3. Wills Report, pp. 50-1, RSA, Bikaner.
4. Tod, vol. III, op. cit., pp. 1378-9.
5. See map of Shekhawati region.
6. *Arhsatta Pargana/Qasbas;* Amarsar, VS 1768/AD 1711, VS 1769/AD 1712; Khatu, VS 1780/AD 1723, VS 1781/AD 1724, VS 1816/AD 1759, VS 1817/AD 1760, VS 1818/AD 1761, VS 1820/AD 1763, VS 1821/AD 1764; Manoharpur, VS 1793/AD 1736; Shahpur, VS 1793/AD 1736; Gaori, VS 1813/AD 1756, VS 1821/AD 1764; Kaawat, VS 1813/AD 1756, VS 1818/AD 1761, VS 1821/AD 1764, VS 1824/AD 1767, VS 1826/AD 1769, VS 1827/AD 1770; Ramgarh, VS 1817/AD 1760, VS 1818/AD 1761; Reengus, VS 1828/AD 1771; Shrimadhopur, VS 1824/AD 1767, VS 1827/AD 1770; Sikarai, VS 1846/AD 1789; Khandela, VS 1862/AD 1805.
7. Ibid.

8. The meaning of *malo-jihat* is explained by S.P. Gupta, *The Agrarian System of Eastern Rajasthan (c. 1600-c. 1750)*, Manohar, New Delhi, 1986, pp. 145 and 153. Also see Irfan Habib, *Agrarian System of Mughal India*, 2nd revd. edn., Oxford University Press, New Delhi, 1999, pp. 283-4.
9. Habib, *Agrarian System of Mughal India*, op. cit., pp. 110 and 300 (also it has been explained in the context of Rajasthan by Gupta, *The Agrarian System of Eastern Rajasthan*, op. cit., p. 156).
10. The term is applied to the assessment in money on lands in which the more valuable products are raised as sugar cane, tobacco, cotton, vegetables and the like. See H.H. Wilson, *A Glossary of Judicial and Revenues Terms*, London, 1968, pp. 561-2.
11. A system of Assessment, Gupta, *The Agrarian System of Eastern-Rajasthan*, op. cit., pp. 39-40.
12. See map of Shekhawati.
13. Mountstuart Elphinstone, *An Account of the Kingdom of Caubul* [*Kabul*], Richard Bentley, London, 1839, vol. I, p. 5. [Elphinstone gives statement regarding the Shekhawati region after visiting different towns. On 21October, he entered Shekhawati region, on the 22 October, he reached Singhana, a handsome town. He marched from Jhoonjhunu to Churu and finally left the Shekhawati region. Conclusively he said that the Shekhawati region contains large towns.]
14. See map of Shekhawati.
15. *Arhsatta, pargana/qasbas*, op. cit.
16. Ibid.
17. *Qarar-ijara* denotes that number of *khalisa* villages or position of the villages. The revenue of which were farmed out. Gupta, *The Agrarian System of Eastern-Rajasthan*, op. cit., p. 145.
18. *Mal* seems to represent the original tax (land revenue). Gupta, *The Agrarian System of Eastern-Rajasthan*, op. cit., p. 145.
19. Gupta, p. 150.
20. *Arhsatta pargana/qasbas*, op. cit.
21. Ibid.
22. *Arhsatta pargana* Ramgarh (*qasba* Khatu), VS 1781/AD 1724, VS 1816/AD 1759.
23. Ibid.
24. *Arhsatta pargana/qasbas*, op. cit.
25. See Watt, *Dictionary*, pp. 282-4.
26. Ibid.
27. Ibid.
28. Ibid.

29. *Arhsatta pargana/qasbas,* op. cit.
30. *Arhsatta pargana* Manoharpur (*qasba* Shahpur), VS 1794/AD 1737.
31. *Arhsatta pargana* Ramgarh (*qasba* Ramgarh), VS 1816/AD 1759, VS 1820/AD 1763.
32. *Arhsatta pargana* Shrimadhopur (*qasba* Kaawat), VS 1816/AD 1759, *qasba* Sikarai, VS 1844/AD 1787.
33. *Arhsatta pargana/qasbas,* op. cit.
34. *Arhsatta qasba* Ramgarh, VS 1816/AD 1759 and VS 1820/AD 1763; *Arhsatta qasba,* Khatu, VS 1816/AD 1759.

CHAPTER 5

Sanganer: A Centre of Textile and Calico-printing in the Eighteenth Century

Sanganer, a famous textile centre of Rajasthan, has come a long way in mastering the art of textile printing and related works. A position which it still enjoys in the textile field, and has emerged as a great centre of textile printing and gained the recognition not only in Rajasthan and India but also in countries such as the USA, Canada, Mexico and in Europe. Thus, through exports it has become a huge earner of foreign exchange.

What were the factors that gave boost to the development of printing industry and artwork in this town? The study would be of great interest not only to the general public and art historians but even to those who are involved in works related with present-day textile manufacturing.

Sanganer is situated at a distance of about 13 km to the south of Jaipur. Its earlier name, as found in inscriptions and *prashastis,* were Sangrampura which is said to have been founded by Sanga, a Kachhwaha prince in the sixteenth century; but its antiquity goes beyond that period.[1] In 1561, Bharmal, the Kachhwaha chief, extended a warm welcome to the Mughal Emperor Akbar at this place, when he was going to Ajmer to pay homage to the shrine (*dargah*) of Khwaja Moinuddin Chishti.[2]

Later, in the sixteenth century Raja Man Singh of Amber had also developed close relation with Akbar and became one of his most trusted and loyal commanders.[3]

The Kachhwaha rulers of Jaipur took keen interest in the development of trade, commerce and industries in the eighteenth-nineteenth century and as a result, Sanganer emerged as one of the calico-printing centres. In the beginning of twentieth century almost all important towns of the State of Jaipur were well-connected by road and a few towns by train also. Jaipur is well connected with most important towns including Sanganer.[4] This strengthened the handicraft manufacturing industry here especially cotton and woollen-cloth, and the capital city in particular was highly developed.

A survey of the existing works on calico-printing and dyeing shows that the majority of scholars have highlighted the centres such as Surat, Dhaka, Chittagong, Sonargaon, Sironj and Chanderi but neglected Sanganer altogether because they mainly relied on Persian chronicles as well as accounts of European travellers. Even some other centres of Rajasthan find place in their writing but not the premier printing centre in eastern Rajasthan. To highlight the real significance and the role of this place in the calico-printing sector we have utilized the *arhsattas*, which offer information on crops, taxes on calico-printing with the names of calico printers and other professional groups. The data on 'cash crops' especially cotton and indigo are extremely useful to know the possibilities of growth of textile industry in the area.

An attempt has been made here to study the importance of agricultural production especially cotton and indigo and the tax collection under *sair-jihat* especially *chhapa*, in the *qasba* during the eighteenth-nineteenth centuries. An effort has also been made to establish a link between cotton and indigo production and the emergence of the *qasba*. The study is based exclusively on the examination of the *arhsattas*.[5] It is divided into three parts: Part I deals with agricultural production; part II with *sair-jihat* (non-agricultural) taxes; while part III deals the size of *qasba* Sanganer.

I

Our documents record the names and number of crops in Sanganer. The *arhsattas*[6] provide total amount of *syalu* and *unhalu* under the heads *mal-o-jihat* and *sair-jihat*. The comparison of the *hasil* figures of both *mal-o-jihat* and *sair-jihat* would show their importance in terms of cash-collection. The figures are depicted in Table 5.1 (also see Graph 5.1).

TABLE 5.1: THE PERCENTAGE OF *MAL-O-JIHAT* (*SYALU* + *UNHALU*) AND *SAIR-JIHAT* (*SYALU* + *UNHALU*) IN *QASBA* SANGANER

Year	Total amount (*Kharif* + *Rabi*) in rupees (A)	*Mal-o-Jihat* (*Kharif* + *Rabi*) in rupees (B)	(B) as % of (A)	*Sair-jihat* (*Kharif* + *Rabi*) in rupees (C)	(C) as % of (A)	Remarks
VS 1772/AD 1715	54,104.37	7,891.37	14.59	46,212.93	85.41	*Kharif* + *Rabi*
VS 1775/AD 1718	49,793.75	7,359.62	14.78	42,434.12	85.22	*Kharif* + *Rabi*
VS 1785/AD 1728	25,707.37	8,400.12	32.67	17,307.31	67.33	*Kharif* + *Rabi*
VS 1790/AD 1733	6,097.56	3,906.87	64.07	2,190.68	35.93	*Kharif* + *Rabi*
VS 1812/AD 1755	9,764.87	8,821.32	90.34	943.50	9.66	*Kharif* + *Rabi*
VS 1817/AD 1760	6,107.56	54,64,125	89.47	64,3132	10.53	*Kharif* + *Rabi*
VS 1820/AD 1763	7,344.42	6,589.99	89.73	754.43	10.27	*Kharif* + *Rabi*
VS 1825/AD 1768	7,621.07	6,909.74	90.66	711.83	9.34	*Kharif* + *Rabi*
VS 1827/AD 1770	7,870.37	6,872.51	87.32	997.74	12.68	*Kharif* + *Rabi*
VS 1828/AD 1771	8,591.75	7,530.87	87.65	1,060.89	12.35	*Kharif* + *Rabi*

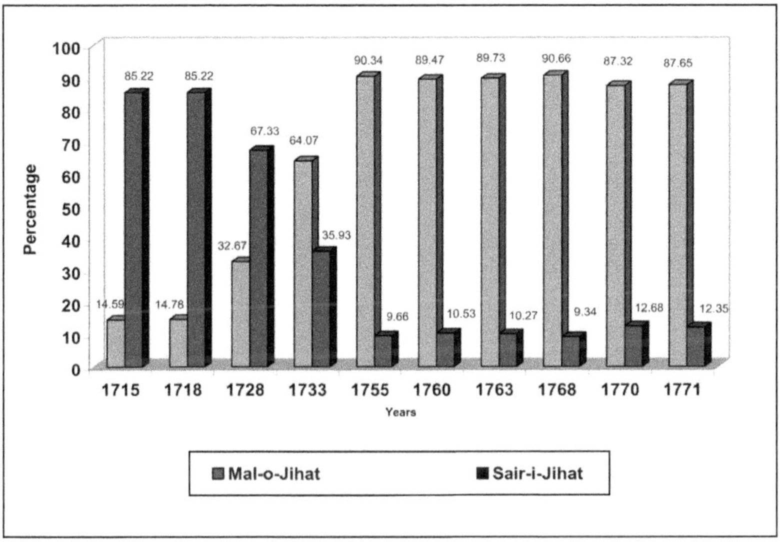

Graph 5.1: A Comparison of the Percentage of *Mal-o-Jihat* and *Sair-i-Jihat* in *Qasba* Sanganer

Table 5.1 shows clearly that the percentage of the *sair-jihat* was higher than the *mal-o-jihat* in VS 1772/AD 1715, VS 1775/AD 1718, VS 1785/AD 1728 and VS 1790/AD 1733 while it is lower in VS 1812/AD 1755, VS 1829/AD 1772, VS 1825/AD 1768, VS 1827/AD 1770 and VS 1828/AD 1771.

Similarly the comparison between the *hasil* figures from *rabi* and *kharif* would be interesting. The data is given in Table 5.2. Two points emerge from the table, that the state income derived from *rabi* was higher than that from *kharif* in seven out of ten years for *qasba* Sanganer and second, the state income was mainly from *zabti* in *kharif* and from *jinsi* in *rabi*.[7]

After studying Tables 5.1 and 5.2, we are able to say that the higher receipts from *sair-jihat* show increase in non-agrarian taxes. It may be inferred from it that the area was developing as an agrarian mart and earned the status of a *qasba*.[8] Besides this, we can say that the enormous collection under *malo-jihat* shows that the *qasba* developed as a food producing centre also.[9]

The *arhsatta* of *qasba* Sanganer shows the crop pattern. The crops

TABLE 5.2: PROPORTION OF REVENUE FROM *KHARIF* AND *RABI* HARVESTS IN *QASBA* SANGANER

Year	% of Total Revenue		% of *Kharif* Revenue		% of *Rabi* Revenue	
	Kharif	*Rabi*	*Zabti*	*Jinsi*	*Zabti*	*Jinsi*
1	2	3	4	5	6	7
VS 1772/ AD 1715	81.01	18.99	76.14	23.86	54.37	45.63
VS 1775/ AD 1718	67.01	32.99	72.09	27.91	27.11	72.89
VS 1785/ AD 1728	48.67	51.33	92.93	7.07	19.59	80.41
VS 1790/ AD 1733	85.84	14.36	95.35	4.66	NA	NA
VS 1812/ AD 1755	33.32	66.68	95.95	4.05	14.60	85.40
VS 1817/ AD 1760	32.58	67.42	74.61	25.39	19.49	80.51
VS 1820/ AD 1763	27.34	72.66	93.67	5.77	17.44	77.69
VS 1825/ AD 1768	32.14	67.86	86.54	3.11	18.32	74.39
VS 1827/ AD 1770	41.25	58.75	94.07	5.93	18.84	70.74
VS 1828/ AD 1771	37.46	62.54	93.30	5.28	12.68	78.32

assessed under *kharif*[10] numbered approximately 20 while as many as 16 were under *rabi*[11] with five crops common to both the harvests.[12]

The data on revenue derived from different crops both in the *kharif* and *rabi* are shown in Tables 5.3(a) and 5.3(b). The crops assessed under *kharif* are: *makka* (maize), *mandawa, vani* (cotton), *varh* (sugar cane), vegetables, *moth, urd, bajra* (millet) and *neel* (indigo); while crops under *rabi* are: oilseed, *dodi* (opium), *makka,* vegetables, *jau* (barley), *gehoon* (wheat), sugar cane and *gojarau.*[13]

TABLE 5.3(a): PERCENTAGE OF REVENUE DERIVED FROM DIFFERENT CROPS IN *QASBA* SANGANER *KHARIF (ZABTI + JINSI)*

Crops	VS 1772/ AD 1715	VS 1775/ AD 1718	VS 1785/ AD 1728	VS 1790/ AD 1733	VS 1812/ AD 1755	VS 1817/ AD 1760	VS 1820/ AD 1763	VS 1825/ AD 1768	VS 1827/ AD 1770	VS 1828/ AD 1771
Makka (maize)	10.43	28.81	17.14	29.32	38.16	13.45	11.41	5.05	6.17	11.68
Mandava	6.24	20.89	4.96	18.78	9.88	13.06	4.97	1.41	2.48	4.39
Vani (cotton)	26.97	28.19	53.27	21.05	13.55	25.51	49.66	19.31	30.95	4.11
Varh (sugar cane)	48.25	13.41	6.74	9.15	22.40	9.40	1.39	28.79	33.12	39.46
Baigan (brinjal)	0.87	0.82	1.22	4.95	6.06	12.73	–	11.56	6.75	–
Sakarkand (sweet potato)	2.75	1.20	8.38	11.11	3.08	2.19	–	–	–	–
Sabzi (vegetable)	4.26	6.20	6.64	5.22	3.61	12.10	–	6.25	3.77	4.27
Karela (vegetable)	0.23	0.36	0.07	0.19	–	–	–	–	–	–
Tambakhoo (tobacco)	–	0.08	–	–	–	–	–	–	–	–
Guwar	–	–	–	0.18	2.60	7.20	–	3.32	2.88	5.17
Jowari (millet)	–	–	–	–	–	2.39	–	–	–	–
Bajra (millet)	6.77	26.17	–	–	–	10.36	–	2.34	38.54	10.48
Moth (pulse)	15.05	11.16	46.52	46.63	25.42	68.14	65.35	92.68	40.39	72.93
Urd (pulse)	3.77	7.09	14.15	15.47	–	14.40	34.16	4.34	21.27	13.05
Moong (kidney beans)	1.02	0.22	7.03	–	–	7.11	–	–	–	3.65
Guwar	0.53	2.72	20.93	6.48	–	–	–	–	–	–
Til (sesamum)	0.02	0.21	–	–	–	–	–	–	–	–
Neel (indigo)	–	–	–	25.87	–	8.39	4.82	–	–	–
Singhara (water chest nut)	27.21	1.73	9.43	3.20	–	–	–	–	–	–
Saal (rice coarse)	–	–	–	2.67	–	–	1.28	–	0.57	0.49
Chola	0.06	–	–	–	–	–	–	–		–
Neelvarhi (indigo)	72.78	50.69	–	–	–	–	–	–	–	–
Saavan	–	–	–	–	–	–	–	–	–	–
Arai (vegetable)	–	–	–	–	–	–	1.97	4.22	2.68	1.97

TABLE 5.3(b): PERCENTAGE OF REVENUE DERIVED FROM DIFFERENT CROPS IN *QASBA* SANGANER *RABI (ZABTI + JINSI)*

Crops	VS 1772/ AD 1715	VS 1775/ AD 1718	VS 1785/ AD 1728	VS 1790/ AD 1733	VS 1812/ AD 1755	VS 1817/ AD 1760	VS 1820/ AD 1763	VS 1825/ AD 1768	VS 1827/ AD 1770	VS 1828/ AD 1771
Sarso (mustard) *Gajar* (carrot) *Rai* (oil seed)	–	27.06	36.30	–	52.31	60.75	48.57	45.96	30.20	32.51
Dodi (opium)	7.71	19.32	20.28	–	0.21	–	6.55	0.81	–	10.53
Makka (maize)	3.62	6.79	3.37	–	10.62	4.82	2.02	11.32	12.15	10.25
Tarbooz/Baigan/ Sabzi (veg.)	35.28	45.96	37.57	–	28.60	–	–	0.62	–	1.97
Kakari (veg.)	–	–	–	–	–	–	–	–	–	–
Methi (veg.) *Sarso* (mustard) *Seen* (veg.) *Gajar* (carrot)	51.51	–	–	–	–	–	–	–	–	–
Tambakhoo (tobacco)	1.02	–	2.76	–	1.15	0.61	–	–	–	–
Cheena (veg.)	0.09	–	–	–	0.22	–	–	–	–	–
Koda/ Ajwain	–	–	–	–	2.96	–	3.88	0.26	17.05	–
Patan (fibre)	–	–	–	–	–	–	–	–	–	–
Jau (barley)	72.13	60.04	60.27	58.99	63.03	46.90	48.14	21.44	27.82	25.12
Gehoon (wheat)	26.40	20.59	6.84	2.63	13.99	14.95	22.82	31.24	18.08	6.83
Chana (gram)	0.67	–	13.53	–	–	–	–	16.34	–	–
Bajra (millet)	–	–	–	–	–	–	–	–	–	–
Sarso/vegetable/*Karela*	–	–	–	–	–	3.11	6.08	3.79	6.61	4.84
Gojarau	0.81	19.41	12.82	–	22.98	27.47	29.05	16.39	–	21.83
Besuri	–	–	6.52	38.43	–	6.96	–	5.18	15.26	31.04
Varh (sugar cane)	–	–	–	–	–	–	21.31	34.57	34.04	39.86
Gochani	–	–	–	–	–	–	–	9.43	2.54	6.83

CASH CROPS

The 'cash crops' of modern classification are practically identical with that in Mughal records and are termed *jins-i-kamil* or *jins-i-ala*[14] 'high grade crops', chiefly grown for the market. Cotton and sugar cane were the major crops belonging to this category.[15] Besides these two, others were: opium, indigo, tobacco, oilseed, and vegetables.[16] In Sanganer nine crops in *kharif* and *rabi* were assessed under *zabti* namely; cotton, sugar cane, sweet potato, vegetables, tobacco, indigo, vegetables *(singhara)*, mustard and opium.[17] The dominance of the production of cotton, indigo, opium, tobacco and sugar cane, etc. demonstrates the preference of peasants for 'cash crops' which indicates the emergence of Sanganer primarily as an open commercial mart and acquiring the status of a *qasba*.

Cotton was produced in large quantities in Sanganer. The revenue derived from the crop is given in Table 5.3(a). The revenue percentage of the crop to that of the total income is worked out which ranged between 4.11 and 53.27 per cent.[18] The lowest 4.11 per cent was for VS 1828/AD 1771 which may have been a famine year. The higher percentage of tax collection from cotton shows potentialities of the development of textile industry in the area.

INDIGO

The *arhasattas* of Sanganer recorded *indigo* cultivation in the *qasba* only for three years. The revenue income from it ranged between 4.82 and 72.78 per cent[19] in the years between VS 1772/AD 1715 and VS 1828/AD 1771.[20] The dyers of Sanganer were using indigo from other places, probably from Bayana. The revenue income from indigo shows its importance and usefulness forlocal dyers.

The *arhsattas* also contains information on opium cultivation for seven years.[21] The revenue income ranged between 0.21 and 20.28 per cent in the years between VS 1772/AD 1715 and VS 1828/ AD 1771.[22]

II

The non-agricultural taxes designated as *sair-jihat* are important for the study of the non-agrarian sector. Keeping in view the importance of *sair-jihat* an attempt has been made in this part to utilize them to trace the development of handicrafts and other industries in *qasba* Sanganer. Craft production for the market seems to have been largely organized in two forms: first, as domestic industry in varying degrees of association with agriculture; and second, as full-fledged autonomous production, mainly in the towns.[23]

Cotton was produced in sufficient quantity in the *qasba* in the eighteenth century.[24] This in turn promoted manufacturing of cotton cloths here. Mention may also be made here of the weaving, dyeing, and printing of cloths which were important branches of the industry in the town.[25] The people were very fond of wearing colour fast cloths such as red, saffron, blue and black.[26] Blue colour was made by dyeing with indigo, which was produced in *qasba* Sanganer itself. The town was renowned for its tie and dye work: *chundaris* and *lahariyas.* There was a great demand for tie and dye work throughout northern India. In chintz production the names of Sanganer and Bagru had by then acquired the status of trade-mark.[27] Fateh Mohammad and Dost Mohammad, as has been mentioned in *arhsatta karkhanazat,* were famous calico printers of Jaipur.[28] *Chhinpas* lived in the *qasba* in large numbers.[29]

The *arhsattas* contain valuable information on *sair-jihat,* i.e. *hasil chhapa, hasil bhet, hasil arairooi, hasil paina, hasil tulai* and *va rooi amal khalsa,* etc. It is important to know the proportion of income from dyeing- related industries.[30] The data is given in Table 5.4.

The documents throw light on prominent *sahukars* such as Sahu Durgadas and Sahu Amarchand in VS 1772/AD 1715;[31] Sahu Ramchand Sobhachand and Sahu Ramchand Man Rai in VS 1775/AD 1718;[32] who were engaged in the collection of revenue from the dyers on dyeing and printing. These taxes were known as *chhapa* (printing), *arai rooi* (raw cotton), *paina* (water), *tulai* (weighing) and *rooi* (cotton).[33] The total revenue from *sair-jihat* collected in the year AD 1715 comes to Rs. 46,213 in round figure,[34] of which Rs. 29,020 came from *Chautra qasba.*[35] Under this head the collection was made from various items such as *chhapa* (printing),

TABLE 5.4: *SAIR-JIHAT* IN *QASBA* SANGANER

Year	Total amount of *Sair-Jihat* in rupees (A)	Collected amount *Chautra Qasba* in rupees (B)		*Baqi Muqarrara Jama Bandi* in rupees (C)		Item of *Sair-Jihat* (in *Chautra Qasba*): Item (D)	Value (E)	(E) as % of (B)
VS 1772/ AD 1715	46,213 (*Kharif* + *Rabi*)	29,020	62.80%	17,193	37.20%	*CHAUTRA QASBA*	29,020	
						1. Amal Sahu Durgadas	626	2.16
						2. Amal Sahu Amarchand	28,394	97.84
						HASIL BHET	8	0.03
						Amal Amarchand	8	0.03
						HASIL CHHAPA (Jama month-12)	9,272	31.95
						1. Amal Sahu Durgadas	126	0.43
						2. Amal Sahu Amarchand	9,146	31.52
						HASIL ARAI ROOI	3,383	11.66
						1. Amal Sahu Durgadas	6	0.02
						2. Amal Sahu Amarchand	3,377	11.64
						HASIL PAINA	3,981	13.72
						1. Amal Sahu Durgadas	300	1.03
						2. Amal Sahu Amarchand	3,681	12.69
						HASIL TULAI	6,530	22.50
						1. Amal Sahu Durgadas	266	0.92
						2. Amal Sahu Amarchand	6.264	21.58
						VA ROOI AMAL KHALSA	355	1.22
						1. Amal Sahu Durgadas	1	0.003
						2. Amal Sahu Amarchand	354	1.22
						Miscellaneous (Name of the *sahukars* are not mentioned)	5,501	18.96

contd.

TABLE 5.4 contd.

Year	Total amount of *Sair-Jihat* in rupees (A)	Collected amount *Chautra Qasba* in rupees (B)		*Baqi Muqarrara Jama Bandi* in rupees (C)		Item of *Sair-Jihat* (in *Chautra Qasba*): Item (D)	Value (E)	(E) as % of (B)
VS 1775/ AD 1718	42,434 (*Kharif* + *Rabi*)	30,323	71.46%	12,111	28.54%	1. Amal Ramchand Sobhachand	3,247	7.65
						2. Amal Ramchand Man Rai		
						CHAUTRA QASBA	39,187	92.35
						1. Amal Ramchand Sobhachand	30,323	
						2. Amal Ramchand Man Rai	1,954	6.44
						HASIL BHET		
						1. Amal Ramchand Sobhachand	28,369	93.56
						2. Amal Ramchand Man Rai	4	0.01
						HASIL CHHAPA	–	–
						(Jama month-12)		
						1. Amal Ramchand Sobhachand	4	0.01
						2. Amal Ramchand Man Rai	4,164	13.73
						HASIL ARAI ROOI		
						1. Amal Ramchand Sobhachand	385	1.27
						2. Amal Ramchand Man Rai		
						HASIL PAINA	3,779	12.46
						1. Amal Ramchand Sobhachand	2,530	8.34
						2. Amal Ramchand Man Rai	28	0.09

						HASIL TULAI		
						1. Amal Ramchand Sobhachand	2,502	8.25
						2. Amal Ramchand Man Rai	4,273	14.09
						VA ROOI	488	1.61
						1. Amal Ramchand Sobhachand		
						2. Amal Ramchand Man Rai	3,785	12.48
						Miscellaneous	617	2.03
						(Names of the *sahukars* are		
						not mentioned)	72	0.24
							545	1.79
							506	1.67
							1	0.003
							505	1.67
							18,229	60.12
VS 1785/	17,307	14,124	81.61%	3,183	18.39%	*CHAUTRA QASBA*	14,124	
AD 1728	(*Kharif* + *Rabi*)					*Hasil bhet*	1	0.007
						Hasil chhapa	7,769	55.01
						Hasil arai rooi	52	0.36
						Hasil paina	–	–
						Hasil tulia	1,874	13.27
						Va rooi	–	–
						Miscellaneous	4,428	31.35

arai rooi (raw cotton), *paina* (water), *tulai* (weighing) and *rooi* (cotton). The revenue from *chhapa* constituted 31.95 per cent of the total collection. It is followed by *tulai* (22.50 per cent), *paina* (13.72 per cent), *arai rooi* (11.66 per cent) and *rooi* (1.22 per cent) and other miscellaneous taxes whose revenue comes to 18.90 per cent.[36] The percentage of these taxes vary in different years.[37] It indicates that the dyeing and textile industries were flourishing and that the revenue collected from *chhapa* was higher than the other items related to dyeing and printing.

III

The study of pre-census urban population is an interesting theme which is attracting the attention of urban historians and economists alike. Direct data on population count before 1881 are elusive. Therefore scholars have adopted different methods to estimate the population of that period. Pioneer among them is Moreland.[38] His methods were refined by Irfan Habib[39] and later on Shireen Moosvi.[40] S.P. Gupta[41] and B.L. Bhadani[42] have worked out the urban population of Marwar on the basis of house as well as plough-count. The researches by the above scholars prove that the different kinds of data on taxes, military, house-plough count and agricultural productivity can be used to have the population estimates.

Sanganer is a *qasba* near Jaipur occupying an important place as an industrial centre in Rajasthan. It had earned a name in the field of textile printing. Large amount of material is available in the form of *arhsattas*[43] which furnish information on tax collection under different heads. The evidence on tax appropriation from the different castes settled in different *pattis* (see Map 5.1). These data can be utilized to estimate the population of those castes in Sanganer.

The *qasba* Sanganer consists of eight *pattis.*[44] The total castes (individuals) recorded comes to one hundred seventy-nine, which are as follows; Mewati (20), Kumbhar (35), Jat-Ahir (22), Vakaichi (16), Jodha (6), Baghara (2), Mali (74) and Gujar (4).[45] The total amount realized from these castes (individuals) comes to Rs. 1,055.[46] The details are given in Table 5.5.

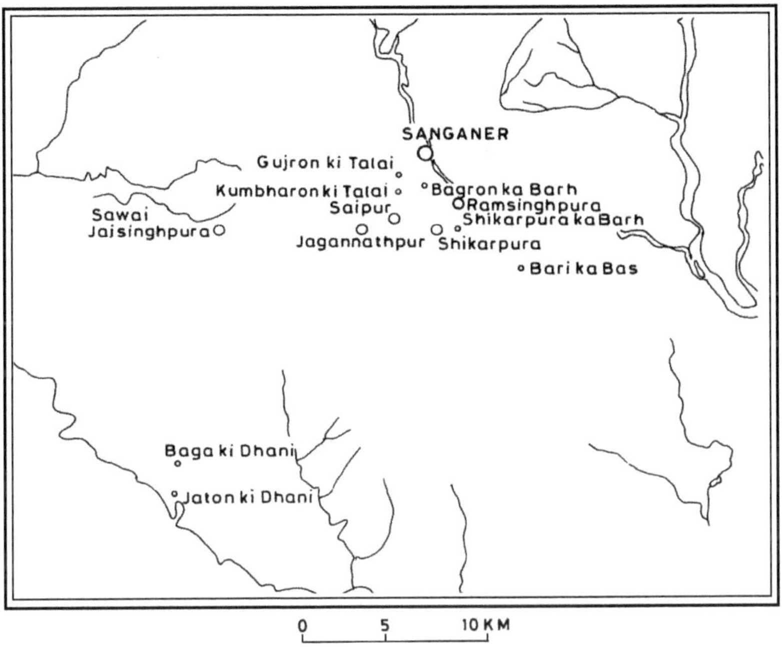

Map 5.1: *Pattis* of *Qasba* Sanganer (Eighteenth Century)

TABLE 5.5: POPULATION OF THE CASTE IN THE *PATTIS* OF *QASBA* SANGANER

Name of the *pattis* with caste	Total Individual	Population (total individual multiplied by 5 which is assumed figure)
Patti Mewati	20	100
Patti Kumbhar	35	175
Patti Jat-Ahir	22	110
Patti Vakaichi	16	80
Patti Jodha	6	30
Patti Bagara	2	10
Patti Mali	74	370
Patti Gujar	04	20
Total	179	895

It would not be unreasonable to assume that a tax-payee was an individual and was headman (owner) of his family. It is generally believed by the demographers that one household contains five persons.[47] If we multiply the number of individuals by this rate (5), then practically we could obtain the population of the entire *qasba*.

Qasba Sanganer consisted of different *pattis* (see Map 5.1). Table 5.5 clearly shows the population of different castes in the different *pattis*. In *patti* Mewati, the total population comes to 100 (20 × 5), others are as follows: *patti* Kumbhar 175 (35 × 5), *patti* Jat-Ahir 110 (22 × 5), *patti* Vakaichi 80 (16 × 5), *patti* Jodha 30 (6 × 5), *patti* Bagara 10 (2 × 5), *patti* Mali 370 (74 × 5) and *patti* Gujar 20 (4 × 5). Of these the dominant *patti* of the composition of caste is *patti* Mali and the lowest is *patti* Bagara. While the total population of *pattis* comes to 895.[48]

Further, Table 5.6 is prepared to know the real dominating position of the caste on the basis of available caste population data in the year VS 1812/AD 1755.[49] Its details are shown in Table 5.6.

From Table 5.6, it is clear which caste is in a dominating position from all the *pattis* in the said *qasba*. The dominating caste was

TABLE 5.6: POPULATION AND PERCENTAGE OF DIFFERENT CASTES IN THE *PATTIS* OF *QASBA* SANGANER

Name of the caste	Total no. of the caste and percentage		Population multiplied by 5 (assumed conventional figure)	
	No.	%	No.	%
Mewati	13	7.26	65	7.26
Kumbhar	21	11.73	105	11.73
Jat-Ahir	5	2.79	25	2.79
Mali	92	51.41	460	51.41
Gujar	5	2.79	25	2.79
Miscellaneous	43	24.02	215	24.02
Total	179	100	895	100

Mali[50] with 51.41 per cent followed by Kumbhars (11.73 per cent), Mewati (7.26 per cent), Gujars and Jat-Ahir (2.79 per cent) each whereas the total miscellaneous castes were 24.02 per cent.[51]

After an examination of the two tables (Tables 5.5 and 5.6), we are in position to say about *qasba* Sanganer that location of *pattis* shows the size of the town. Beyond this, we cannot say much at this point of time. More evidence would enable us to study it in more detail.

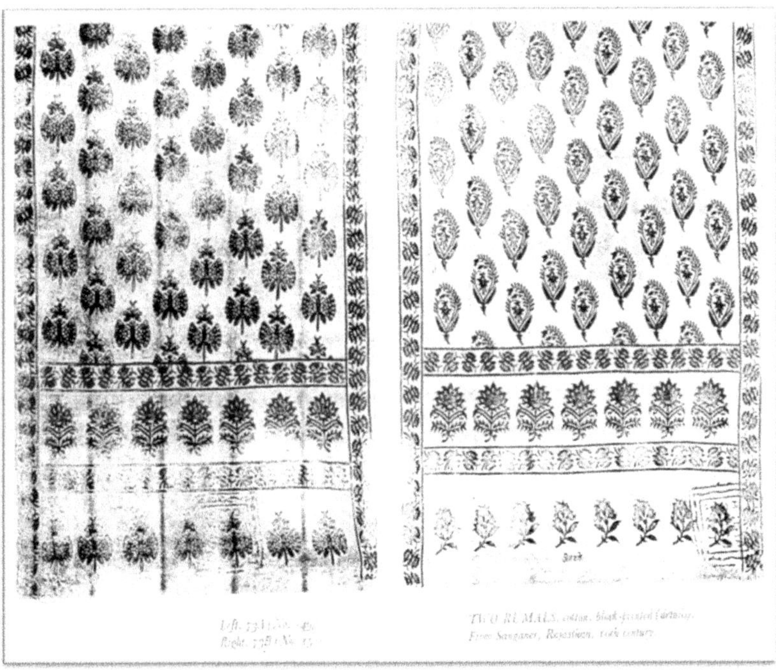

Figure 5.1: Two *Rumals*, Cotton, Block-printed (details) from Sanganer, Rajasthan, Eighteenth Century

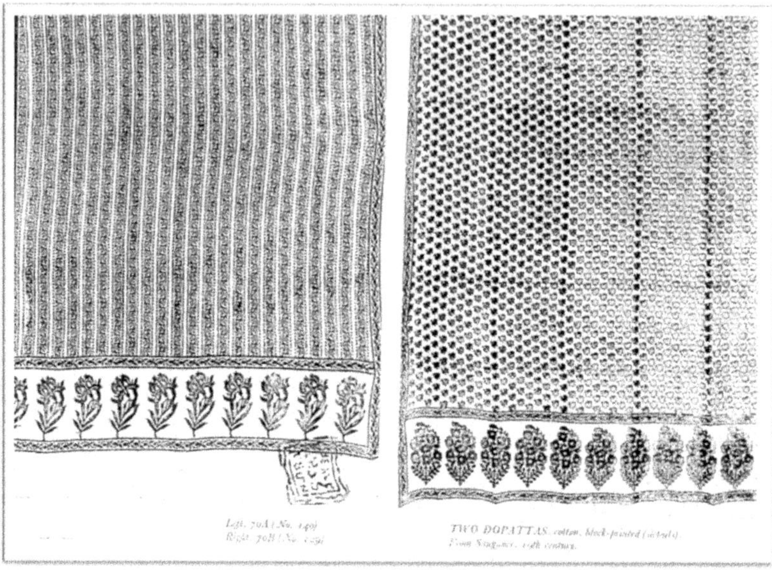

Figure 5.2: Two *Dupattas*, Cotton, Block-printed (details) from Sanganer, Rajasthan, Eighteenth Century

NOTES

1. K.C. Jain, *Ancient Cities and Towns of Rajasthan*, Motilal Banarsidass, Delhi, 1972, p. 455.
2. Abul Fazl, *Akbarnama*, translated into English by H. Beveridge, vol. II, rpt., Low Price Publication, Delhi, 1993, pp. 510-11.
3. John Irwin and Margret Hall, *Indian Painted and Printed Fabrics*, vol. I, Calico Museum, Ahmadabad, 1971, p. 110, cf. R.N. Prasad, *Raja Man Singh of Amber*, World Publication, Calcutta, 1966, pp. 106-19.
4. *Rajasthan District Gazetteers*, ed. Savitri Gupta, Government of Rajasthan, Jaipur, 1987, pp. 318-19.
5. *Arhsatta mujmali*, and *Arhsatta ek harfi*, *Arhsatta* of different years of Sanganer. VS 1772/AD 1715, VS 1775/AD 1718, VS 1785/AD 1728, VS 1750/AD 1733, VS 1812/AD 1755, VS 1817/AD 1760, VS 1820/AD 1763, VS 1825/AD 1768, VS 1827/AD 1770, VS 1828/AD 1771.
6. *Arhsatta qasba* Sanganer, VS 1772/AD 1715.
7. Ibid.
8. Ibid.
9. *Arhsatta qasba* Sanganer, VS 1812/AD 1755.

10. See different years of *Arhsattas* of *qasba* Sanganer, op. cit.
11. Ibid.
12. Ibid.
13. Ibid.
14. These two terms are very frequently encountered in the revenue literature of the period from the *Ain* onwards, but the sense seems everywhere to have been regarded as self-evident, Khafi Khan classifies crops as *jins-i-ghalla* (food grains) and *jins-i-ala* such as sugar cane, etc. (I, 156, 735n. In a late eighteenth-century *glossary* of revenue terms (MS Add. 6603, f. 57a) the *jins-i-kamil* is stated to include sugar cane, betel leaf, cotton, etc., as distinct from the *jins-i-adna* defined as crops fetching low prices, such as the various kinds of millets. See Irfan Habib, *The Agrarian System of Mughal India*, Oxford University Press, New Delhi, 1999, p. 43.
15. Ibid.
16. *Arhsatta qasba* Sanganer, op. cit.
17. Ibid.
18. Ibid.
19. 72.78 per cent value is for *neelvarhi* (bundle of indigo a type of indigo called *gatth* of *neel*).
20. *Arhsatta qasba* Sanganer, op. cit.
21. *Arhsatta qasba* Sanganer, VS 1772/AD 1715, VS 1775/AD 1718, VS 1785, AD 1728, VS 1812/AD 1755, VS 1820/AD 1763, VS 1825/AD 1768 and VS 1828/AD 1771.
22. Ibid.
23. B.L. Bhadani, *Peasants, Artisan and Entrepreneur: Economy of Mewar in the 17th Century*, Rawat Publications, Jaipur, 1999, p. 360.
24. *Arhsatta qasba* Sanganer, op. cit.
25. *Rajasthan District Gazetteers*, Jaipur, op. cit., p. 318.
26. B.L. Gupta, *Trade and Commerce in Rajasthan during 18th Century*, Jaipur Publishing House, Jaipur, 1987, p. 57. [The saffron colour was dyed with the flower of a tree named *kasooli* the red with a kind of timber dust named *kasoomb*. Whereas, blue was dyed with indigo]. Indigo was being very much produced in Sanganer. See different years of *Arhsattas* of Sanganer, op. cit.]
27. Gupta, *Trade and Commerce in Rajasthan during 18th Century*, op. cit., p. 57.
28. *Arhsatta karkhanazat (chhapa khana), Bhadrapad Sudi* 3, VS 1794/AD 1737; Jaipur records available in RSA, Bikaner. Also see Sumbul Halim Khan, *Art and Craft Workshops under the Mughals: A Study of Jaipur Karkhanas*, Primus Books, New Delhi, 2015.
29. *Arhsatta karkhanazat* (*chhapa khana*), VS 1823/AD 1766.

30. *Arhsatta qasba* Sanganer, op. cit.
31. Ibid., VS 1772/AD 1715.
32. Ibid., VS 1775/AD 1718.
33. *Arhsatta qasba* Sanganer, op. cit.
34. Ibid., VS 1772/AD 1715.
35. Ibid.
36. Ibid.
37. *Arhsatta qasba* Sanganer, VS 1772/AD 1715; VS 1775 AD 1718 and VS 1785/AD 1728.
38. The pioneer attempt was made many decades ago by W.H. Moreland, *India at the Death of Akbar*, Low Price Publications, Delhi, rpt., 1962 (1990), p. 21.
39. *Cambridge Economic History of India*, vol. I, ed. Tapan Raychaudhuri and Irfan Habib, op. cit.
40. Shireen Moosvi, 'Production Consumption and Population in Akbar's Time', *IESHR*, vol. X, no. 2, 1973, pp. 181-95.
41. S.P. Gupta, 'Evidence for Urban Population and its Composition from the 17th-18th Century Rajasthan', *Proceedings of Indian History Congress* (hereafter, *PIHC*), Calicut, 1976, pp. 179-80.
42. Bhadani, *Peasants, Artisans and Entrepreneurs*, op. cit., pp. 20-33. Also see his article 'Population of Marwar in the Second Half of the Seventeenth Century', *IESHR*, vol. XIV, no. 4, pp. 115-27.
43. *Arhsatta qasba* Sanganer, VS 1812/AD 1755.
44. Ibid.
45. Ibid.
46. Ibid.
47. Scholars assumed this figure for the estimation of population. For instance; James Tod assumed this figure 4 and 5; S.P. Gupta and B.L. Bhadani both assume this conventional figure 4.5 for the estimation of population to the region of Marwar. Author of the book finally adopted 5 as a conventional (assumed) figure for the estimation of population.
48. *Arhsatta qasba* Sanganer, VS 1812/AD 1755.
49. Ibid.
50. Ibid. (presence of Malis in a large number and in dominating position shows their significance in the economic set up and we could say that they were not only gardeners but were involved in agriculture and could call them as 'agriculturist castes'.
51. *Arhsatta qasba* Sanganer, VS 1812/AD 1755.

APPENDIX 5.1

Qasba Sanganer: Sample of *Arhsatta* Documents

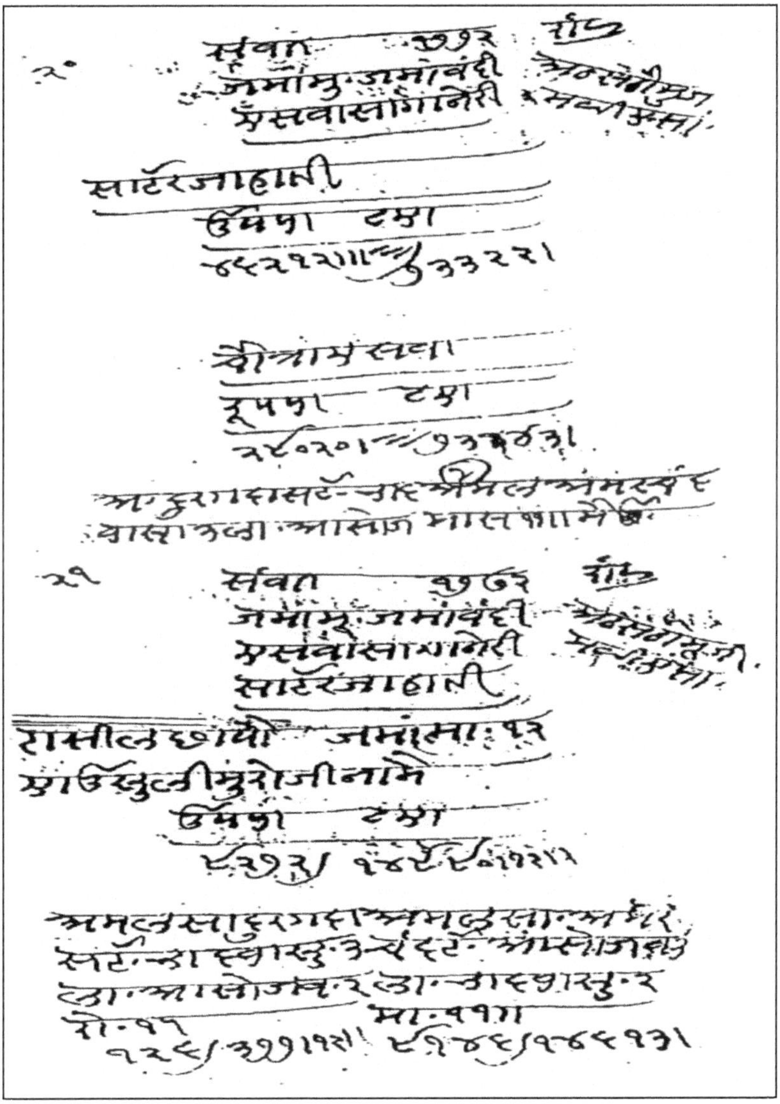

१० संवत १७७२ सं॰

जमा मुजमा अठस्योमुज

वंदी जमा सत्तीआसो

मुसवासगावेरी

रुपया टका

५६१०४।ना ७३७३८१२॥

मालजराती

रुपया टका

७९८१।ना ४१५८८०

११ संवत १७७२ सं॰

जमामु. जमावदी अठस्यौमु

मुसवासागावेरी सत्मलमुसा

मालजारातीफू

जमा परिजवनी म्हाणे

बी.पा॥३८ बी.पा॥१८ बीघ्या॥३ बीघ्या७५८

मा॥ ८० ४॥८० रु.मा॥ ८० रु. ७॥८०

५ ६॥ ६॥ ७

बीघा॥८ बीघा२९॥३ बीघा२९ २८

रु.पा॥ ८० रु.पा॥ ८० रु.१॥ ८०

२१॥ ४९॥॥ २९५

बाकिनीघ्या ६१॥३८ बाकीबीघा ५२६१

८०

१३१२॥ २३८९८

१६

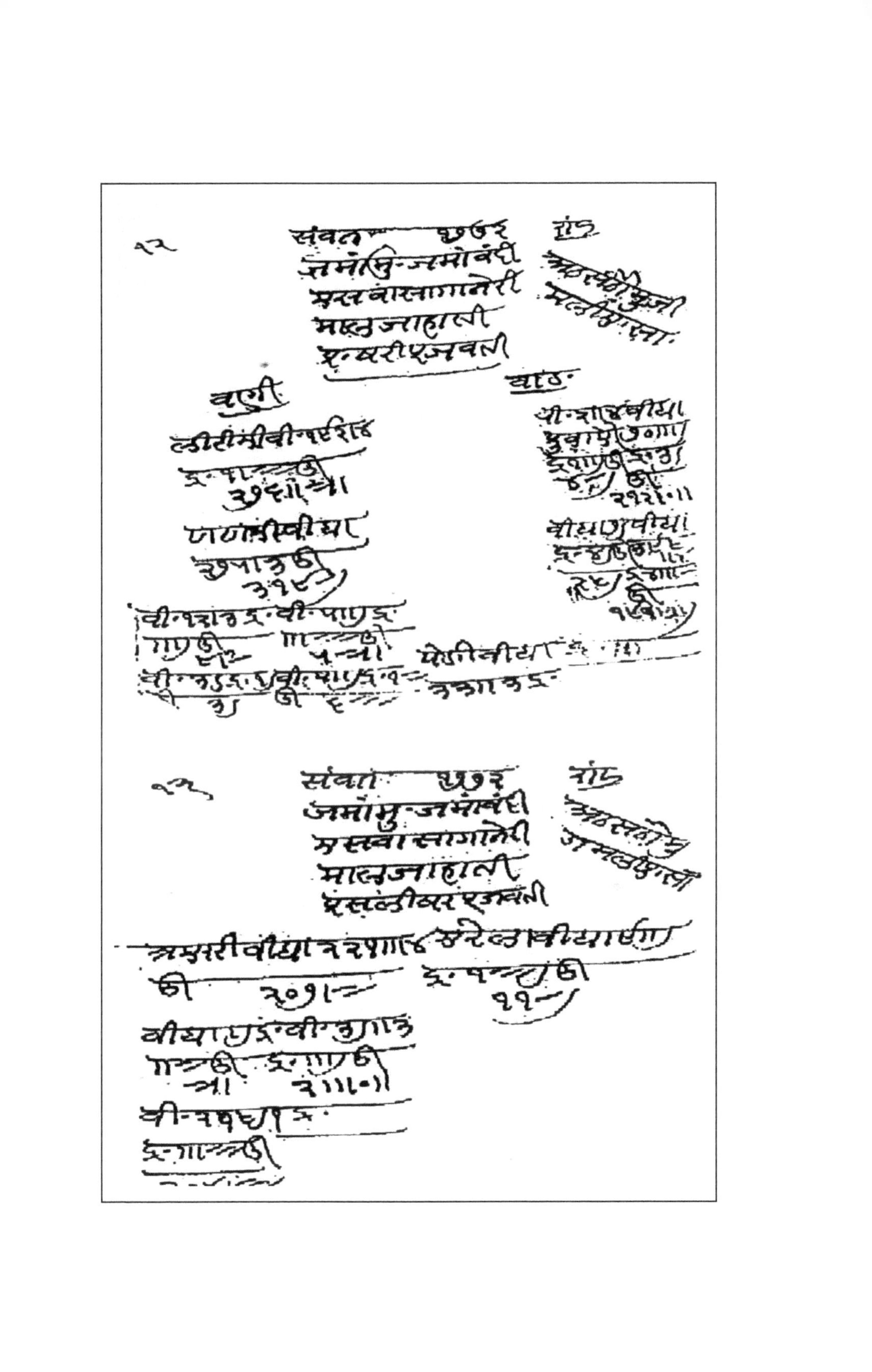

२२

संवत १७७२ [illegible]

जमांमु-जमांबंदी

मसवासागानेरी

माल्जाहाली

[illegible]री[illegible]ज्वती

[illegible]

[illegible]

वाढ

[illegible]

[illegible]

[illegible]

[illegible]

२९२।०॥

[illegible]

[illegible]

[illegible]

१६॥

[illegible]

[illegible]

३५७॥

[illegible]

[illegible]

३१८

[illegible]

[illegible]

[illegible]

[illegible]

[illegible]

२२

संवत १७७२ [illegible]

जमांमु-जमांबंदी

मसवासागानेरी

माल्जाहाली

[illegible]ली[illegible]रजवती

[illegible]

[illegible]

[illegible]

[illegible] २०१।=

[illegible]

११=

[illegible]

[illegible]

२॥।०॥

[illegible]

[illegible]

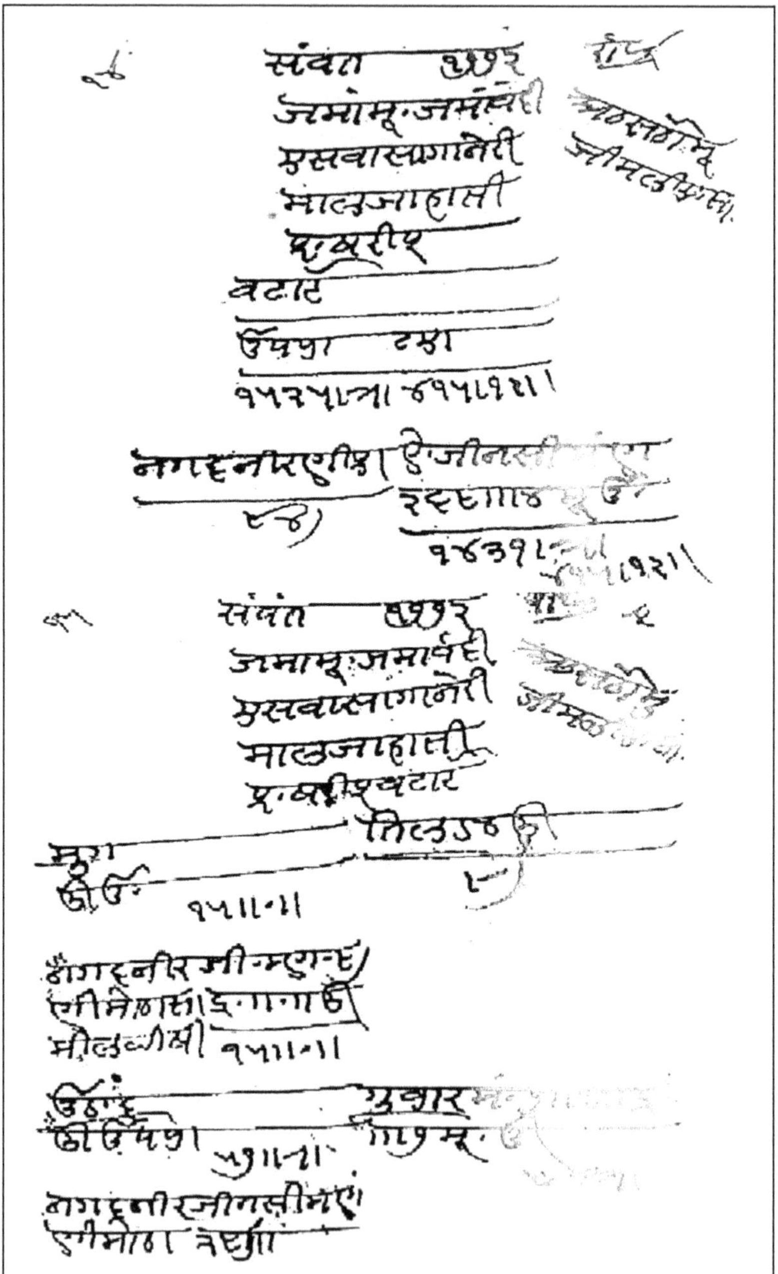
संवत १७७२
जमा मु. जमाबंदी
मुसवास गानेरी
माल जाहासी
रु. खरीफ
बटाई
उपज टका
संवत १७७२
जमा मु. जमाबंदी
मुसवास गानेरी
माल जाहासी
रु. खरीफ बटाई
तिल
मुग
१५॥।

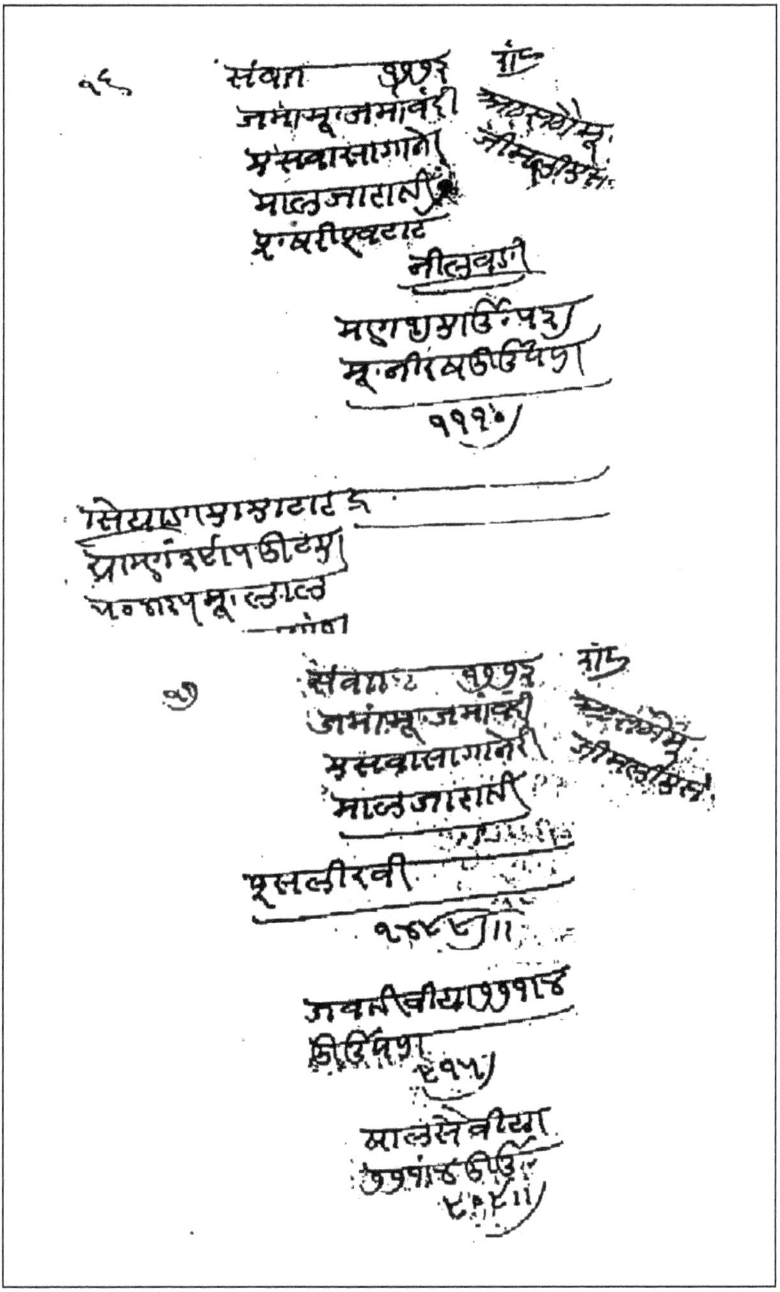

१८ संवत १७७२ सांद
जमा मू जमावंदी
मसवासागानो
माल जारानी
ग्रंवरीएवटाट
नीलवड़ी
महगाण्णाउ पर
मू नीरवडउपडा
१११०

सियाणगण्गटाटड़
प्राम्गरपाडीम्
५० गरप मू लाल
ओषा

संवत १७७२ सांद
७ जमा मू जमावंदी
मसवासागानेरी
माल जारानी
फूलडीरवी
२६८०॥
जवतीवीय १७७५८
डीउपश
२१५
मालसेवीया
७७५ाडउडउ
४५४॥

श्री   राम

सवत १७९२

वार्कोश्रग नांमेदैहाय   अब्दस्ठौ गु

मुन्सांगानेर   सांगानेर

पटीमाली

२३५॥।८।

मान्होसीश्रा मालत्रौहीस मीसनोमे युस्यालीरौ

मीमाली रामोमाली हामोमाली लामोमा-

॥।८।   ६॥।८।   ॥।=   २॥।

सुवोक्सलारेमोफ्स युस्यालोस्स वीस्योजीश्रा

कोमाली लामोमाली रामोमा- कोमाली

२।ऽ   ३॥ऽ   ६=॥   ७॥।

यास्योडीम नेतोठोमा नेतोरेमा नेतीलाल

मीमाली माली माली कीमाली

॥।=   ६=   ३॥   ७॥ऽ

नेतोठाजू नाथोमूधरा भत्रोमा नन्देलोमूय

कोठामुरामो मीमाली मीमाली कोमाली

मोगो   ११॥ऽ   ६॥   २।ऽ
६॥।

२३ सवत १६१२ राठ
वामी मठस्वामी
प्रगनांमे वमै फोजीव्ह ३।।। सांगानेर
मुकासदिवापी माल्व जोपजीश
पतकों सय।
१६८३।।
देहाय माल्व जोय कीफो
तकों स्ठय १५५७४ ४१।५८
१५८५
मुसवासांगानेर माल्वजोय कीर्को
पुतस्ठया
१०५५। ।
यटीमे पाती

२३८ सवत १६१२ राठ
वामीप्रगनानी देहाय मठस्वामी
मु.सांगानेर यटीमे पाती सांगानेर
जोयती कैसास्वांमी हरी उदैराव पांमी डेलीसा कु
मो अहदे ग्रास पागपान मुसल्मान
३।। ११।। ३। १।।
यटीमुमहार
१४।।।
कैसो गौयाक सलौरपा माल्मौ स्यौरां कुस्याल्हो दे
कौसा जी मीमू ममौमू दामौमू
छीत्र मलम्हा १। १।। ४।।।
५।
नराय रमां कुस्याल्ही का नानीगौ देदा नेतोस्वाणा
जेदमी मू हल्ला मीमू मीमू मू
११।।। ।। ३।। ।।।
नारायण भीम झूमौ देदु मी सीतो मेल्ठछा देल्हो भीम
नाम मू मू मीमू मीमू
।।। ७।। २।। ३।

१३८ सवत १८१२ रुं
वामीप्रगनांमे हैठो अठस्य मौमु
पक्र-सांगानेर सांगानेर

पटीजाट अहीर

१२०॥।
कालोमोहं नानीगोओ जोतीपुरामौजीयोरामअ
नभी सामीमाली माली मोमा-
१।। ३॥। ॥।= १॥।
जीवोरीषवाजीयो सुखामौ जीयोसापु जीदेमोहन
कोमाली मा-दै योमीयौ मोमाली मोअहीर
३ ॥ ८।। ३॥। ५॥।
टीकू खेताको टेकू मेसांमौ टेकूपुरा छोमा दे दोखेतर
मा- मा- ३२= १॥।= मोमा- २।।
२॥ स्या- ३
८॥ २५॥

...पीरमीमीनाम्ब मीमौदीपामी रूपोगोयापु

६० सवत १८१२ रुं
वाकीप्रगनामे देहापु अमस्य मौमु-
म-सांगानेरपटीपुर सांगानेर
ग्रांमी
मोतीराम म्हा-अमरो खीखोलो पली जगतो भूगं
अमोमाली मोगूजर दमोया-
५॥। ८॥ ॥ ५॥=
यास्तीमीयां रूपोखीवामौ सदे देपाल लालचंद
वा-नाजारांम माली मोया- पटी
चंदपुरवामे १॥। ॥। १०॥।
खेलआपो
३॥।

पटीओयामी

३८॥।=।
पीरखां चौदे दोलौनाम्बू मदराम गम जागजीबुलद
मू- मोहाल छागर सवायवडे
दोलामो १॥। २॥
८॥ ७। मूअल नगराज मू-म-टीड
मीरपद्मा॥ ८॥ ५॥

CHAPTER 6

Population of Artisans and Menial Castes in *Qasbas* Sangod and Mangrol in Kota: A Decline in Textile Professions

A fifteenth-century inscription about Kumbha's conquests described the area around Bundi as Hadavatim[1] which later on came to be known as Hadauti.[2] Abul Fazl employs the term 'Hadauti' and describes it as one of the three main constituents of *suba* Ajmer, the other two being Mewar and Marwar.[3] The region lies in the greener belt of south-east Rajasthan, and had been agriculturally an important principality.[4] This chapter is mostly based on revenue records of Kota preserved at the Rajasthan State Archives, Bikaner. Through the Kota records, especially *toji taqsim* and *toji-do-varkhi-parchajat-baje-talke*, we come to know of approximately 90 *qasbas* in the region.[5]

An attempt has been made in this chapter to study the non-agricultural production and a tax known as *kholari,* levied upon menials pursuing different professions, e.g. *chamars, kumbhars, dhobis, sunars, lakheras, mahajans, jolahas,* etc. It was collected house-wise under both the *kharif* and *rabi* harvests at varying rates. The *kholari* was component of the *sair* which was in essence a house-tax collected from the artisans. This in fact is an enumeration of artisan castes of different *qasbas* which enables us to make an estimation of population and caste composition. Besides this, we can also assess the position of individual crafts in a town in Kota. We have selected, viz., Sangod and Mangrol because of detailed information available about them. On the basis of this tax we can work out the population of artisans and menial castes in both the *qasbas.*

Pattern of non-agricultural production and its overall significance in the economy of 'pre-colonial' India has been a subject of several scholarly studies, but the focus has been primarily on the capital cities like Agra, Delhi, Lahore, etc., and the coastal regions.[6] It is true that these areas occupied an important place in the politics and economy of the country but to be able to discuss 'growth of an integrated market covering extensive parts of *Hindustan*',[7] one needs to know a lot more about the level of non-agricultural production in the interior regions of the country. In this context the information contained in the Kota records is of immense value. It can be used to ascertain the size of the non-agricultural sector in the economy of eighteenth century, Hadauti. It covers the different branches and organization of production in the *qasbas,* forms of labour organization in the productive and unproductive spheres, and gives a general idea about the earnings of the artisans and menials of a *qasba.* An estimate of the size of non-agricultural sector and its proportion to the agricultural population can be made on the basis of such taxes and cesses which were realized at a fixed rate from an individual household.[8]

The *toji-do-varkhi-baje-talke* offers the numbers and the names of the non-agriculturist households such as artisans and menial castes under the head *kholari.*[9] This was realized at fixed rate from the non-agricultural population of both rural as well as urban sector, while peasants paid land revenue and *bighori.*[10] This tax was being realized from the artisans and menials living in rural and urban areas, even in seventeenth century and was continued throughout the eighteenth century.[11]

For a systematic analysis of the available data we have divided our study into four sections: I, II, III and IV. Section I discusses the commercial crops of *qasba* Sangod. In sections II and III, number of houses and estimation of population of Sangod and Mangrol is made; and in section IV, a comparison is made between the worked-out population with the 1931 census and the position of textile workers of eighteenth century is also discussed.

I. COMMERCIAL CROPS

Data on the commercial crops in *qasba* Sangod is of extreme significance. These are *vani* (cotton), *til* (sesamum), *kosumbo* (opium), *tambakhu* (tobacco), *sunn* (Indian hemp or a source of fibre), *neel* (indigo) and *anju* (unidentified).[12] Out of these, cotton, hemp, opium and indigo are related to the textile industry. Besides this, the oilseeds grown in the region were *til* (sesamum) and *alsi* (linseed) in both the harvests and covered a good number of *bighas.*[13]

There is variable evidence about the availability of opium and indigo in the eighteenth century which shows that those crops were raised in the region. For instance, in *qasba* Sangod, in 1741, opium was produced on 14.18 *bighas* while indigo covered 95.07 *bighas.*[14]

Cotton was a major crop in the Kota region.[15] In *qasba* Sangod, it was cultivated on 457.12 *bighas* which constitute 29.84 per cent of the total area in 1741.[16]

The other commercial crops in the said *qasba* were *anju* (unidentified), tobacco and *hemp*[17] in *kharif* harvests, sown on 15.06, 0.15 and 62.17 *bighas* respectively.[18] *Anju* was produced both in *kharif* and *rabi.*[19]

Besides it, the food crops were also produced in large areas. Those were wheat (*gehoon*), gram (*chana*) and *saal* (coarse rice).[20] The details about them are shown in Tables 6.1 and 6.2.

TABLE 6.1: *KHARIF* (VS 1798/AD 1741)

Name of the Commercial Crop	Land in *Bighas/ Biswas*		Realized amount in rupees	
	Total	%	Total	%
Vani (cotton)	457.12	29.84	431.00	19.73
Saal (coarse rice)	606.13	39.56	1,456.00	66.67
Til (sesamum)	218.05	14.23	36.00	1.65
Sund (unidentified)	64.006	4.18	36.00	1.65
Anju (unidentified)	15.06	0.98	5.00	0.23
Kasumbho (opium)	14.18	0.93	10.00	0.46
Tambakhu (tobacco)	0.15	0.01	3.00	0.74
Sunn (source of fibre)	62.17	4.06	53.00	2.43
Neel (indigo)	95.07	6.21	154.00	7.05
Total	1,532.00*	100	2,184.00*	100

Note: *In round figure

TABLE 6.2: *RABI* (VS 1798/AD 1741)

Name of Crop	Land in *Bighas/ Biswas*		Realized amount in rupees	
	Total	%	Total	%
Gehoon (wheat)	358.00	64.39	223.00	72.88
Chana (gram)	117.07	21.04	27.00	8.82
Alsi (linseed)	76.13	13.69	51.00	16.67
Anju (unidentified)	3.02	0.54	2.00	0.65
Others	2.04	0.37	3.00	0.98
Total	556.00*	100	306.00*	100

Note: *In round figure

From the perusal of the Tables 6.1 and 6.2, three points emerge; first, the occupation of large areas under these crops probably was to feed the large number of people in the *qasba;* second, the development of the place into a big agrarian mart; and lastly, the cultivation of commercial crops related to textile show the possibility of emergence of the *qasba* as a centre of textile industry.

II. *QASBAS* SANGOD AND MANGROL

Sangod is situated on the right bank of River Ujar, a tributary of river Kali Sindh, 75 km south east of Kota town with which it is connected by road[21] (see Map 6.1: *Qasbas* Sangod and Mangrol).

The series of the *toji-do-varkhi-baje-talke* furnish information on artisans, menial castes and their number of houses[22] (see Appendix 6.1a & b). They enable us to estimate the population of the *qasba* in the eighteenth century. The statistical data of the year 1741 and 1751 on tax collection (*kholari*) and number of houses contained in the document are compiled in the Tables 6.3 and 6.4.

The castes recorded in 1741 are twenty while nineteen in 1751. Of these, eighteen are common in both the years. Dhobi and Gadarias were present in both the years while Ghosis was an addition in 1751 but not present in 1741.[23]

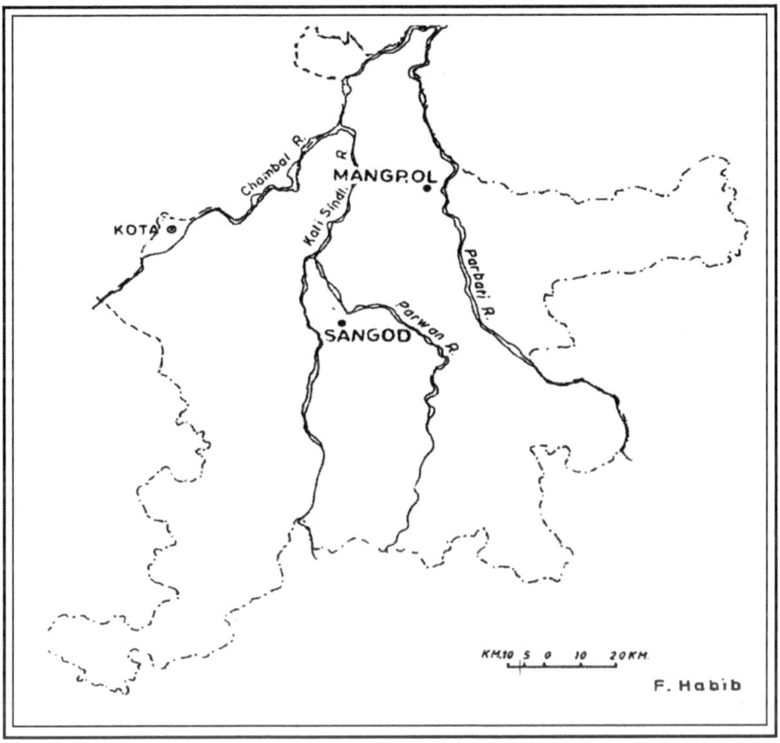

Map 6.1: *Qasbas* Sangod and Mangrol

Now we have prepared two tables for index (Tables 6.5 and 6.6) to know the rate per *asami* and the real position of the castes.

In Table 6.5 the total collection under the tax *kholari* and the number of *asamis* of *qasba* Sangod is recorded. The tax *kholari* signifies the house tax which was imposed on the different occupational groups.

The term *asami* indicates an individual.[24] But our records do not mention the rate of tax; therefore we have divided the total amount by the number of *asamis* to obtain the house tax per head. Then we have made an index of the rate of house tax. Assuming the number of *telis* as 100, we have prepared an index (Table 6.5). If we accept 20 per cent plus-minus range then all will fall in the same category except six, three in lower and three in higher.

TABLE 6.3: *QASBA* SANGOD (VS 1798/AD 1741)

Name of the Caste	Total realization in *Takas* (*sair-kholari* tax)	*Asami's Ghar* (no. of houses)	Population (no. of houses multiplied by 5)
Teli (oil man)	175	15	75
Dhobi (washerman)	127	12	60
Gadaria (shepherd)	43	4	20
Kharol	95	13	65
Chhinpas (calico printer)	111	7	35
Mehar	51	5	25
Khatik (leather worker)	42	3	15
Kumbhar (potter)	97	12	60
Gujar	70	5	25
Tamoli (betel seller)	29	3	15
Khati (carpenter)	137	8	40
Julaha (weaver)	588	53	265
Lohar (blacksmith)	63	4	20
Chamar (leatherworker)	93	7	35
Koli	113	12	60
Lakhera (lac worker)	66	5	25
Kalal (wine distiller)	265	22	110
Pinjara (cotton carder)	95	12	60
Sunar (goldsmith)	83	6	30
Lilgar (indigo dyer)	102	8	40
Total	2,445	216	1,080

Making the same assumption for the *telis* in the same *qasba* for 1751 (Table 6.6), if we accept 20 per cent plus-minus range then almost all fall in the same category except one which is lower than others.

The number of houses belonging to each caste is given, which can help us to estimate the population of that region. It means that if we multiply the number of houses by 5 (assumed conventional figure for each household),[25] we can obtain a population for practically all the artisans and menial castes in *qasba* Sangod. Already we have prepared Tables 6.3 and 6.4 to show the estimation of population in the said *qasba* for the years 1741 and 1751 respectively. It is quite clear that in 1741, the population of the

TABLE 6.4: *QASBA* SANGOD (VS 1808/AD 1751)

Name of the Caste	Total realization in *Takas* (*sair-kholari* tax)	*Asami's Ghar* (no. of houses)	Population (no. of houses multiplied by 5)
Kumbhar (potter)	110	10	50
Chhinpas (calico printer)	155	11	55
Lakhera (lac worker)	55	5	25
Tamoli (betel seller)	36	4	20
Gujar	107	9	45
Khati (carpenter)	124	9	45
Lohar (blacksmith)	59	4	20
Sunar (goldsmith)	89	7	35
Kharol	92	8	40
Kalal (wine distiller)	244	17	85
Teli (oilman)	169	13	65
Ghosi (milk seller)	88	8	40
Pinjara (cotton carder)	98	8	40
Khatik (leather worker)	52	5	25
Nilgar (indigo dyer)	79	6	30
Mehar	31	3	15
Koli	79	8	40
Julaha (weaver)	366	39	195
Chamar (leather worker)	54	5	25
Total	2,087	179	895

20 castes was 1080 (no. of houses 216 × 5), and in 1751, the population of the 19 castes was 895 (no. of houses, 179 × 5). In both tables (6.3 and 6.4) the leading professional castes were the Julahas (weavers), followed by Kalal (wine distiller), Teli (oil man), Kharol (salt workers) and Kumbhars (potters), etc.[26]

Qasba Mangrol is situated at a distance of 89 km to the east of the town of Kota. It is the headquarters of a *tehsil* of the same name. The town is situated on the right bank of the river Banganga, a tributary of river Parbati[27] (see Map 6.1: *Qasbas* Sangod and Mangrol).

For the study of *qasba* Mangrol, we have the same sources that of *qasba* Sangod and found more or less same castes, applying the

TABLE 6.5: *QASBA* SANGOD (VS 1798/AD 1741)

Name of the Caste	Total realization in *Takas* (*sair-kholari* tax)	Asami's Ghar (no. of houses)	Worked out rate per *asami**	Index (assumed value of Teli=100)
Teli (oil man)	175	15	11.67	100
Dhobi(washerman)	127	12	10.58	90.66
Gadaria (shepherd)	43	04	10.75	92.12
Kharol	95	13	07.31	62.64
Chhinpas (calico printer)	111	07	15.86	135.90
Mehar	51	05	10.2	87.40
Khatik (leather worker)	42	03	14.00	119.97
Kumbhar (potter)	97	12	08.08	69.24
Gujar	70	05	14.00	119.97
Tamoli (betel seller)	29	03	09.67	82.86
Khati (carpenter)	137	08	17.13	146.79
Julaha (weaver)	588	53	11.09	95.03
Lohar (blacksmith)	63	04	15.75	134.96
Chamar (leather worker)	93	07	13.29	113.88
Koli	113	12	0.9.42	80.72
Lakhera (lac worker)	66	05	13.20	113.11
Kalal (wine distiller)	265	22	12.05	103.26
Pinjara (cotton carder)	95	12	07.92	67.87
Sunar (gold smith)	83	06	13.83	118.51
Lilgar (indigo dyer)	102	08	12.75	109.25
Total	2,445	216	11.32	97.00

Note: *Rate per *asami* = Total realization/Total number of houses.

same method to know the rate per head and to estimate the population. The available information for the years 1731 and 1786 is put in Tables 6.7 and 6.8.[28]

The total number of castes recorded in 1731 is fifteen, while twenty-three in 1786.[29] Under both the years the total common castes are twelve, where Lakhera (lac worker), Bhutikhara and Lilgar (indigo dyer) are present in 1731 and absent in 1786.[30] The additional castes available in 1786 are eleven, viz. Mahajan, Golavar, Varagaon Vasan, Brahman (Sanawar and Gujar Gaur), Mali, Julaha, Darzi, Nai, Pinjara, Balaiand Vajepot[31] (see Appendix 6.1b & c.)

TABLE 6.6: *QASBA* SANGOD (VS 1808/AD 1751)

Name of the Caste	Total realization in *Takas* (*sair-kholari* tax)	Asami's Ghar (no. of houses)	Worked out Rate per *asami*	Index (assumed value of Teli=100)
Kumbhar (potter)	110	10	11.00	84.62
Chhinpas (calico printer)	155	11	14.80	108.38
Lakhera (lac worker)	55	5	11.00	84.62
Tamoli (betel seller)	36	4	09.00	69.23
Gujar	107	9	11.89	91.46
Khati (carpenter)	124	9	13.78	106.00
Lohar (blacksmith)	59	4	14.75	113.46
Sunar (goldsmith)	89	7	12.71	97.77
Kharol	92	8	11.50	88.46
Kalal (wine distiller)	244	17	14.35	110.38
Teli (oilman)	169	13	13.00	100.00
Ghosi (milk seller)	88	8	11.00	84.62
Pinjara (cotton carder)	98	8	12.25	94.23
Khatik (leather worker)	52	5	10.40	80.00
Nilgar (indigo dyer)	79	6	13.17	101.31
Mehar	31	3	10.33	79.46
Koli	79	8	09.88	76.00
Julaha (weaver)	366	39	09.38	72.15
Chamar (leather worker)	54	5	10.80	83.08
Total	2,087	179	11.66	89.69

We have prepared two tables (6.9 and 6.10) to work out the rate per head and their position is shown in index.

We have prepared Table 6.9 and applied the same method as that of *qasba* Sangod to calculate the rate and then we have made the index of the rate of house tax. We assumed the amount of Telis as 100, as earlier, and prepared tables of index. If we accept 20 per cent plus-minus range then all will fall in the same category except five, where four are higher and only one is lower.

For the year 1786 (Table 6.10) we have assumed the number of Telis again as 100. And if we accept 20 per cent plus-minus ranges then almost half of them are in the same category. Among the rest ten, three are higher and seven are lower in their position. Already, in Tables 6.7 and 6.8 we have worked out the population (Applying

TABLE 6.7: *QASBA* MANGROL (VS 1788/AD 1731)

Name of the Caste	Total realization in *Takas* (*sair-kholari* tax)	*Asami's Ghar* (no. of houses)	Population (no. of houses multiplied by 5)
Gujar	215	11	55
Dhobi (washer man)	81	6	30
Kalal (wine distiller)	111	6	30
Lakhera (lac worker)	62	4	20
Chhinpas (calico printer)	218	11	55
Khati (carpenter)	159	8	40
Kumbhar (potter)	178	8	40
Shudra (leather worker)	79	5	25
Teli (oilman)	130	8	40
Tamoli (betel seller)	43	4	20
Bhutikhara	102	6	30
Khatik (leather worker)	75	5	25
Lohar (blacksmith)	44	2	10
Lilgar (indigo dyer)	34	2	10
Chamar (leather worker)	365	25	125
Total	1,899	111	555

the method which we used in Section II) of *qasba* Mangrol. In year 1731 castes were 15 with their total number of houses 111 and the population in round figure is 555 (no. of houses 111 × 5).[32] While in 1786, it became 23 and their number of houses 427 and total population 2,195 (no. of houses 427 × 5).[33] In 1731, the numerically leading caste was Chamar followed by Chhinpa, Gujar, Kumbhar, Telis, Kalal, Dhobi, etc.[34] While in 1786, the leading caste was Mali followed by Julaha, Golawar, Mahajan, Gujar, Chamar, Nai and Brahamin, etc.[35] The striking thing is that Mahajan and Julaha are present in 1786 while absent in 1731 in the same *qasba*.[36]

III. POSITION OF TEXTILE WORKERS

The study of the position of textile workers in the towns of Kota is quite interesting. Though information about them is compiled in the combined tables (6.3, 6.4, 6.7 and 6.8) but to highlight their

TABLE 6.8: *QASBA* MANGROL (VS 1843/AD 1786)

Name of the Caste	Total realization in *Takas* (*sair-kholari* tax)	*Asami's Ghar* (no. of houses)	Population (no. of houses multiplied by 5)
Mahajan	75	32	160
Golavar	117	54	270
Varagaon Vasan	7	8	40
Brahman (Sanavar + Gujar Gaur)	18	13	65
Mali (gardener)	212	96	480
Julahas (weaver)	152	67	335
Darzi (tailor)	5	4	20
Shudra (leather worker)	13	10	50
Kumbhar (potter)	30	8	40
Dhobi (washerman)	25	8	40
Chhinpas (calico printer)	18	7	35
Teli (oilman)	15	7	35
Lohar (blacksmith)	21	5	25
Nai (barber)	32	18	90
Pinjara (cotton carder)	7	8	40
Gujar	47	24	120
Balai (leather worker)	22	12	60
Tamoli (betel seller)	7	6	30
Kalal (wine distiller)	22	11	55
Khati (carpenter)	28	–	–
Vejepot	5	6	30
Khatik (leather worker)	4	3	15
Chamar (leather worker)	37	20	100
Total	919	427	2195

strength, we have formulated a separate table (Table 6.11) stating their number of houses and the population obtained through multiplying with the conventional rate five (5). This would highlight the strength of individual textile castes.

The *toji-do-varkhi-baje-talke* contains approximately 22 castes in *qasba* Sangod and 26 castes in *qasba* Mangrol of craftsman and menial castes. Documents also record the total number of houses of each professional group and class of mentioned castes for both of the towns. It will be worthwhile to use the data on the number of houses of each professional caste for two *qasbas* in a tabular

TABLE 6.9: *QASBA* SANGOD (VS 1798/AD 1741)

Name of the Caste	Total realization in *Takas* (*sair-kholari* tax)	Asami's Ghar (no. of houses)	Worked out rate per *asami**	Index (assumed value of Teli=100)
Gujar	215	11	13.00	120.31
Dhobi	81	6	19.55	83.08
Kalal	111	6	13.50	113.85
Lakhera	62	4	18.50	95.38
Chhinpas	218	11	15.50	121.97
Khati	159	08	19.82	122.34
Kumbhar	178	08	19.88	136.92
Sudar	79	5	22.25	97.23
Teli	130	08	15.80	100.00
Tamoli	43	04	16.25	66.15
Bhutikhara	102	06	10.75	104.62
Khatik	75	05	17.00	92.31
Lohar	44	02	15.00	135.38
Lilgar	34	02	22.00	104.62
Chamar	365	25	17.00	89.85
Total	1,899	111	17.11	105.29

Note: *Rate per *asami* = Total realization/Total number of houses.

form. In putting castes under the heading of 'Textile Workers',[37] we have selected only those castes which are easily identifiable with a particular profession.

The comparison of the population figures of textile workers[38] in the two periods which leads to some very interesting results (see Table 6.11 and also Graph 6.1 and 6.2). In 1741 and 1751 in *qasba* Sangod, the leading professional class is Julahas (weavers) with their population 265 and 195 respectively followed by Pinjara, Lilgars, Chhinpas, Lakheras, etc., and their total population is 425, while in 1751 the dominating positions is again of Julahas followed by Chhinpas, Pinjaras, Nilgars, Lakheras, etc., and their total population comes to 345. There is a decline of population of these castes between 1741 and 1751 and completely disappeared in1931.[39]

TABLE 6.10: *QASBA* MANGROL (VS 1788/AD 1731)

Name of the Caste	Total realization in *Takas* (*sair-kholari* tax)	Asami's Ghar (no. of houses)	Worked out rate per *asami*	Index (assumed value of Teli=100)
Mahajan	75	32	2.34	109.35
Golavar	117	54	2.17	101.40
Varagaon Vasan	7	8	0.88	41.12
Brahman (Sanavar + Gujar Gaur)	18	13	1.38	64.49
Mali (gardener)	212	96	2.21	103.27
Julahas (weaver)	152	67	2.27	106.07
Darzi (tailor)	5	4	1.25	58.41
Sudra (leather worker)	13	10	1.30	60.75
Kumbhar (potter)	30	8	3.75	175.23
Dhobi (washerman)	25	8	3.12	145.79
Chhinpas (calico printer)	18	7	2.57	120.09
Teli (oilman)	15	7	2.14	100.00
Lohar (blacksmith)	21	5	4.20	196.26
Nai (barber)	32	18	1.78	83.18
Pinjara (cotton carder)	7	8	0.88	41.12
Gujar	47	24	1.99	92.99
Balai (leather worker)	22	12	1.83	85.51
Tamoli (betel seller)	7	6	1.17	54.67
Kalal (wine distiller)	22	11	2.00	93.46
Khati (carpenter)	28	–	–	–
Vejepot	5	6	0.83	38.79
Khatik (leather worker)	4	3	1.33	62.15
Chamar (leather worker)	37	20	1.85	86.45
Total	919	427	2.15	100.47

In 1731 and 1786 in *qasba* Mangrol, it is seen that the leading professional caste is Chhinpas with its population at 55 followed by Lakheras, Lilgars, etc. Here Julahas, Nilgars, Pinjaras are not available in AD 1731, while in 1786 Julahas are in, dominating position with their population at 335 followed by Pinjaras, Chhinpas, etc. Their total population in 1731 is 85, and in 1786 it is 470, which shows an increase. But they have altogether disappeared by 1931.[40]

TABLE 6.11: *QASBA* SANGOD AND MANGROL: A COMPARISON OF CASTE POPULATION WITH CENSUS 1931 (TEXTILE WORKERS)

Name of the Caste	*Qasba* Sangod			*Qasba* Mangrol		
	Urban Population AD 1741	Urban Population AD 1751	Urban Population AD 1931	Urban Population AD 1731	Urban Population AD 1786	Urban Population AD 1931
Chhinpa (calico printer)	35	55	DA*	55	35	DA*
Julaha (weaver)	265	195	DA	–	335	DA
Lakhera (lac worker)	25	25	DA	20	–	DA
Lilgar (indigo dyer)	40	–	DA	10	–	DA
Nilgar (indigo dyer)	–	30	DA	–	–	DA
Pinjara (cotton carder)	60	40	DA	–	40	DA
Total	425	345	DA	85	470	DA

Note: *DA denotes disappeared.

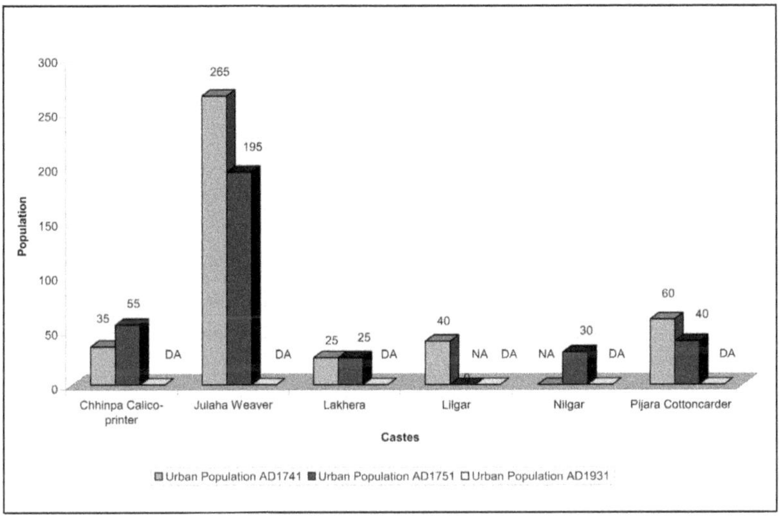

Graph 6.1: A Comparison of the Population of Textile Workers in *Qasba* Sangod

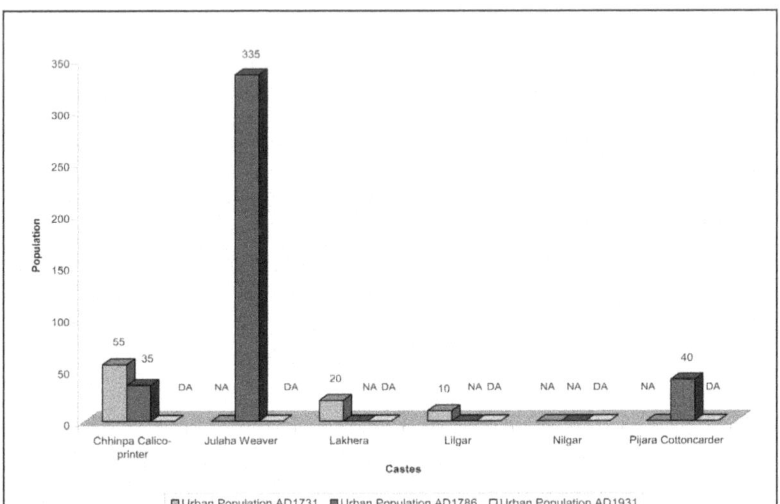

Graph 6.2: A Comparison of the Population of Textile Workers in *Qasba* Mangrol

After an examination we are conclusively able to say that approximately six textile workers and other professional groups like Kalal and Lakheras had completely disappeared from both the *qasbas* Sangod and Mangrol by 1931.[41] The decline or disappearance of Julahas (weavers) and Chhinpas (calico printer) including Nilgars, Pinjaras, etc., was clearly an outcome of the impact of the competition of British cloth in the nineteenth century. The weavers and calico printers suffered in the nineteenth century because probably British cloth and yarn became cheaper, and also the demand for British cloths cheapened their product and British cloth production increased.[42] Gradually the number of textile workers declined and ultimately they vanished from the scene by the first quarter of the twentieth century, which is clear from the census of 1931. The fading-out of Kalals (wine distillers) also indicates the import of English wine from England.

The above study shows de-industrialization as well as de-urbanization at least in these two towns. We can also infer a similar kind of phenomenon in the entire state of Kota.

NOTES

1. *Kumbhalgarh Inscriptions* IV slab (264) text given by Shyamaldas in *Vir Vinod*, vol. 1, rpt., 1986, Delhi, pp. 411-16.
2. Madhu Tandon Sethia, *Rajput Polity: Warriors, Peasants and Merchants, (1700-1800)*, Rawat Publications, Jaipur, 2003, p. 20.
3. *Ain.* II, tr. Corrected and annotated by J.N. Sarkar, New Delhi, p. 273.
4. *Rajasthan District Gazetteers,* Jaipur, ed. Savitri Gupta, Government of Rajasthan, Kota, 1982, p. 78.
5. *Toji taqsim* and *Toji-do-varkhi-baje-talke* of different years of different *parganas.*
6. H.K. Naqvi, *Urban Centres and Industries in Upper India* (*1556-1803*), Asia Publishing House, Bombay, 1968; and *Urbanization and Urban Centres under the Great Mughals*, Indian Institute of Advanced Study, Simla, 1972.
7. *Inland Trade in the Cambridge Economic History of India, c. 1200-1750*, ed. Tapan Raychaudhuri and Irfan Habib, vol. I, Orient Longman in Association with Cambridge University Press, 1982; rpt. 2004, p. 338.

8. Sethia, *Rajput Polity: Warriors, Peasants and Merchants*, op. cit., p. 231.
9. *Toji-do-varkhi-baje-talke, qasba* Sangod and *qasba* Mangrol of years VS 1798/AD 1741, VS 1808/AD 1751 and VS 1788/AD 1731, VS 1843/AD 1786.
10. Sethia, *Rajput Polity*, op. cit., pp. 91-2. Literally a *kholari* is a house tax on a professional who was engaged in production in a village or a town.
11. Sethia, *Rajput Polity*, pp. 91-2. Cf. *Toji-do-varkhi-baje-talke* for Kota state.
12. *Toji-do-varkhi-baje-talke, qasba* Sangod, VS 1798/AD 1741.
13. Ibid.
14. Ibid.
15. Ibid.
16. Ibid.
17. *Sunn* (a plant is a source of fibres), H.H. Wilson: *A Glossary of Judicial and Revenues Terms*, compiled and published under the authority of the Honorable the Court of Directors of the East India Company, Munshiram Manoharlal, Oriental Publishers & Booksellers, Delhi, 2nd edn., 1968, p. 460.
18. *Toji-do-varkhi-baje-talke, qasba* Sangod, VS 1798/AD 1741.
19. Ibid.
20. *Saal* (coarse rice). See *Rajasthani Shabd Kosh*, part 3, p. 1453.
21. *Rajasthan District Gazetteers*, Kota, op. cit., pp. 508-9.
22. *Toji-do-varkhi-baje-talke, qasba* Sangod, op. cit.
23. *Toji-do-varkhi-baje-talke, qasba* Sangod, VS 1798/AD 1741 and VS 1808/AD 1751.
24. Ibid.
25. S.P. Gupta and B.L. Bhadani assumed conventional Figure 4.5 for the estimation of population of the Marwar region. Tod assumed 4 and 5 at different places such as Jaisalmer and Bikaner respectively.
26. *Toji-do-varkhi-baje-talke, qasba* Sangod, op. cit.
27. *Rajasthan District Gazetteers*, Kota, op. cit., p. 507.
28. *Toji do-varkhi-baje-talke, qasba* Mangrol, VS 1788/AD 1731 and VS 1843/AD 1786.
29. Ibid.
30. Ibid.
31. *Toji do-varkhi-baje-talke, qasba* Mangrol, VS 1843/VS 1786
32. Ibid., VS 1788/AD 1731.
33. Ibid., VS 1843/AD 1786.
34. Ibid., VS 1788/AD 1731.
35. Ibid., VS 1843/AD 1786
36. Ibid.

37. Six castes are included in the textile profession: *julahas* (weavers), *chhinpas* (calico printers), *lakheras* (lac workers), *lilgars* (indigo dyers), *nilgars* (indigodyers) and *pinjaras* (cotton carder).
38. Ibid.
39. B.L. Cole, *Census of India*, 1931 (Rajputana Agency), rpt., Manohar, Delhi, 1992, pp. 216-17.
40. Ibid.
41. Ibid.
42. *Kalals* (wine distillers) also disappeared probably due to sale of British wine in that region.

APPENDIX 6.1

Name of the Professional Groups, Artisans and Menial Castes in the Kota Documents: *Toji-do-varkhi-baje-talke*

A. *QASBA* SANGOD (VS 1798/AD 1741)

Teli (15)

1. Hemo Kanha	2. Jaudo	3. Veno
4. Chhajau	5. Natho	6. Ghasi Patal
7. Dharmo Phuda	8. Uro Sudar	9. Khemo Vavan
10. Upo Galari	11. Hemo Dharma	12. Puro Dalu
13. Puro Dharma	14. Nani Gatharalai	15. Pri Rago

Dhobi (12)

1. Bakhto	2. Ramkhadalu	3. Gokal Padharat
4. Nangoh Lakhman	5. Peetho Mundala	6. Kewal
7. Khemo Fakeer	8. Jodho Jeetha	9. Sovara Medala
10. Ramovasi	11. Lachho Sergarh	12. Amradev

Gadaria (4)

1. Devo Bhagta	2. Bhopo Chaju	3. Netau
4. Modi		

Kharol (13)

1. Thakursi	2. Khemo	3. Deva Hemo
4. Deepo	5. Aaso	6. Khemo Dore
7. Kheewasi	8. Devo Nandgaon	9. Cheekho
10. Nango	11. Mano Devo	12. Bhagato
13. Khemo Gidhra		

Chhinpa (7)

1. Bhovo	2. Kisano	3. Khemo
4. Todu	5. Amro	6. Nango
7. Rupo Udi		

Mehar (5)

1. Kheevasi	2. Ido	3. Kheevo
4. Chutro	5. Nango	

Khatik (3)

1. Bhagirath	2. Bhodar	3. Gego

Kumbhar (12)

1. Moto Patal	2. Pramadi	3. Keso
4. Keelani	5. Nango	6. Ramji
7. Vachhau	8. Isar	9. Lalu
10. Lalo Vavan	11. Vandhu Ghasi	12. Bhovo

Gujar (5)

1. Jeevo	2. Vaiso	3. Hedaro
4. Keso	5. Ghasi	

Tamoli (3)

1. Kubho	2. Lalu	3. Hairani

Khati/Khatri (8)

1. Laluasa	2. Kisanau	3. Devo
4. Puro	5. Jedo	6. Geedho
7. Dudo	8. Gangaram	

Julaha (53): There are two *pattis*, one is Patti Saru with 28 names and second is Patti Habib with 25 names.

1. Fakir Servadi	2. Khanu Chauhan	3. Jamal Multani
4. Dadu Arsi	5. Tadar Gori Javda	6. Bheekhe Murmah
7. Tadar Gori Sera	8. Haji Meratwal	9. Barihavavaseed
10. Melu	11. Khanu Manglo	12. Nathu Jaijato
13. Khadar Agwan	14. Nuro Vaseeh	15. Haji Agwan
16. Sah Mahatra	17. Jamal Lakharo	18. Jedovara
19. Bheekho Aravi	20. Ghasi Gori	21. Nathu Salulo
22. Hanse Nagori	23. Gariva Ghori	24. Bandhu Sarvadi Fakira
25. Jamal Bheekha	26. Bridam Viyavar	27. Bridam Ajmeri
28. Lalu Mahetri	29. Habib Mahetri	30. Madaro Vagsu
31. Nuro Jaijuto	32. Mahmud Barmu	33. Rahim Vasu
34. Fakirau	35. Haji Jalavan	36. Geedho Maretuval
37. Peeru Aadhau	38. Nathu	39. Karim

40. Tadar Deidhera	41. Iso	42. Bhovilji
43. Karimi Khokhar	44. Kimal Varuval	45. Chad
46. Vagru	47. Kasu Agwan	48. Danu
49. Lalu Gori	50. Sailemanai	51. Medo
52. Medhu Sergarh	53. Chade Mahi.	

Lohar (4)

1. Nango	2. Savji	3. Gangaramai
4. Kisanai		

Chamar (7)

1. Gangolau Godhra	2. Kisanai	3. Jairamai
4. Lalau	5. Lakhmanau	6. Savalau
7. Nangau		

Koli (12)

1. Manoro	2. Ramaiji	3. Udi
4. Netau	5. Bhamau	6. Udhau
7. Hemau	8. Ramau Hema	9. Sago
10. Ghasinau	11. Nathau	12. Gogalau

Lakhera (5)

1. Ramchand	2. Vagsu	3. Lalji Derikhera
4. Gangaramai	5. Sevochhetra	

Kalal (22)

1. Jaudo deili	2. Ramaiji	3. Soramai
4. Bhaigvanai	5. Gharivo Naharo	6. Karamchand
7. Narharau	8. Godau	9. Lalu
10. Ramji	11. Ramansagi	12. Jeevo
13. Modinai	14. Harajai	15. Nathu
16. Bakhatau	17. Bheevo Teji	18. Nango Deevo
19. Natho Bharma	20. Lodore Kavaru	21. Dharmo
22. Jaramo Saga		

Pinjara (12)

1. Davahai	2. Ghazi	3. Ramo Nadar
4. Sedhu	5. Nathu	6. Haji
7. Ghasau	8. Methu	9. Bheekhao
10. Khanu	11. Methau	12. Khradarai

Sonar (6)

1. Kaso Ghasee	2. Udo Sahe	3. Peermai
4. Udo Narsaug	5. Charanau	6. Nangau

Lilgar (8)

1. Dathu	2. Gothu	3. Sama ki Bahu
4. Jamalau	5. Nangau ki Bahu	6. Isai
7. Naharau	8. Vandhu	

B. *QASBA* SANGOD (VS 1808/AD 1751)

Kumbhar (10)

1. Keso	2. Lalo	3. Isar
4. Lachhai	5. Vachhai	6. Vailu
7. Voitho Ramji	8. Ramo Ajnava	9. Fakiro
10. Veeram		

Chhinpa (11)

1. Kisanau	2. Devidas	3. Khemo
4. Amaro	5. Nango	6. Udho
7. Devakersa	8. Keso	9. Bhopo
10. Dugo	11. Harajai	

Lakhera (5)

1. Ghasi	2. Kusali	3. Bhopo
4. Vagasu	5. Dhepo	

Tamoli (4)

1. Kumho	2. Lalu	3. Bhopau
4. Soji		

Gujar (9): There are five Gujars and 4 Gadari, therefore this is Gujar Gadari.

1. Gujar Jeevo	2. Gujar Vodho Dahara	3. Gujar Purokeso
4. Gujar Ghasi	5. Gujar Nanrano	6. Bhopo Gadari
7. Modu Gadari	8. Khemo Gadari	9. Puro Gadari

Khati/Khatri

1. Khati Jedo	2. Khati Deepo	3. Khati Vali
4. Khati Girdhar	5. Khati Mekhu	6. Khati Puro
7. Khati Maru	8. Khati Narnaugi	9. Khati Tulo Nandgira

Lohar (4)

1. Nango	2. Kisno	3. Gangaram
4. Soj		

Sunar (7)

1. Ghasi	2. Udho Navsada	3. Charnau
4. Mekhbhara	5. Peermo	6. Hemo
7. Udho Sedho		

Kharol (8)

1. Keso	2. Bhopon Fursi	3. Devo Mono
4. Deva ki Bahu	5. Dolaram	6. Deepo
7. Pemo Furas	8. Mano	

Kalal (17)

1. Naatho Deepo	2. Nango Deva	3. Harajai Heera
4. Bheepo	5. Jado Dali	6. Soranau
7. Bakhto	8. Teki Lahu	9. Jarana Keevas
10. Dharma Gangaram	11. Bheekho	12. Bhagvanam Gangaramai
13. Uvoruwo	14. Jeevo Deva	15. Udo Neeraj
16. Ramji	17. Natho	

Teli (13)

1. Ghasi	2. Venau	3. Soj Debho
4. Prasau	5. Nathau	6. Dharmau
7. Veerago	8. Namvanau	9. Hema
10. Rupa	11. Dalo	12. Jaramau
13. Nangau		

Ghosi (8)

1. Jodho	2. Lachhau	3. Asau
4. Sothdhiya	5. Gokalo	6. Khamako
7. Ramo Dasu	8. Kasali	

Pinjara (8)

1. Dayad	2. Chand	3. Methu
4. Harikho	5. Dolo	6. Kaji Lada
7. Prataro	8. Kumal Vakulodavad	

Khatik (5)

1. Bhodar	2. Gego	3. Nanago
4. Bheevado	5. Dhanau	

Neelgar (6)

1. Dathau	2. Guto	3. Jamal
4. Bheekho	5. Datau	6. Chadau

Mehar (3)

1. Kheevasau	2. Thakuro	3. Ghasi

Koli (8)

1. Ram Jamau	2. Bhamau	3. Ramau Tila
4. Udhau	5. Dhole	6. Hemo
7. Dalai	8. Natho Nadargau	

Julaha (39): Two *pattis*, Patti Saru (22) and Patti Habib (17)

1. Rahim Gori	2. Dadu Aarsi	3. Sero Savaj
4. Bheekhe Aarvi	5. Bheekho Gori	6. Natho naram
7. Tadar Gori	8. Tadar Jeedo Su Gori	9. Jedo Chauhan
10. Bhan Chauhan	11. Tejo Sarvo	12. peero Kacharo
13. Mahatri Saru	14. padhu Saafadi	15. Mahasam Niti
16. Hasan Gori	17. Peero Sagval	18. Noor Deeva Sadi
19. Lala Saru	20. Nadaro Gori	21. Khanau Gori
22. Teko Karal	23. Habi Mahatri	24. Chad
25. Karamo	26. Mahemado Karim	27. Nuri-Jajalo
28. Medano Merativale	29. Malai Chauhan	30. Rahimo vad
31. Bhikho khal	32. Natho Chauhan	33. Fakiro Alalgas
34. Haji Jajan	35. Iso Latar	36. Garadio Desus
37. Tadar Mohi	38. Dhrata Majtas	39. Mehar Khachu

Chamar (5)

1. Gango Lamori	2. Lakhmanau Pakhri	3. Sudhagra
4. Veermau	5. Lakhmanau	

C. *QASBA* SANGOD (VS 1788/AD 1731)

Gujar (11)

1. Lakhman	2. Dugo	3. Narain
4. Jadho	5. Kalu	6. Geehho
7. Bhagato	8. Bhagato	9. Lalu
10. Samo	11. Herau	

Dhobi (6)

1. Kuliro	2. Chojo	3. Nango
4. Puro	5. Natho Bihadi	6. Dharmo

Lakhera (4)

1. Rauda	2. Lalu	3. Meeda
4. Kasinophar		

Kalal (6)

1. Jeeva	2. Udho Fakira	3. Parmadai
4. Udho Bheeja	5. Keso	6. Kanha Mojram

Chhinpa (11)

1. Jeto	2. Deepo	3. Ghasi
4. Ramo	5. Feto	6. Chhitra
7. Kharhat	8. Mohan	9. Pemo
10. Kilano	11. Keso	

Khati (8)

1. Dikhra Das	2. Mudo	3. Jaganath
4. Mukandai	5. Lachhiram	6. Jairamau
7. Voitho	8. Tulachhi	

Kumbhar (8)

1. Jeto	2. Rasji	3. Jairam Umoji
4. Jedo	5. Sudrai	6. Chhitra
7. Jeto Jairam ki Javai	8. Rekho	

Sudar (5)

1. Laloo	2. Peetho	3. Natho
4. Sukho	5. Divradasi	

Teli (8)

1. Kisanai	2. Hathai	3. Hedro
4. Kheevasi	5. Sukho	6. Manai
7. Lalau	8. Hatho kisana	

Tamoli (4)

1. Tilok	2. Dayaram	3. Raudo
4. Bhakhro		

Bhutikhara (6)

1. Bheno	2. Ruko	3. Kaso

4. Reudo	5. Manau	6. Ratnau

Luhar (2)

1. Harjai	2. Devo	

Khatik (5)

1. Bhopo	2. Kisanau	3. Taro
4. Naraino	5. Pemo	

Leelgar (2)

1. Lilgar Havato	2. Dikhualo Bhadbhuj	

Chamar (25)

1. Gego	2. Neto Bhivalu	3. Kheevo
4. Maheso	5. Khusalo	6. Polau
7. Pemo Parsaku	8. Nathan	9. Lohatau
10. Mohano	11. Chutra	12. Beerbhan
13. Grarso	14. Gangoli	15. Harajval Khadag
16. Keelano	17. Sramo	18. Ghano
19. Peero Gaga	20. Gadho Pola	21. Lalo Vadha
22. Harajai	23. Pemo Gadar	24. Pemo Gadar
25. Pemo Damodar		

D. *QASBA* MANGROL (VS 1843/AD 1786)

Mahajan (32)

1. Nanaj	2. Vajato	3. Sojoda
4. Karso	5. Ratano Veeje	6. Amro Sarawaji
7. Soji Sogani	8. Magni Parewada	9. Dalo Parwad
10. Adar Bhoj Pamsari	11. Venomuch	12. Narotham Dhorwad
13. Josal Mangado	14. Choji Porwad	15. Moti Bhigarwali
16. Jeevasi Bhuch	17. Kaniram Miti	18. Dudi Jeevan Sogaji
19. Maniram Sarraf	20. Bhilara Madhorwad	21. Teelo Sarawagi
22. Hatu Sogaji	23. Lalu Sogaji	24. Neto Bhaso
25. Hathi Jasu	26. Cheeto Bhuch	27. Devo Bhadsal
28. Rodu Porwal	29. Kalu Bhopo	30. Nihalchand Bajaj
31. Harchand	32. Moti Nanaj	

Golavar (54)

1. Hatiram Maharo	2. Karso Kandoi	3. Ghasi Naik

4. Bhagirath Chaudhari
5. Peetho Choparo
6. Sitaram Kandoi
7. Maharam Kaichi
8. Lilo Sethi
9. Lal kakar
10. Ghasi Kandoi
11. Karso Madara
12. Sambharam Kuti
13. Hataram Sethi
14. Sevo Kukarni
15. Pemo Dudilo
16. Udhau Kalu
17. Maharam tudilo
18. Deepo Katukaicho
19. Umado Dudilo
20. Pusal Kai
21. Subho Mahralau
22. Dheno Chopado
23. Bhilo Kaicho
24. lalu Bharatiya
25. Bhopo Naiko
26. Sujram Guj
27. Chhitar Naiko
28. Gomado Naiko
29. Kalu Chopalo
30. Veniram Madarko
31. Nango Diharo
32. Gardhar Mandarsiko
33. Nango Diharo
34. Cheto Mandarako
35. Ghasi Kataro
36. Holo Chopado
37. Heero Kakad
38. Jeevasi Kakad
39. Peetho Naik
40. Kuko Bhojar
41. Nathu Dikhawadi
42. Keso Naik
43. Diyaram Dudido
44. Tulo Naik
45. Aadhau Mehali
46. Thakur Siktarau
47. Bholo Naik
48. Lalu Kaludju
49. Ruko Neto Dudilo
50. Mau Kaicho
51. Deepo Sethi ko
52. Mahu Kaicho
53. Jeelasi Naik
54. Sabhu Hunak Tilo

Varagaon Vasan (8)

1. Meetharam Bras
2. Leelo Judiko
3. Gago Mahralo
4. Nanaj
5. Sama Katwari
6. Leelo Jeevasi
7. Sankar Cheetra
8. Nango Raja

Brahman (Sanawar and Gujar Gaur 13)

1. Raman Jodha
2. Duve Ramau
3. Rati Ram Mahsar
4. Lalan Pasai
5. Kusal
6. Chedu
7. Joshi Peejo
8. Pandit Dayalro
9. Dodraj
10. Pandit Hariram
11. Pandit Jheetu
12. Pandit Khusale Sovaro
13. Pandit Surto

Mali (96)

1. Mali Tara Amara
2. Mali nivej
3. Mali Teko
4. Chatro Sitachha
5. Pemo Melkhani
6. Minali
7. Bhopo Raman
8. Karso Lilrora
9. Mano Devara
10. Heero Karsa
11. Girdhar Dharmo
12. Rejo Bhavar
13. Sadi Madali
14. Tulachho Badgaou
15. Jeto Bhopo
16. Hemo Golo
17. Udo Tara
18. Bhojo Ram
19. Rejo Siloro
20. Modi Jairam
21. Bhaga
22. Jusalo Sawa
23. Lilo Jadga
24. Sevo Sitala
25. Jodho Musa
26. Todo Bhiva
27. Rupo Bhavar
28. Gothu Radi
29. Pura Ugra
30. Godho Dhara

31. Chatro Mohan
32. Sambhu Mantila
33. Bhopo Mantila
34. Taro Silora
35. Harlo Mantila
36. Natho Ramchand
37. Gordheno Devidas
38. Ghasi Geedha
39. Tejo Nathu
40. Dadko Mochki
41. Teelo Rupa
42. Mulo Karama
43. Kali Deva
44. Malodeer
45. Nego Devidas
46. Nango
47. Karvo Asal
48. Cholo Maluka
49. Neto Bhavar
50. Pemo Peevasi
51. Jeto Gola
52. Voitho Vagkar
53. Heero Manadarai
54. Soji Mantila
55. Chhito Kalu
56. Jaksandari
57. Hemo Devra
58. Jusalo Vagvaan
59. Bhopo Neta
60. Khemo Devra
61. Bhavali Lira
62. Jusala
63. Parovoith
64. Jeevan Dela
65. Ramkisan
66. Chanko Doli
67. Pemo Devidas
68. Bhopa Devra
69. Mafi Soja
70. Bhojo Vajari Kodi
71. Para Malan
72. Teki Keso
73. Kusalo Mandawar
74. Patal Kesu
75. Taralav
76. Malan Soji
77. Udo Sitala
78. Isro
79. Kilo
80. Peetho
81. Soj
82. Gego
83. Dudo
84. Javonath
85. Jeevasi Choja
86. Veejo Ghasi
87. Dolo Karso
91. Bhilo Mau
92. Ghasi Vagvaan
93. Bhotomuvo
94. Mali Dhen Bhopo
95. Devo Tola
96. Taloni Moda

Julaha (67)

1. Kesaro Barod
2. Bharojuva Javagas
3. Mabhar Jairaj
4. Rahmat Juvajvas
5. Jusal
6. Datokeera
7. Iso Bhaisa
8. Jeevo Rahmat
9. Hakani Padila
10. Jamo Sera
11. Raju Mamrej
12. Jusalo Mamroj
13. Lalaj Bhaveju
14. Javo Ido
15. Bhivo Soi
16. Lalaj Kanayai
17. Jivan Soi
18. Dan Sa Karmala
19. Juvasi Karmala
20. Jusal Ichhan
21. Peero Isau
22. Isau
23. Janukatu
24. Jusal Karmala
25. Padadunath
26. Pahram Nahar
27. Mathur Jusal
28. Ruhmato Ajoit
29. Bholo Soi
30. Dalvar Pada
31. Jeevo Kama
32. Kesaro Bhaisa
33. Haleelo Mamrej
34. Abdullo Inait
35. Sarak Lalso
36. Abdullo Karmala
37. Khuwaj Khanus
38. Khusal Kasam
39. Hate Atrava
40. Maan Savar
41. Paro Karmava
42. Rahmat Mumarakh
43. Madarisara
44. Koju Madan
45. Nathu Bhura
46. Khuwaja Rahmat
47. Khusal Atra
48. Bahadurakhtu

49. Gulabo Iso	50. Hatho Nath	51. Ghaji Mumabarak
52. Mathu Sisva	53. Madari Bahadu	54. Kahal Jeeva
55. Bhapu Kama	56. Khuwaja Ghaji	57. Manasakam
58. Mamarajo	59. Danudehhan	60. Khusal Nai
61. Iso Vadaigo	62. Khuwaja Anata	63. Madari Mamrej
64. Khansatara	65. Rahmat Kanay	66. Nuro
67. Khuwaja Madan		

Darzi (4)

1. Devo Raghunath	2. Harkasan	3. Khusal Raghunath
4. Khusal Hema		

Sudar (19)

1. Jeevan	2. Vachhi	3. Chapo
4. Ratano	5. Kano Bharavao	6. Rupo Peetha
7. Harajai	8. Lalun	9. Bharavo Chetan
10. Bharavo Maharam		

Kumbhar (8)

1. Hemovol Kasan	2. Narsangho Narain	3. Chutro Rupa
4. Heero Vasana	5. Veno Vasana	6. Gangaram
7. Rupo Raman	8. Bhivonu	

Dhobi (8)

1. Kusalo	2. Dugo	3. Sambha
4. Dhena Ki Bahu	5. Pemo Todi	6. Bhagirathro
7. Dolo	7. Dolo Judad	

Chhinpa (7)

1. Jodho	2. Ratano	3. Nango Maghi
4. Narotam	5. Kusal Narotam	6. Dharmo
7. Kavo		

Teli (7)

1. Ghaso	2. Vajto	3. Mano
4. Amra Ki Bahu	5. Khelo	6. Gokalo
7. Chhitaro		

Luhar (5)

1. Vajato Darau	2. Pemo	3. Hemo Dipas
4. Bhopo	5. Vajatosukh	

Nai (18)

1. Khusalo Amra	2. Nango Vacha	3. Ghasi Har Ram
4. Khacho Uda	5. Lalo Amra	6. Chayo Gango
7. Varago Bhara	8. Sambhu Rupovachra	9. Thakursi Nango
10. Ghasi Goda	11. Chhito Shankar	12. Thakur Sitodi
13. Neto Sadaram	14. Shivram	15. Mahari
16. Bhagvan	17. Khusalo Dudo	18. Ghaso

Pinjara (8)

1. Kadaro Khusali	2. Jamali	3. Natho
4. Peeru Ki Pat	5. Khusalo Peeru	6. Kadaro Kisano
7. Pajaro Vali	8. Mal Pajaro	

Gujar (Gujar Gadari 24)

1. Nango Muthra	2. Kusalo Muthra	3. Ajodh Reva
4. Goodaro Gujar	5. Dija Ramdas	6. Darwasi
7. Vajatodas	8. Teko Bhagata	9. Chhito Bhopo
10. Jeevano	11. Kesaro Vasaro	12. Natho Srama Gadra
13. Pemo Raman Godara	14. Udo Raman Godra	15. Deepa Gadara
16. Subho	17. Kato Rama	18. Chhamo
19. Dalo Lachhiram	20. Nago Gadari	21. Gujar Pemo
22. Rupo Gadari	23. Bhuvano Gadari	24. Khemo Gadari

Balai (Bhagat Balai 12)

1. Makud Ram	2. Ram Chand	3. Teekaram
4. Garib Das	5. Balai Cheto	6. Kes Balai
7. Sambhu Balai	8. Bhasi Balai	9. Narsangh Todu
10. Narotam	11. Taro Anata	12. Balai Vagas

Tamoli (6)

1. Ghaso	2. Keso	3. Narain
4. Khemo	5. Khusalo	6. Kheevasi

Kalal (11)

1. Lalu Rupa	2. Chauthi	3. Khusal Darvai
4. Bhagirath	5. Bhivadi	6. Lachhi
7. Jeevano	8. Diyaram	9. Nilali
10. Ghasi Barod	11. Nango Khusal	

Vajepot (6)

1. Lakharo Ghasi	2. Dheno Bhadvajo	3. Lakharo Sankari
4. Rangrej Mamorej	5. Made Bhopo	6. Leelag Rehesan

Khatik (3)

1. Bhau	2. Lalo	3. Mano

Chamar (20)

1. Deepalobol	2. Lalo	3. Samo
4. Lalee	5. Devodhana	6. Natho Magho
7. Isari	8. Sadovoli	9. Kevalo
10. Kusala	11. Natho Mardha	12. Pemo Lala
13. Pemlo Sabhvara	14. Todi	15. Bhura Ko Bhopa
16. Heero Todi	17. Harajai Dayaram	18. Nango
19. Soram	20. Ghasi	

APPENDIX 6.2

Qasbas Sangod and Mangrol: Sample of Documents
Toji-do-varkhi-parchajat-baje-talke

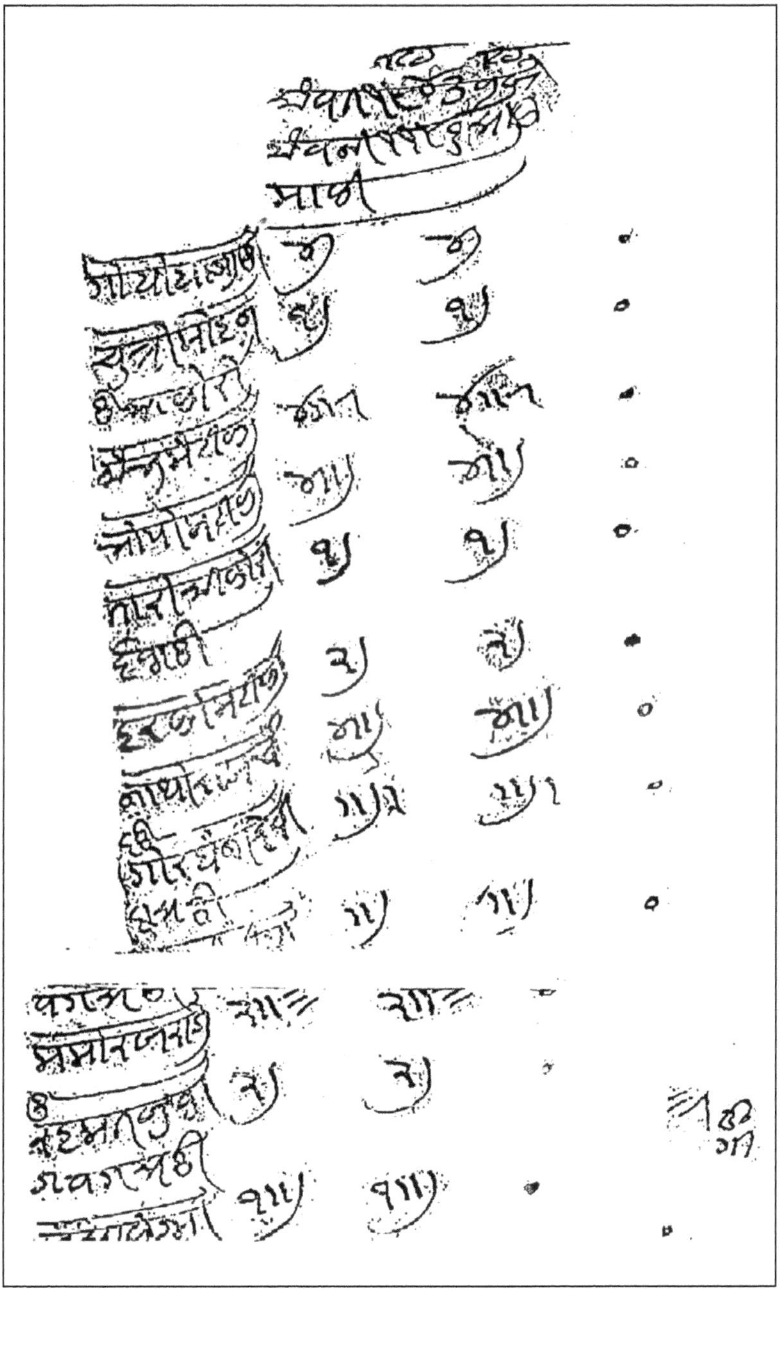

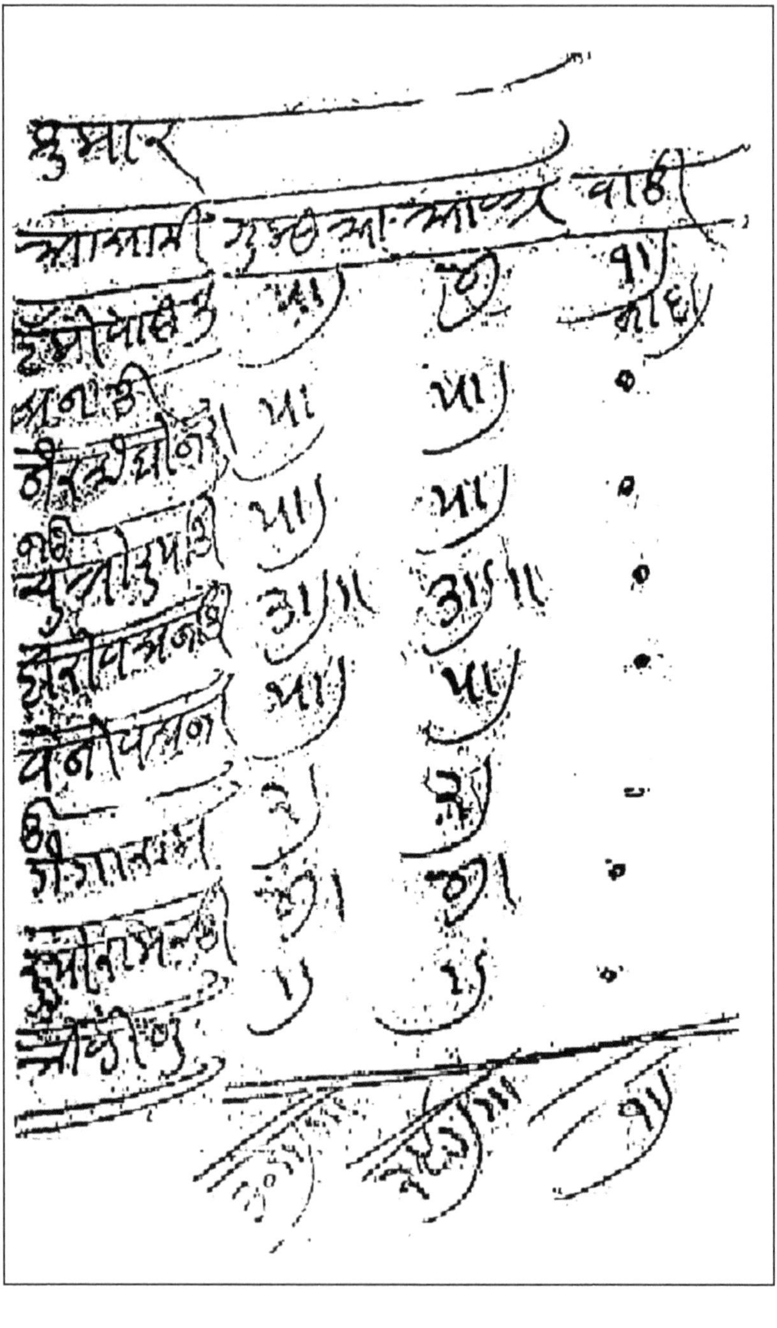

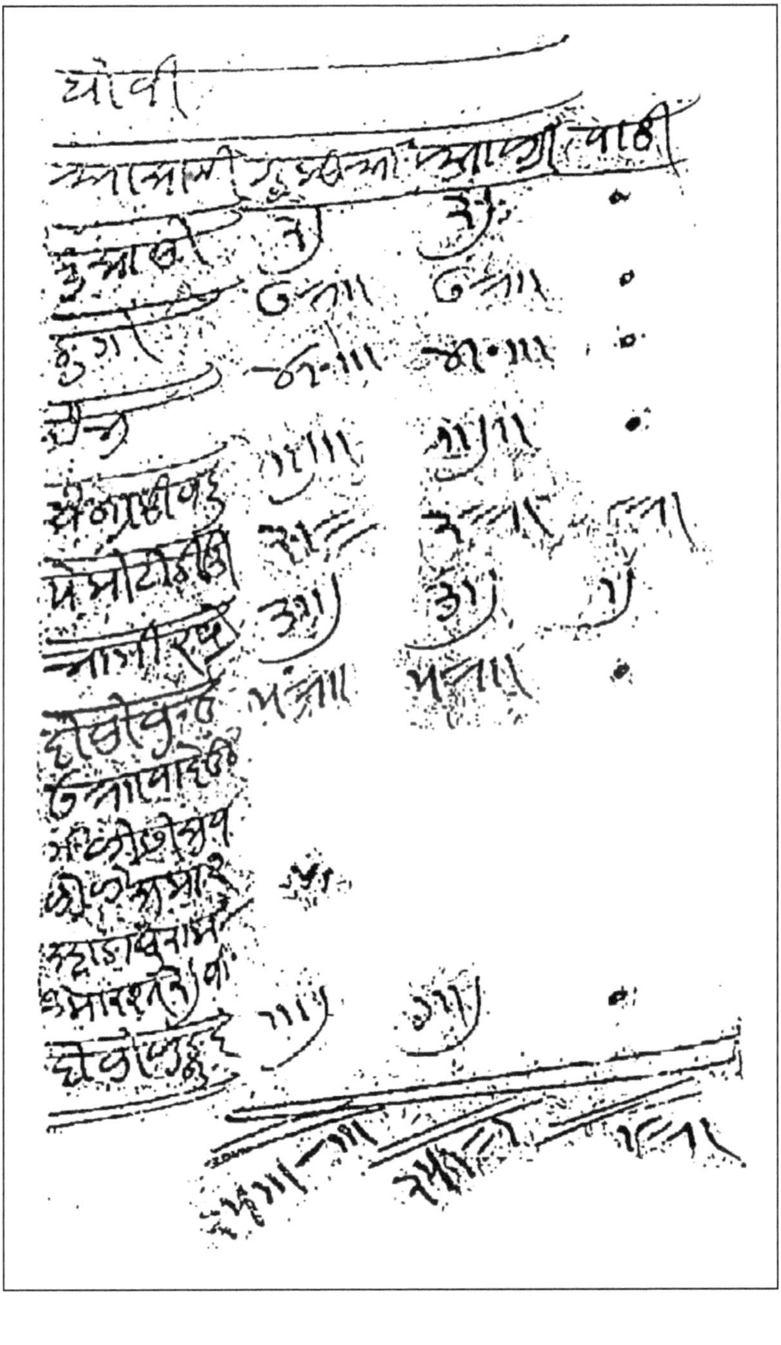

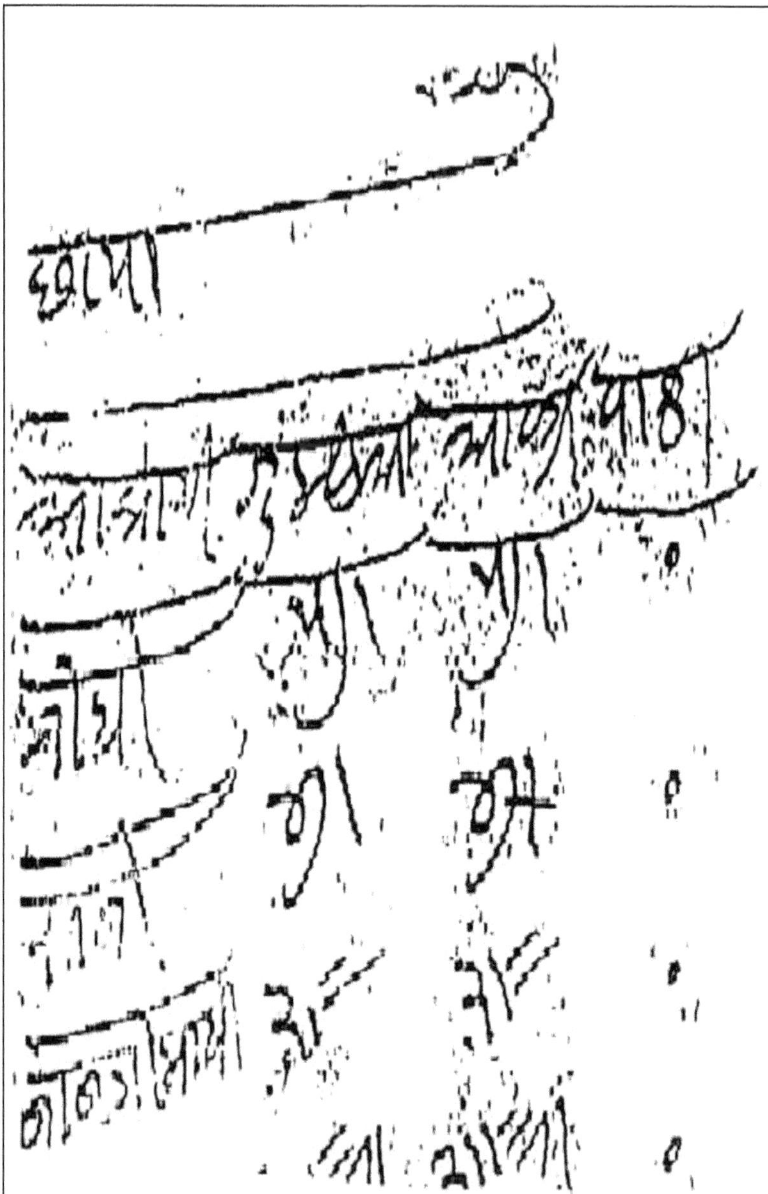

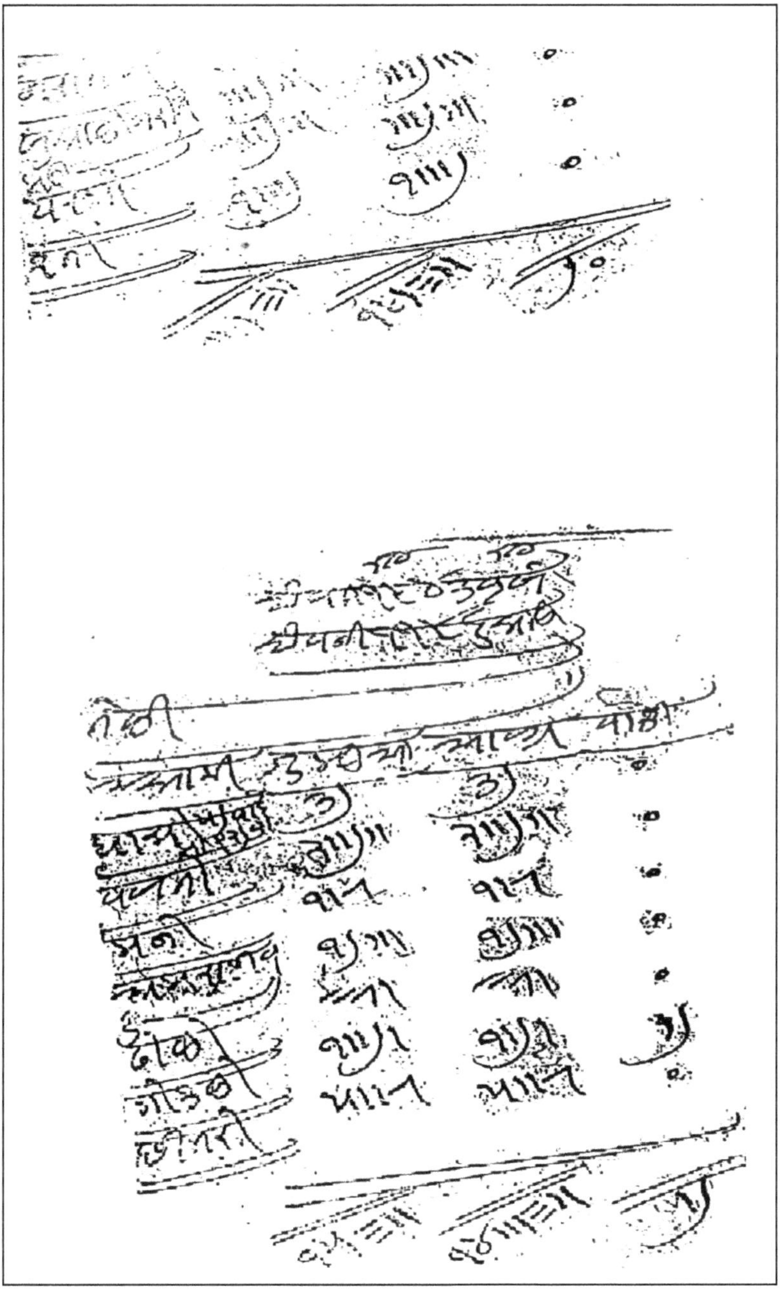

कुहार

[illegible]	[illegible]	[illegible]	[illegible]
[illegible]	३॥	३॥	
[illegible]	३॥	३॥	०
[illegible]	३	३॥	१॥
[illegible]	५॥	३॥।	१=
[illegible]	५॥	५॥	०
	[illegible]	१८॥।	१॥=

गाडी

[illegible]	[illegible]	[illegible]	
[illegible]	१॥।	१॥	
[illegible]	२	२	०
[illegible]	१॥।	१॥	०
[illegible]	३॥	३॥	[illegible]

३०

श्री रामजी

श्री पंडित जी ... लिखी

जैमांम्हे छिपी

... दरखास्त

ढीर खाडीरखो

तीरीजे

आसामी	कलांमा	पढ़ती	पाछा	नाके
तरिक	१५	.	१७	१७॥२५
घोवी	१२	२	१०	१२॥...
गाडरीया	४	.	४	४३
बारोठ	१२	४	८	८॥१॥
छीपा	६	.	६	११॥२५
मेहर	५	२	३	३५
खटीक	३	.	३	८॥१५
सुनार	१२	३	८	८॥२५
...जार	५	.	५	६०॥२५

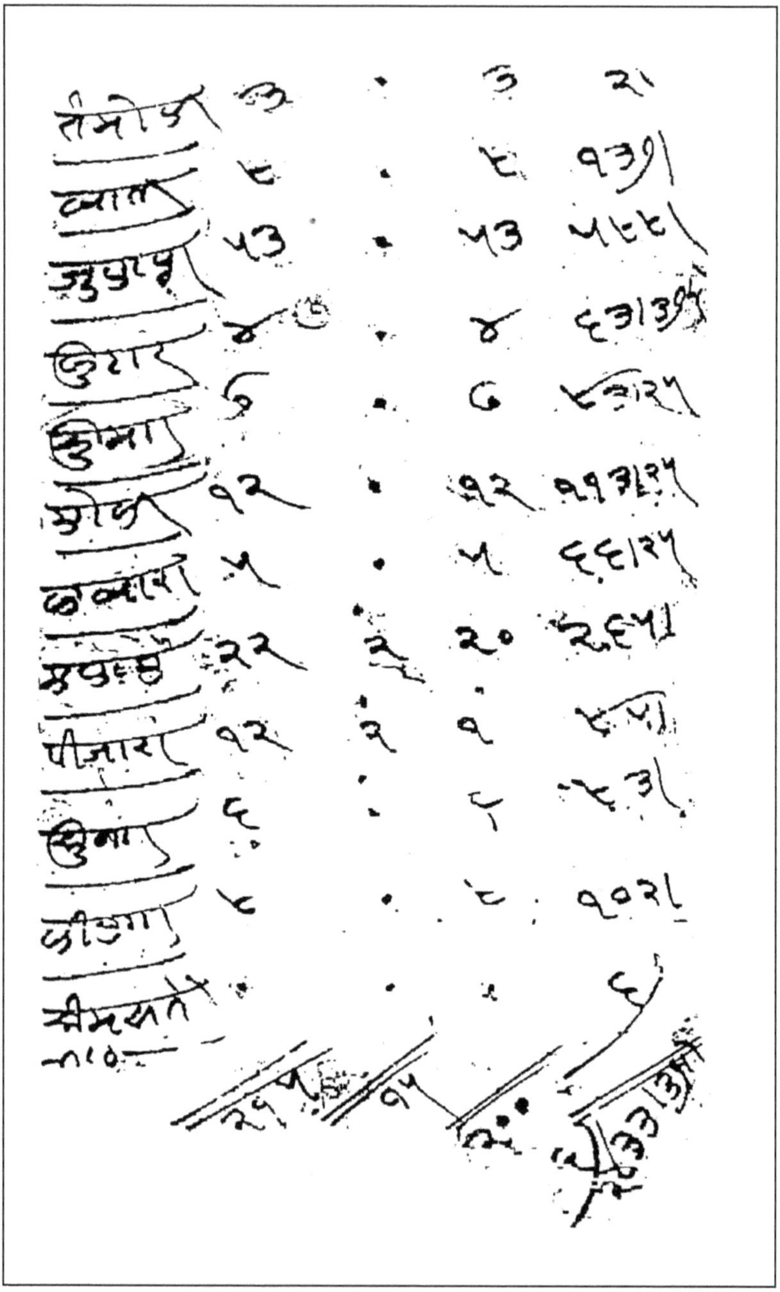

तीसोद्र	३	·	३	२।
ब्यात	८	·	८	१३।
जुग्पड	५३	·	५३	५६८।
कुंदार	४	·	४	६३।३
कुंभा	७	·	७	८३।२५
मोक	१२	·	१२	११३।२५
कमार	५	·	५	६६।२५
मुपह	२२	२	२०	२६५।
पींजारा	१२	२	१	८५।
कुंभा	६	·	५	८३।
कीरा	८	·	८	१०२।
सीमद्याते	·	·	·	६।
	२५५	१५	२००	३३।३

CHAPTER 7

Professional Groups, Textile Workers, Labour and Menial Castes in *Qasba* Churu

The pre-census data for *qasba* Churu is available in varied forms such as *dhuan* tax[1] (house tax) and the name of individual householders in urban areas. For knowing the population of professional groups of this township we have taken the information about the Banias (*sahukars*) and non-Banias (other castes) with their number of houses.[2]

The town of Churu is said to have been founded by a Jat called Chuhru in about AD 1620.[3] Later on it became a *pargana* headquarter which broadly corresponds with the modern district of the identical name. It is situated in the middle portion of north east Rajasthan between 20°24' and 29°00' latitude and 73°40' and 75°41' longitude.[4] Surrounded by sand-dunes,[5] it is bound on the north by Ganganagar district, on the east by Sikar and Jhunjhunu districts of Rajasthan and Hisar district of Haryana; on the south by the district of Nagaur and on the west by district Bikaner.[6] Churu had been one of the important towns in the eighteenth century Rajasthan, specifically in the Rathor principality of the Bikaner State.[7] It emerged as a prominent trading centre during the eighteenth-nineteenth century because of its location on the Delhi-Sindh and Delhi-Kabul routes.[8] It had served as a trade junction. The traders from northern India used to bring goods to sell here and passed through it to reach other destinations.[9]

Some traders also exchanged their goods here with goods from European, Persian, and African countries.[10] The traders ordinarily used the following routes which traversed through Churu (see Map 7.1):

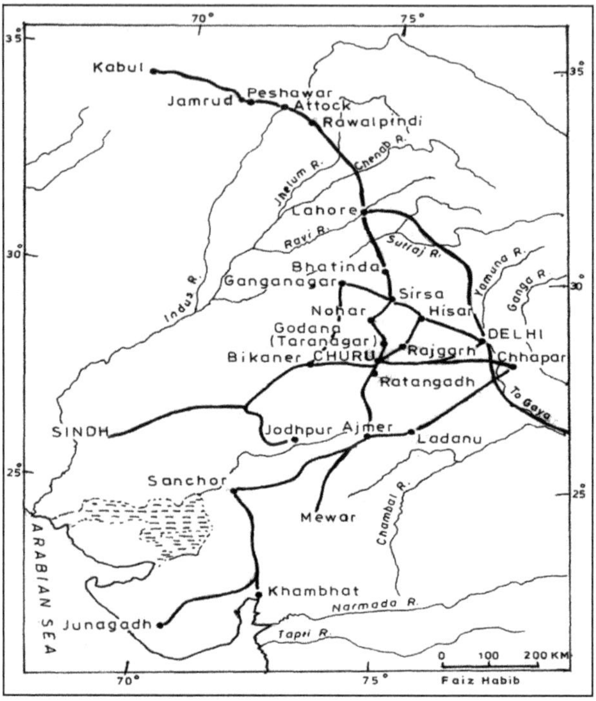

Map 7.1: Trade-routes (Eighteenth-Nineteenth Centuries)

- Bikaner-Agra[11]
- Delhi-Sindh and Delhi-Kabul[12]
- One of the most important route that was connected was Shakhambari and Ajmer to Sirsa and Bhatinda via Churu, Nohar.[13]
- Godana (Taranagar), a village of Churu connected with the district Junagarh (Girnar) via Chhapar, Ladanu, Sanchor, etc.[14]
- Khambhat-Lahore route was the other most important route which passed through Churu.[15]
- An important route leading from Churu connected Rawalpindi, Attock, Peshawar and Jamrud.[16]
- Mewar-Gaya route via Churu.[17]
- One of the routes from Churu was connected to Delhi, Hisar, Ganganagar, and Jodhpur.[18]
- Ratangarh-Rajgarh via Churu.[19]

The connecting link of the place with major cities of India brought it into prominence in the trading world. The important factor which contributed to the growth of Churu as a large commercial mart in northern Rajasthan was its situation on the routes from Multan to Sindh to Jaipur and Delhi and its internal and external trade connections. This helped to augment the population of this *pargana*-headquarter to develop into a town with appreciable number of persons. Thus, flourishing trading and commercial activities attracted traders and artisans towards this trading junction which is attested by documents of the pre-census period specifically of the nineteenth century. The *zakat* (*jagat*) *bahis* further strengthen the above evidence which indicate the emergence of many *qasbas* in this area because of intense trading activities, namely, Churu, Nohar, Reni, and Rajgarh, etc.[20]

HOUSE COUNT OF BANIAS AND NON-BANIAS

The evidence of house-count enables us to make an estimation of the population of the Banias and non-Banias. This means that if we multiply the number of houses by 5 (the conventional figure for each householder),[21] we can obtain a figure for practically the entire population of Baniasand non-Banias in *qasba* Churu.[22]

In Tables 7.1 and 7.2 are shown the caste-wise break up of houses owned by individual members are added together, i.e. houses of individuals belonging to the same caste have been put under one caste designation. The tables show castes, number of houses, population and percentage of houses to that of total owned by individual castes.

I

The evidence of house-count of Banias and non-Banias have been compiled from the *Sava bahis* of VS 1880/AD 1823, VS 1899/AD 1842, VS 1907/AD 1850 and VS 1928/AD 1871 (see Appendices 7.1, 7.2, 7.3, 7.4). The document of AD 1871 provides the enumeration of the Bania castes only while remaining *bahis* offer data both for Banias and non-Banias. Tables 7.1 and 7.2 have been prepared from these *bahis*.

TABLE 7.1: NUMBER OF HOUSES, WORKED OUT POPULATION AND PERCENTAGE OF BANIAS (SAHUKARS: MAHAJAN, MAHESWARI, OSWAL AND AGARWAL) IN *QASBA* CHURU IN THE PRE-CENSUS PERIOD

Name of Caste	VS 1880/AD 1823			VS 1884/AD 1827			VS 1899/AD 1842			VS 1907/AD 1850			VS 1928/AD 1871		
	No. of houses	Population × (5)	%	No. of houses	Population × (5)	%	No. of houses	Population × (5)	%	No. of houses	Population × (5)	%	No. of houses	Population × (5)	%
Agarwal	1	5	0.55	1	5	0.48	5	25	4.42	8	40	5.03	1	5	0.41
Bajaj	7	35	3.83	4	20	1.92	2	10	1.77	7	35	4.40	14	70	5.74
Baghla	3	15	1.64	7	35	3.37	1	5	0.88	1	5	0.63	4	20	1.64
Baghariye	–	–	–	2	10	0.96	1	5	0.88	1	5	0.63	1	5	0.41
Bharatiye	–	–	–	5	25	2.40	–	–	–	2	10	1.26	1	5	0.41
Bhagirath	3	15	1.64	1	5	0.48	2	10	1.77	1	5	0.63	4	20	1.64
Chamadiye	–	–	–	3	15	1.44	1	5	0.88	2	10	1.26	1	5	0.41
Chaudhari	–	–	–	3	15	1.44	–	–	–	1	5	0.63	3	15	1.23
Goyandak	7	35	3.83	6	30	2.88	3	15	2.65	5	25	3.14	10	50	4.10
Kothari	4	20	2.19	10	50	4.81	4	20	3.54	7	35	4.40	9	45	3.69
Kandoi	5	25	2.73	–	–	–	4	20	3.45	5	25	3.14	6	30	2.46
Khemaka	12	60	6.56	11	55	5.29	4	20	3.45	6	30	3.77	13	65	5.33
Lakhotiya	–	–	–	11	55	5.29	2	10	1.77	5	25	3.14	1	5	0.41
Lohiye	3	15	1.64	10	50	4.81	1	5	0.88	3	15	1.89	8	40	3.28
Manada	2	10	1.09	2	10	0.96	1	5	0.88	1	5	0.63	6	30	2.46
Mitari	7	35	3.83	13	65	6.25	4	20	3.54	4	20	2.52	9	45	3.69
Modi	–	–	–	1	5	0.48	–	–	–	–	–	–	1	5	0.41
Parakh	7	35	3.83	9	45	4.3	3	15	2.15	1	5	0.63	7	35	2.87
Pasari	–	–	–	3	15	1.44	1	5	0.88	–	–	–	1	5	0.41
Potdar	9	45	4.92	26	130	12.5	6	30	5.31	8	40	5.03	10	50	4.10
Sarapa	–	–	–	–	–	–	2	10	1.77	–	–	–	1	5	0.41
Sarraf	3	15	1.64	3	15	1.44	1	5	0.88	5	25	3.14	9	45	3.69
Sarawagi	10	50	5.46	9	45	4.33	8	40	7.08	7	35	4.40	11	55	4.51

Sighimiti	2	10	1.09	2	10	0.96	1	5	0.88	2	10	1.26	2	10	0.82
Singhaniye	–	–	–	8	40	3.85	–	–	–	–	–	–	2	10	0.82
Surana	4	20	2.19	5	25	2.40	4	20	3.54	4	20	2.52	3	15	1.23
Sekhsariye	4	20	2.19	1	5	0.48	–	–	–	1	5	0.63	–	–	–
Banthiye	7	35	3.83	12	60	5.77	–	–	–	2	10	1.26	8	40	3.28
Baid	2	10	1.09	1	5	0.48	1	5	0.88	2	10	1.26	4	20	1.64
Bothera	2	10	1.09	2	10	0.96	1	5	0.88	2	10	1.26	–	–	–
Pediwal	1	5	0.55	–	–	–	1	5	0.88	1	5	0.63	1	5	0.40
Dagi	1	5	0.55	2	10	0.96	1	5	0.88	–	–	–	–	–	–
Bavari	8	40	4.37	–	–	–	7	35	6.19	6	30	3.77	–	–	–
Tai	5	25	2.73	1	5	0.48	5	25	4.42	7	35	4.40	4	20	1.64
Kasera	2	10	1.09	–	–	–	–	–	–	–	–	–	2	10	0.82
Jalan	1	5	0.55	2	10	0.96	–	–	–	–	–	–	2	10	0.82
Bhadsariye	–	–	–	–	–	–	1	5	0.88	–	–	–	–	–	–
Jasrasariye	–	–	–	–	–	–	1	5	0.88	–	–	–	–	–	–
Hirawat	–	–	–	3	15	1.44	1	5	0.88	1	5	0.63	2	10	0.82
Gopalpuriye	–	–	–	–	–	–	1	5	0.88	–	–	–	–	–	–
Kejariwal	–	–	–	–	–	–	1	5	0.88	–	–	–	3	15	1.23
Sariye	–	–	–	–	–	–	6	30	5.31	–	–	–	–	–	–
Luniye	–	–	–	–	–	–	1	5	0.88	–	–	–	4	20	1.64
Jaluka	–	–	–	–	–	–	2	10	1.77	–	–	–	4	20	1.64
Rajgarhiye	–	–	–	–	–	–	–	–	–	–	–	–	1	5	0.41
Kago	–	–	–	–	–	–	–	–	–	–	–	–	5	25	2.05
Ramgarhiya	–	–	–	–	–	–	–	–	–	–	–	–	2	10	0.82
Dudhwala	–	–	–	–	–	–	–	–	–	–	–	–	2	10	0.82
Khandelwala	–	–	–	–	–	–	–	–	–	–	–	–	1	5	0.41
Miscellaneous	61	305	33.33	29	145	13.94	91	155	19.50	43	215	27.04	63	315	25.82
Total	183	915	100	208	1,040	100	113	265	100	159	795	100	244	1,200	100

TABLE 7.2: NUMBER OF HOUSES AND WORKED OUT POPULATION OF NON-BANIAS IN *QASBA* CHURU IN THE PRE-CENSUS PERIOD

Name of Caste	VS 1880/AD 1823			VS 1884/AD 1827			VS 1899/AD 1842			VS 1907/AD 1850		
	No. of houses	Population × (5)	%	No. of houses	Population × (5)	%	No. of houses	Population × (5)	%	No. of houses	Population × (5)	%
Ahir	–	–	–	1	5	0.86	–	–	–	–	–	–
Banjara	–	–	–	–	–	–	–	–	–	8	40	2.11
Brahman	–	–	–	–	–	–	–	–	–	30	150	7.92
Chand	–	–	–	–	–	–	–	–	–	15	75	3.96
Chhinpa	5	25	2.28	3	15	2.59	9	45	3.46	–	–	–
Churigar	4	20	1.83	–	–	–	5	25	1.92	4	20	1.06
Darzi	–	–	–	1	5	0.86	6	30	2.31	8	40	2.11
Dhobi	–	–	–	–	–	–	13	65	5.00	10	50	2.64
Gujar	–	–	–	–	–	–	2	10	0.77	4	20	1.06
Jat	18	90	8.22	–	–	–	5	20	1.92	4	20	1.06
Jogi	–	–	–	–	–	–	–	–	–	12	60	3.17
Kalal	4	20	1.83	1	5	0.86	4	20	1.54	4	20	1.06
Khati	8	40	3.65	1	5	0.86	9	45	3.46	10	50	2.64
Khatik	3	15	1.37	–	–	–	7	35	2.69	4	20	1.06
Kumbhar	–	–	–	–	–	–	9	45	3.46	8	40	2.11
Lilgar	2	10	0.91	–	–	–	3	15	1.15	5	25	1.36
Luhar	–	–	–	–	–	–	7	35	2.69	–	–	–
Mali	36	180	16.44	–	–	–	–	–	–	48	240	12.66

Manihar	8	40	3.65	–	–	–	9	45	3.46	13	65	3.43
Meghwal	14	70	6.39	–	–	–	–	–	–	–	–	–
Mochi	15	75	6.85	–	–	–	–	–	–	9	45	2.37
Nai	–	–	–	4	20	3.45	13	65	5.00	8	40	2.11
Pijara	8	40	3.65		–	–	9	45	3.46	11	55	2.90
Purohit	–	–	–	1	5	0.86	–	–	–	–	–	–
Rajput	–	–	–	–	–	–	25	125	9.62	–	–	–
Rangrez	21	105	9.59	–	–	–	13	65	5.00	11	55	2.90
Sunar	16	80	7.31	6	30	5.17	–	–	–	19	95	5.01
Teli	41	205	18.72	–			–	–	–	36	180	9.50
Miscellaneous	16	80	7.31	98	490	84.48	112	560	43.08	83	415	2.89
Total	219	1,095	100	116	580	100	260	1,300	100	379	1,895	100

From Tables 7.1 and 7.2, it is apparent that the population of the non-Banias was larger than the Banias in the year AD 1823, 1842 and 1850[23] (also see Graph 7.1). Though Banias were in the leading position in the year AD 1827[24] in the *qasba*, among the non-Banias the major castes were Teli (18.72 per cent), Mali (16.44 per cent) and Rangrez (9.59 per cent) in AD 1823;[25] Sunar (5.17 per cent), Nai (3.45 per cent) and Chhinpa (2.59 per cent) in AD 1827;[26] Rajput (9.62 per cent), Dhobi (5 per cent), Rangrez and Nai (5 per cent each) in AD 1842;[27] and Mali (12.66 per cent), Teli (9.50 per cent) and Brahman (7.92 per cent) in AD 1850.[28] The other non-Bania castes in the *qasba* were Ahirs, Banjaras, Chands, Churigars (bangle makers), Darzis (tailors), Gujars, Jats, Jogis, Kalals (wine sellers), Khatis, Khatiks, Kumbhars (potters), Lilgars, Luhars (blacksmiths), Manihars (bracelet makers), Meghwals, Mochis (shoemakers/leather workers), Pinjaras and Purohits.[29] While the miscellaneous non-Bania castes represent 7.31 per cent in AD 1823; 84.48 per cent in AD 1827; 43.08 per cent in AD 1842 and 21.89 per cent in AD 1850.[30]

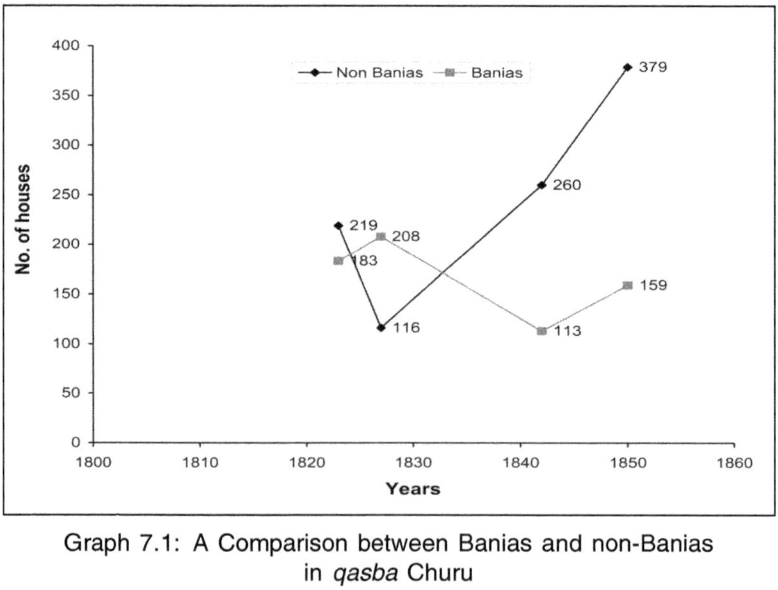

Graph 7.1: A Comparison between Banias and non-Banias in *qasba* Churu

The Banias consisted of Khemakas (6.56 per cent), Sarawagis (5.46 per cent) and Potdars (4.92 per cent) in AD 1823.[31] But in this year the miscellaneous professional groups were one-third (1/3) of the total castes[32] such as Potdars (12.50 per cent), Mitaris (6.25 per cent) and Banthiyas (5.77 per cent) in AD 1827.[33] Sarawagis (7.08 per cent), Bavaris (6.19 per cent) and Potdars (5.31 per cent) in AD 1842.[34] The percentage of various castes in different years is as follows: Potdars and Agarwals (5.03 per cent each), Bajajs, Kotharis and Sarawagis (4.40 per cent each) and Khemakas (3.78 per cent) in AD 1850;[35] Bajajs (5.74 per cent), Khemakas (5.33 per cent), Sarawagis (4.51 per cent) and Potdars (4.10 per cent) in AD 1871.[36] The other castes of Banias available in the *qasba* are: Baghela, Baghariya, Bharatiye, Bhagirath, Chamadiya, Chaudhari, Goyandak, Kandoi, Lakhotiya, Lohiya, Manada, Modi, Parakh, Pasari, Sarapa, Sarraf, Sighimiti, Singhaniya, Surana, Sekhsariya, Banthiya, Baid, Bothara, Pediwal, Daga, Tai, Kasera, Jalan, Bhadsariya, Jasrasariya, Hirawat, Gopalpuriya, Kejariwal, Sariyo, Luniyo, Jaluka, Rajgarhiya, Kago, Ramgarhiya, Dudhwala and Khandelwala.[37] The miscellaneous Bania castes represent 33.33 per cent in AD 1823, 13.94 per cent in AD 1827, 19.50 per cent in AD 1842, 27.04 per cent in AD 1850 and 25.82 per cent in AD 1871.[38]

II

A private record of Mirjamal Potdar (*poddars*), a well-known business family of the area provides us the house-count[39] and shop-count[40] of Banias and non-Banias in the *qasba*. The census was carried out in VS 1884/AD 1827. It records the names of individual owners with their caste designation.[41] In addition it also enters the specific size of open plots owned by individuals. For shops it gives the number and name of owner with caste and their location in the market.[42] In Section I, the details of house-count, had been explained. However, in Section II we are concerned to explain about shop-count of Banias and non-Banias only. The details are given in Tables 7.3 and 7.4.

TABLE 7.3: SHOP-COUNT OF BANIAS (VS 1884/AD 1827)

Name of the Caste	No. of Shops	Percentage of Shops
Potdar	38	15.2
Baghala	23	9.2
Mitari	18	7.2
Pasari	13	5.2
Khemka	13	5.2
Bhagirath	11	4.2
Sarawagi	09	3.6
Singhaniye	09	3.6
Murarka	09	3.6
Parakh	09	3.6
Mudda	09	3.6
Manada	09	3.6
Banthiya	08	3.2
Goyandak	07	2.8
Sekhsariye	07	2.8
Kothari	06	2.4
Lohiya	04	1.6
Bajaj	04	1.6
Sankhen	04	1.6
Chaudhari	03	1.2
Sankhuwala	03	1.2
Kanodiya	03	1.2
Fatehpuriya	03	1.2
Bihani	03	1.2
Dhoot	02	0.8
Modi	02	0.8
Surana	02	0.8
Lakhotiya	02	0.8
Kalindiya	02	0.8
Sarahiya	02	0.8
Jaluka	02	0.8
Sarraf	01	0.4
Joga	01	0.4
Rinya	01	0.4
Bothara	01	0.4
Muhnot	01	0.4
Jaju	01	0.4
Tai	01	0.4
Nahta	01	0.4
Sarabhsukh	01	0.4
Minani	01	0.4
Boghra	01	0.4
Total	250	100

TABLE 7.4: SHOP-COUNT OF NON-BANIAS
(VS 1884/AD 1827)

Name of the Caste	No. of Shops	Percentage of Shops
Mohant	4	8.33
Oje	3	6.25
Permian Hasantu	3	6.25
Lilgar Peeru	2	4.16
Sunar	2	4.16
Jatiye	2	4.16
Kyal	1	2.08
Darzi	1	2.08
Dadupanthi	1	2.08
Miscellaneous	29	60.40
Total	48	100

As mentioned earlier, the document contains the shop-count for the *qasba*. The location and the arrangement of the shops in the market is also recorded.[43] The shop-count enables us to know the kind of business carried out in the town by the Banias. Among the Banias, Potdars occupied the first place who owned above 15 per cent of shops. Then followed the Baghala (9.2 per cent), Mitari (7.2 per cent), Pasari/grocers (5.2 per cent), Bhagirath (4.4 per cent), Sarawagi (3.6 per cent) and Goyandaka (2.8 per cent), etc.[44] Among the non-Banias, the leading castes are Mahant (8.33 per cent), followed by Ojha, Hasantu, Lilgar, Sunar, Jatiya, Kayal, Darzi, etc. While miscellaneous castes occupied 60.40 per cent shops.[45]

III

It would be interesting to study the position of textile workers in the nineteenth century.[46] For this we have reformulated Table 7.5 from the data furnished in Tables 7.1-7.4. There were six castes involved in the textile industry,[47] whose number of houses and worked out population (obtained by multiplication of number of houses/shops by 5) for different years along with the population of 1931 is given in Table 7.5.

TABLE 7.5: TEXTILE WORKERS: A COMPARATIVE FIGURE OF URBAN POPULATION AD 1823, 1827, 1842, 1850 WITH CENSUS 1931

Name of Caste	Population of *qasba* Churu								
	VS 1880/ AD 1823		VS 1884/ AD 1827		VS 1899/ AD 1842		VS 1907/ AD 1850		Census 1931
	Total population	%	Total population	%	Total population	%	Total population	%	
Chhinpa (calico printer)	25	14.71	15	50.00	45	16.98	NA*	–	DA**
Darzi (tailor)	NA	–	5	16.67	30	11.32	40	17.78	DA
Dhobi (washer man)	NA	–	NA	–	65	24.53	50	22.22	DA
Lilgar (indigo dyer)	NA	–	10	33.33	15	5.66	25	11.11	DA
Pinjara (cotton carder)	40	23.56	NA	–	45	16.98	55	24.44	DA
Rangrez (dyer)	105	61.76	NA	–	65	24.53	55	24.44	DA
Total	170	100	30	100	265	100	225	100	DA

Notes: *Not available; **Disappeared. Julahas (Weavers) are one of the important textile workers but it is surprising to note that they were not seen, in *qasba* Churu.

Table 7.5 is a comparison of the population figures of the textile workers in the available years with that of the caste census of 1931, leads to some very interesting results. From the 1931 census,[48] we have the names of at least six textile castes/professional groups, which practically completely disappeared or got wiped out from the *qasba* (see Graph 7.2).

Table 7.5 shows that the dominating textile workers of the *qasba* were Rangrezs. In AD 1823, they comprised 61.67 per cent of the textile workers of Churu, and were followed by Pinjaras (23.56 per cent) and Chhinpas (14.71 per cent).[49] In AD 1827 Chhinpas made up 50 per cent of the workers, followed by Lilgars (33.33 per cent) and Darzis (16.67 per cent).[50] In AD 1842 the position of the Dhobis and Rangrezs was same, each accounting for 24.53 per cent of the textile worker population of Churu, followed by Chhinpas (16.98 per cent), Pinjaras (16.98 per cent), Darzis (11.32 per cent) and Lilgars (5.66 per cent).[51] In AD 1850, the first position was enjoyed by the Rangrezs and Pinjaras who comprised 24.44 per cent each, followed by Dhobis (22.22 per cent), Darzis (17.78 per cent) and Lilgars (11.11 per cent).[52] The absence of Julahas (weavers) in the documents is surprising.

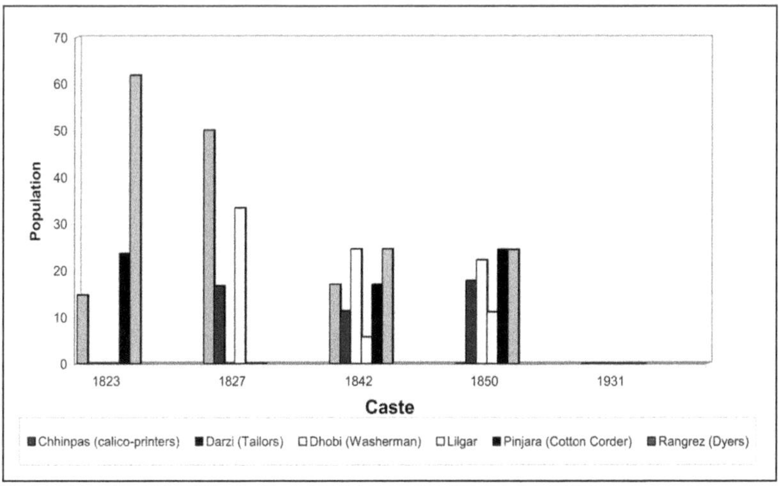

Graph 7.2: A Comparison of Population of Textile Workers in *Qasba* Churu

After an examination of the above data we can conclusively say that there was a clear and sharp decline or disappearance of the number of Chhinpas (calico printers), Darzis (tailors), Dhobis (washerman), Lilgars (indigo dyer), Pinjaras (cotton carder) and Rangrezs (dyers). One credible presumption could be that this sharp decline was an outcome of the impact of the competition of British cloths in the nineteenth century. The textile workers especially Chhinpas (calico printers) suffered heavily in the nineteenth century, because probably the British cloth and yarn became cheaper, and at the same time the British cloth merchants cheapened their product and therefore British cloths gradually generated larger demand and thus affected the demand for locally made cloths, so far so that gradually the number of the textile workers in Churu declined and ultimately disappeared. This is attested by the census of 1931. This study shows the symptom of de-industrialization and consequently de-urbanization in *qasba* Churu.

NOTES

1. *Dhuan* cess also called hearth or houses tax. James Tod, *Annals and Antiquities of Rajasthan*, vol. II, Humphrey Milford, Oxford University Press, London, 1920, pp. 1128-9
2. *Sava bahi*, VS 1880/AD 1823, VS 1884/AD 1827, VS 1899/AD 1842, VS 1907/AD 1850, VS 1928/AD 1871.
3. *Rajasthan District Gazetteers, Churu*, ed. K.K. Sehgal, Government of Rajasthan, Jaipur, 1970, p. 1.
4. Ibid., p. 1.
5. Ibid., p. 4.
6. Ibid., p. 1.
7. Govind Agrawal, *Churu Mandal ka Shodhpurna Itihas*, Lok Sanskriti Shodh Sansthan, Churu, 1974, p. 1.
8. Mountstuart Elphinstone, *An Account of the Kingdom of Caubul*, Richard Bentley, London, 1939. Also see Agrawal, *Churu Mandal ka Shodhpurna Itihas*, op. cit., p. 478.
9. *Rajputana ka Itihas*, cover 1, pp. 117-18. Also see Agrawal, *Churu Mandal ka Shodhpurna Itihas*, op. cit., p. 477.

10. Ibid., pp.117-18.
11. *Rajasthan District Gazetteers, Churu*, op. cit., p. 139.
12. Agarwal, *Churu Mandal ka Shodhpurna Itihas*, op. cit., p. 478.
13. *Art and Architecture, Bikaner State*, pp. 49-50, cf. Agarwal, *Churu Mandal ka Shodhpurna Itihas*, op. cit., p. 478.
14. Agarwal, *Churu Mandal ka Shodhpurna Itihas*, ibid., p. 478.
15. *Yugpradhan Shri Jin Chandra Suri*, pp. 66-7 (as quoted by Agrawal, ibid., p. 478).
16. Agarwal, *Churu Mandal ka Shodhpurna Itihas*, op. cit., p. 478.
17. Ibid.
18. Ibid.
19. Ibid., p. 479.
20. *Zakat/jagat bahis* (VS 1800/AD 1743, VS 1820/AD 1763) of different years for Bikaner State.
21. 'The conventional figure for each householder', this method for estimation of population has was adopted by S.P. Gupta, B.L. Bhadani, M.S. Ranawat and James Tod, as 4.5, 4.5, 5 and 5 respectively.
22. See all the prepared tables of Banias and non-Banias and all the graphs (Tables 7.1, 7.2, 7.3, 7.4 and 7.5; Graphs 7.1 and 7.2).
23. *Sava Bahis*, VS 1880/AD 1823, VS 1899/AD 1842, VS 1960/AD 1903, RSA, Bikaner.
24. Govind Agrawal, 'Churu Me Gharon, Noharon Ki Prachin Vigat', in *Marushri*, January-June 1979, part III, vols. 2 and 3, pp. 19-30.
25. *Sava Bahi qasba* Churu, VS 1880/AD 1823.
26. Agrawal, 'Churu Me Gharon, Noharon Ki Prachin Vigat', op. cit.
27. *Sava Bahi qasba* Churu, VS 1899/AD 1842.
28. *Sava Bahi qasba* Churu, VS 1907/AD 1850.
29. *Sava Bahis qasba* Churu, op. cit., and Agrawal, 'Churu Me Gharon, Noharon Ki Prachin Vigat', op. cit.
30. Ibid.
31. *Sava Bahi qasba* Churu, VS 1880/AD 1823.
32. Ibid.
33. Agrawal, 'Churu Me Gharon, Noharon Ki Prachin Vigat', op. cit.
34. *Sava Bahi qasba* Churu, VS 1899/AD 1842.
35. *Sava Bahi qasba* Churu, VS 1907/AD 1850.
36. *Sava Bahi qasba* Churu, VS 1928/AD 1871.
37. *Sava Bahi qasba* Churu, and Agrawal, 'Churu Me Gharon, Noharon Ki Prachin Vigat', op. cit.
38. Ibid.
39. Agrawal, 'Churu Me Gharon, Noharon Ki Prachin Vigat', op. cit.

40. Agrawal, 'Churu Me Haton Ki Prachin Vigat', in *Marushri*, December 1973, part 1, vol. II, pp. 43-7.
41. Agrawal, *Marushri*, op. cit., pp. 19-30.
42. Ibid., pp. 43-7.
43. Ibid.
44. Ibid.
45. Ibid.
46. *Sava Bahis qasba* Churu, VS 1880/AD 1823, VS 1899/AD 1842, VS 1907/AD 1850, VS 1907/AD 1850, VS 1928/AD 1871 and Agarwal, *Marushri*, op. cit., pp. 19-20 and 43-7.
47. There are six castes or professional groups included in the textile crafts: Chhinpas (calico printers), Darzis (tailors), Dhobis (washermen), Lilgar (indigo dyers), Pinjaras (cotton carders) and Rangrezs (dyers).
48. B.L. Cole, *Census of India 1931* (*Rajputana Agency*), rpt., Manohar, Delhi, 1992.
49. *Sava Bahi qasba* Churu, VS 1880/AD 1823.
50. Agrawal, *Marushri*, op. cit.
51. *Sava Bahi qasba* Churu, VS 1899/AD 1842.
52. *Sava Bahi qasba* Churu, VS 1907/AD 1850.

APPENDIX 7.1

Sample of *Sava Bahi* Documents:
Information of House Count in *Qasba* Churu
(A part of sources for the year of VS 1880/AD 1823)

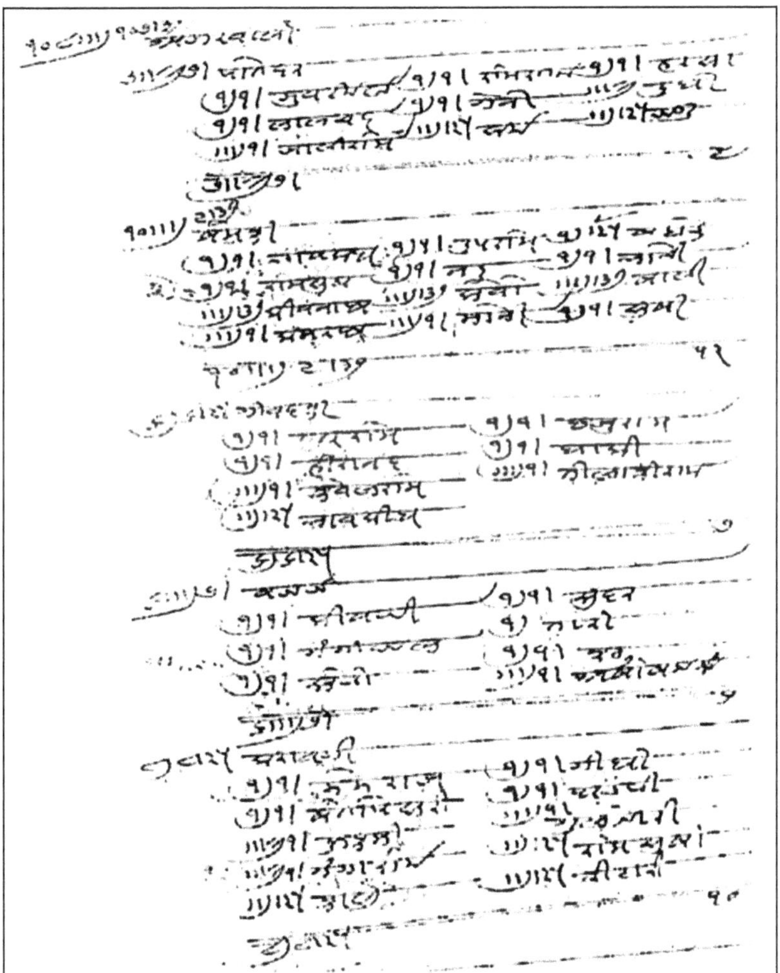

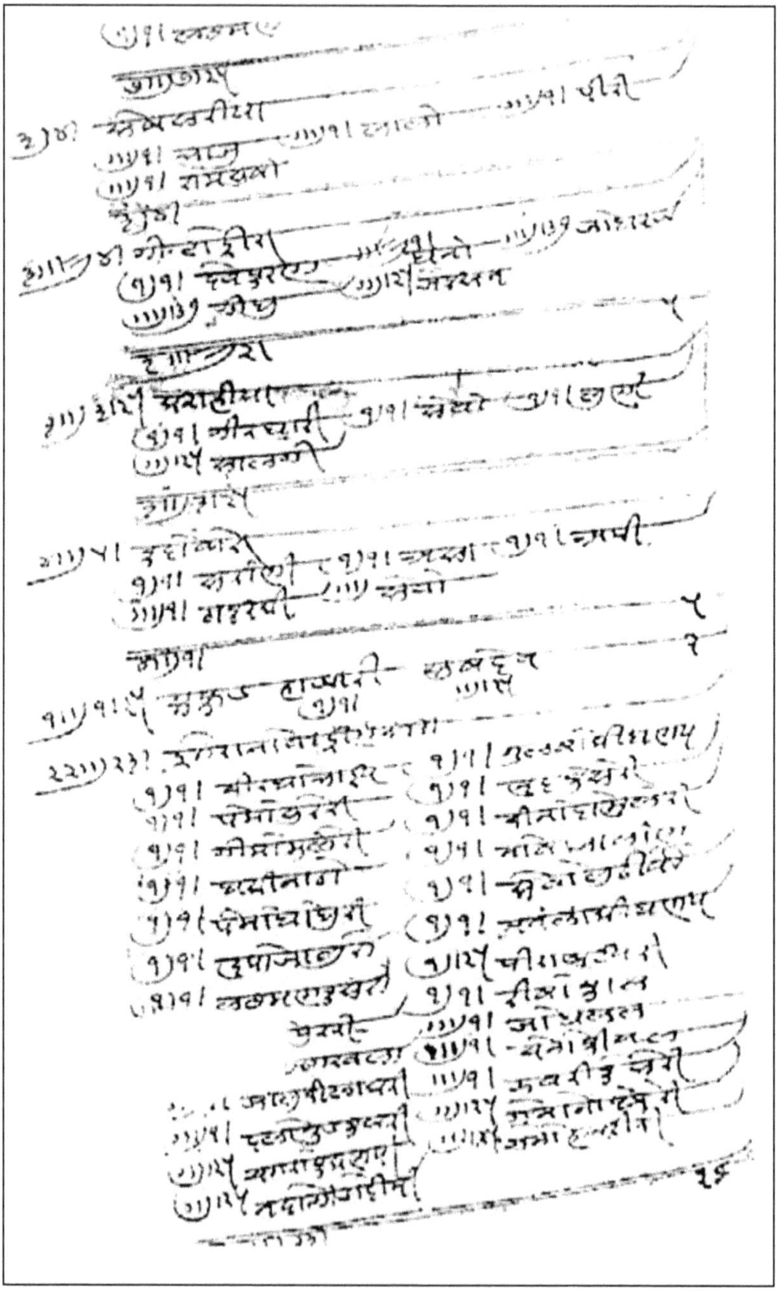
(।)१। स्वरूप
३)४। ।।)१। पीरी
।।)१। रामख्ञो
।।)१३ जोधा
।।)१२ जसवन्त
।।)१। चोखो
।।)१। कासीदो ।।)१। ञ्रापी
।।)१। माइरपी ।।)१। सन्तो
(१)१। बीसायदा
(१)१। बुपाजी
(१)१। जी सवा
२६

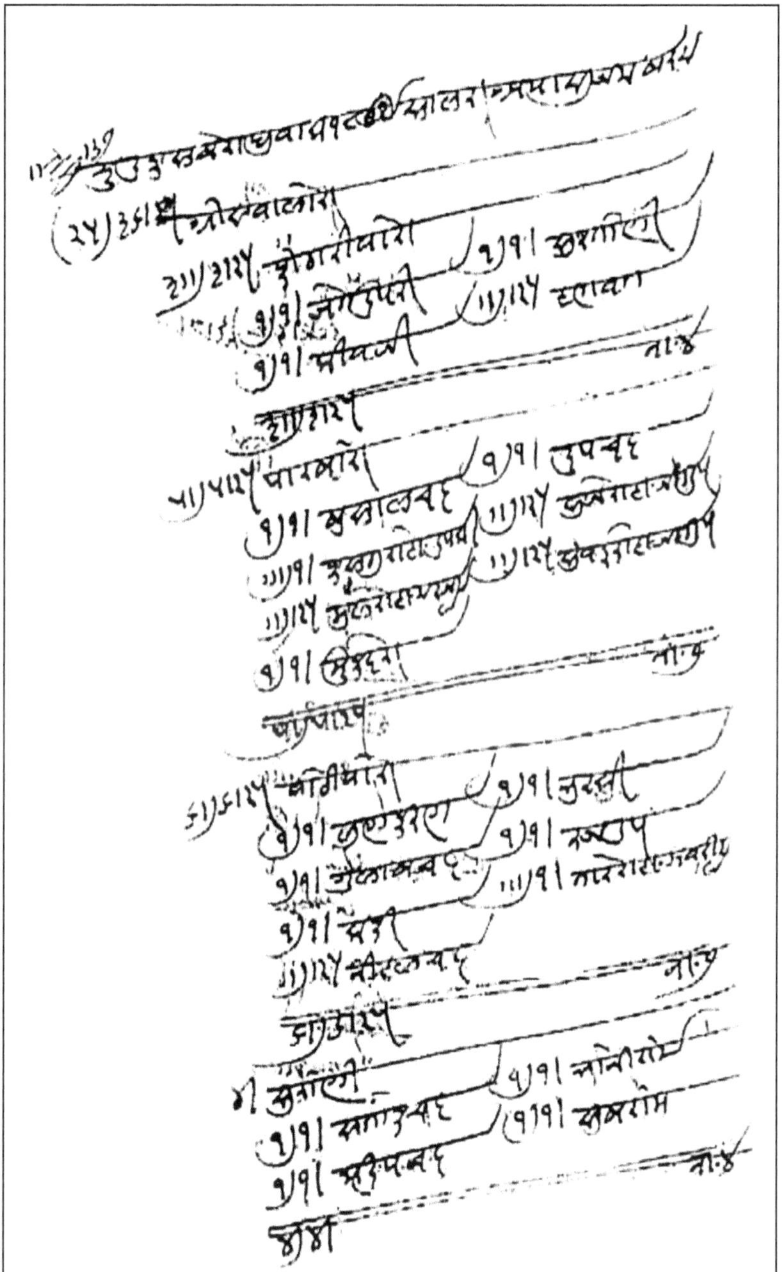

ना.४
१।१। रुपचंद
ना.५
ना.५
ना.४

APPENDIX 7.2

Qasba Churu (VS 1899/AD 1842): House Count of Banias

Sahukars (Kheti khadvodiyo: 141)

1. Devi Dutt Potdar
2. Pannalal Khemak
3. Rampratap
4. Hukamo Dhodhuro
5. Dhuchar Bothra
6. Sivlal Chamadiye
7. Hadvanto Goyandak
8. Sukhlal Suwano
9. Ukali Lunaro
10. Jeevan Kesan
11. Hero Vagasiyo
12. Phal Bhagirathro
13. Jogi Khemako
14. Rupo Bhansariyo
15. Nathee Sakud
16. Udeebhan Saraff
17. Udlan Bhagirathro
18. Rupo Bajaj
19. Ram Sukh Karni
20. Vashrishi Lakhotiyo
21. Mamati Soni
22. Sapano Goyandako
23. Jeevan Bhimji
24. Pemi Surano
25. Chandu Potdar
26. Khuchi Tikara
27. Kheto Pediwal
28. Sambhu Mitari
29. Puran Sukhano
30. Baliraj Chadag
31. Asu Bavari
32. Dedi Bavari
33. Nango Bavari
34. Dasu Agrawal
35. Ramkaran Bavari
36. Nathu Bavari
37. Ramkisan Prathsasi
38. Ramup Mitari
39. Bhopat Kuthiro
40. Mino Toiro
41. Chumi Kandoi
42. Chanduli Lohiyo
43. Udi Toiro
44. Har Gopal Sarraf
45. Manasi Palaiko
46. Harsukh Toiro
47. Sambholasarvo
48. Sivnath Kandoi
49. Vaali Kandoi
50. Vamdayal Mitri
51. Dhani Daliwal
52. Bhipo Sidhi
53. Aadu Bavara
54. Murali Bajaj
55. Mani Kothari
56. Rupo Daliwal
57. Minaro Goga Pasari
58. Shaghu Veepaliro
59. Gama Toiro
60. Vali Mandawaro
61. Gulajada Sarwagi
62. Phagusar Salro

63. Ram Sarwargi
64. Ramsukh Sarwagi
65. Rupasi Khemak
66. Sarwan Surana
67. Udi Sarawagi
68. Aabhi Kandoi
69. Dedi Sarawagi
70. Vaali Sarawagi
71. Rato Sarawagi
72. Sanchar Kripal
73. Savaro Goyandako
74. Manado Dadodiyo
75. Kiti Safud
76. Khemo Kothari
77. Sasano Sasari

78-82 not available

83. Pranapo Parakh
84. Ghazi Parakh
85. Mehiro Bhasi
86. Sevo Saraipo
87. Devi Potdar
88. Devo Nahadi
89. Kalu Barad
90. Peni Surano
91. Hadavato Sarawagi
92. Deepo Toiro
93. Seri Dago
94. Hadavato Khejari
95. Lakshman Sarawagi
96. Koni Agrawal
97. Sebouth Valparo
98. Padmi Budvo
99. Saav Jeejabhan
100. Gopi Agrawal
101. Jeevan Romuro
102. Navali Potdar
103. Ramkaran Jakhan
104. Jevrajal Lakhotiye
105. Veero Agrawal
106. Cheeros Jasrasariye
107. Nathmol Bavari
108. Jeevan Bavari
109. Heero Agrawal
110. Heero Agrawal
111. Lunraj Sarapo
112. Sultano Gopalpuryo
113. Dosi Hirawat
114. Sambhu Potdar
115. Khetopeero Mitari
116. Mamdino
117. Manika Kadechharo
118. Pari Pondariro
119. Kasroji Vanaro
120. Manyoji Peri
121. Alawag Saswanapuro
123. Choinmal
124. Upali Motiro
125. Kheti Podinaro
126. Moti Porajaro
127. Khetiye Nejaro
128. Mutalo Bajro
129. Padu Nimro
130. Isi Sadharo
131. Masi Potairo
132. Jalu Jayro
133. Para Lolasuro
134. Bahariyo Gonari
135. Guman Potajani
136. Isma Patajiparo
137. Sarad Mamro
139. Jeeji Majoparo
140. Manao Rajathiyo
141. Lalipojiparo

Gujar (2)

1. Fato Sukharo
2. Sevi Shaatu

Jat (5)
1. Mohan Mehali
2. Hirapo Jat
3. Udi Mehali
4. Mewaliyo Veeraje
5. Phurasi Kheechad

Lilgar (3)
1. Vaje Pateduryo
2. Motiyo Lilgar
3. Sardaro Siraparo

Pinjara (9)
1. Kuti Posalro
2. Parto Chonuro
3. Kuti Potisaro
4. Matirdaro Vakhuro
5. Peerpo Varkhuro
6. Vaji Pobhinaro
7. Imam Fakiro
8. Maniyo
9. Kasim Piduro

Manihar Sasgarn (9):
1. Peeru Sasgar
2. Khujusi Sanem
3. Peeru Varomaro
4. Salim Manihar
5. Kuliro Askaro
6. Nathi Porajaro
7. Lali Rehimkaro
8. Vaji Pogusaro
9. Sali Manihar

Darzi (6)
1. Sawai
2. Tamli
3. Mohaniyo
4. Ajityo
5. Luniyo
6. Puraniyo

Khati (9)
1. Hadvato
2. Vegali
3. Devo
4. Komi Kudasaro
5. Sudiyo
6. Kasiyo
7. Manas Poduparo
8. Kursayo
9. Udi Sukharan

Chinpa (9)
1. Lakhiyo
2. Suwair
3. Nath Rao
4. Padami
5. Vaua
6. Dayarimayo
7. Amodivato
8. Moshri
9. Devali

Vaya Pora: (NA)

Rangapara (13)

1. Rajuko Saraki
2. Karsa
3. Suwai Kusalro
4. Vasu Kusalro
5. Pemi
6. Vavata Variyo
7. Jumin Yogelpuro
8. Veniyo
9. Tejiyo
10. Lolyogigaro
11. Terijo Asadaro
12. Udayo Jerimaro
13. Puro Pulalko

Khatikira/Khatik (7)

1. Arkojaro
2. Kadarri magatiyo
3. Kadar Daliro
4. Ismap Laktaro
5. Dini Majro
6. Paru
7. Karim Monuro

Khumbharira/Khumbhar (9)

1. Mulacho Tira
2. Shivji Vaduro
3. Vemi
4. Bhato Gopalro
5. Kirni Pemro
6. Dudo Gopalro
7. Kusali Gopalro
8. Jhodhyo Rupro
9. Ghasi Rogarau

Bhacha Pora (7)

1. Kasaliyo
2. Bagasiyo
3. Deviyo
4. Vasilro Kasaliyo
5. Gagala Idaro
6. Ukmalo Pusaro
7. Not available

Kalal (4)

1. Mavaliyo
2. Bhali
3. Aliyo
4. Chimaniyo

Chungarira/Churigar (5)

1. Doli
2. Mirak Gasparjaro
3. Vaju
4. Meraliyo
5. Vada Vagasiyo

APPENDIX 7.3

Sample of *Sava Bahi* Documents: Information of House Count in *Qasba* Churu (A part of sources for the year of VS 1907/AD 1850)

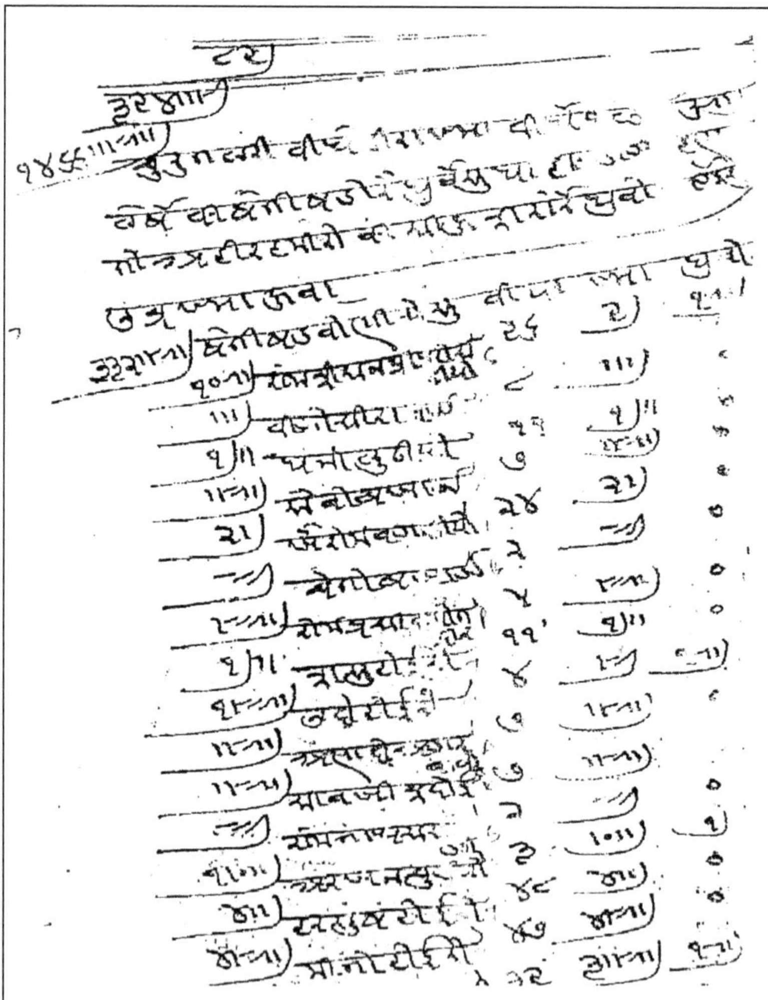

८८२॥=)

१८६॥=)

	माली	बीघा	जमा	सुबी
७॥४)	नाथ्यावोन्वेगरो	६२	६॥=॥)	१=॥)
३।=)	नीमजीपीवीजरी	२८	२॥=)	॥४)
२॥४)	देदोम्याघफरो	२३	८॥४=॥	१=॥)
१३॥४=)	वाउम्याघमो	१२३	१२॥।=॥)	१=॥)
६४=)	ओघीजोमरूशर्व	५७	५॥=॥)	१=॥)
२॥४=॥	जाहुन्लाजेरी	२४	८॥४)	१=॥)
१२॥४=॥	नगवीनवीज	१२६	११॥४)	१=॥)
११४=॥	जोनरा जेरोमरी	११०	१०४)	१=॥)
६॥४)	वीवरोम तुलसीरी	६१	५॥=॥)	१=॥)
२=॥	जीपाटोघमरो	१२	९=)	१=॥)
१॥=॥	जोजीपोतुरी	३	॥४)	१=॥)
६॥४)	उपोराम कलरतु	६२	६=॥)	॥०॥)
४=४	हरागोजगोरी	३२	३॥=॥	।=॥)
६॥०॥	उदोजोजरी	६४	६)	०
॥।	तीमीयोरामप्रसा	८	॥।)	
६॥०॥	रेतु	५८	५४=)	१=॥)
५॥४=)	मतुरामकलारेतु	५१	७॥०॥	१=॥)
४=)	तुटजरापोरी	३२	३=॥)	१=॥)
७॥४)	नरमोघाममरा गादरो	४३	३॥४=)	।४=)
	जालुमालरी			
५=॥	पीटरेतु	४४	४=)	१=॥)
॥।	मेघोवोझरजी	८	॥।)	०
२॥॥=॥	जोनडोरामपरी	१९	१॥=)	१=॥)
॥।	तुलारामयारी	८	॥।)	०

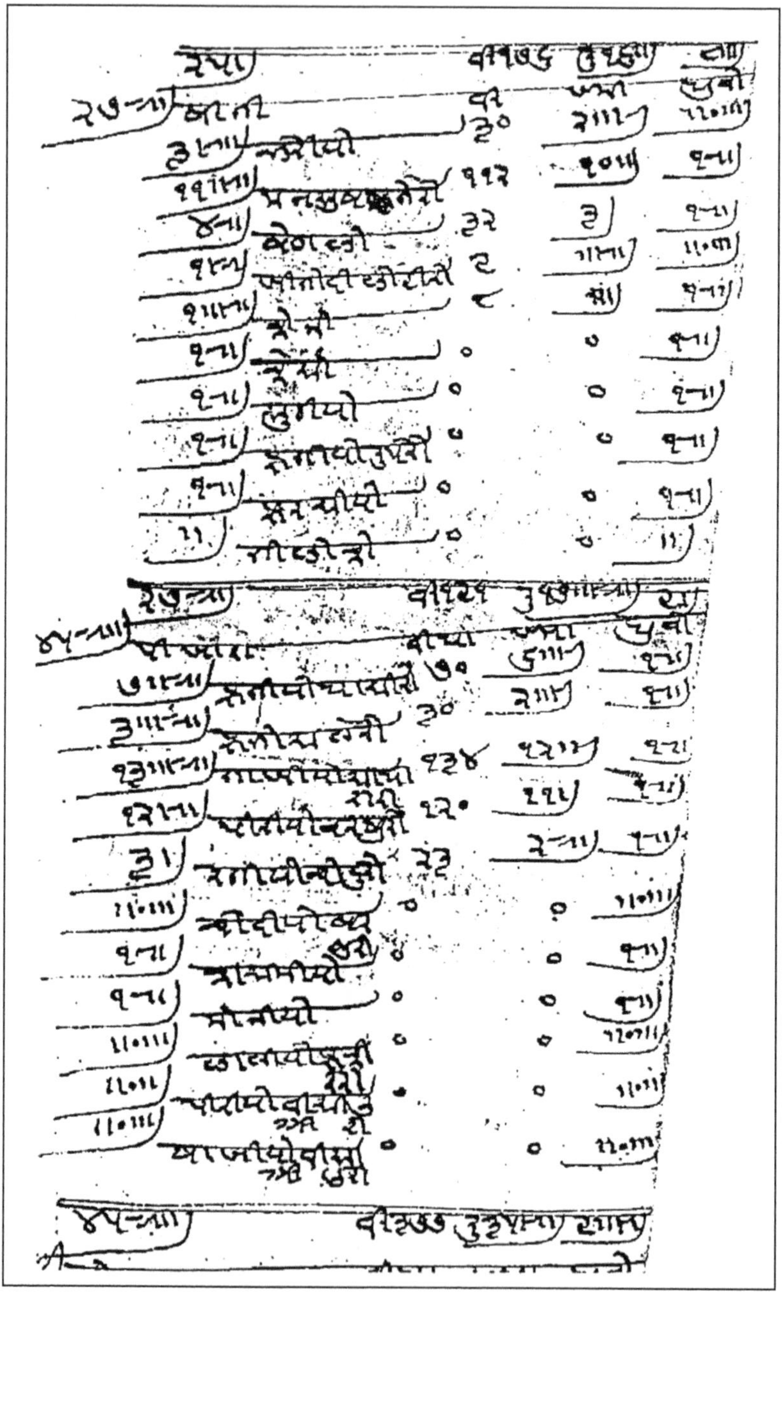

गामरो — बी१८ ३१॥ ३॥॥

६॥ — बीघा जमा घुवी

३॥॥ कुल ३ — ३॥ १॥

५॥॥ नाथाघोमालरे ५० ३॥ १॥

५॥॥ नवचीपो ५० १॥ ३॥॥

१॥ धीराघोअमबीरे ३ ० १॥

१॥ सीलुजो ० ०

बी १८३ ३ ३॥ ४॥

१२॥॥ — बीघा जमा घुवी

१०॥ हरजी ३६ ३॥ १॥

३॥ — सीवजीकोपुसो ३ १॥ ११॥॥

॥॥ हेमी ४ १॥ ११

३॥ — अजीतीयरो ० ० ११॥॥

११॥॥ जुहन ० ० १॥

१॥ हुलाछीपी ० ० ३॥॥

॥॥ वालीयोअयपरे — — ३॥॥

॥॥ चुरला ० ० ११॥॥

११॥॥ हरसुखीयरो ०

बी १४२ ३४॥ ६

१०॥ — बीघा जमा घुवी

११॥॥ हुमागर ५३ ५॥॥ ११॥॥

६॥ फतापरोअबीवाररे ५ १॥ ॥

१॥॥ रामजीनाराजुरा १२ १॥ १॥

२॥॥ रूपचीयरो १० १॥ ५॥

[illegible] ३॥॥

APPENDIX 7.4

Qasba Churu (VS 1928/AD 1871): House Count of Banias

Sahukars (Oswal, Mahesari and Agrawal)

1. Multanchand Banthiye
2. Ramchand Banthiye
3. Harkhu Kothari
4. Kaluram Mohasi
5. Omchand Chopamal Surano
6. Guturam Banthiya
7. Uma Baid
8. Sevaram Surana
9. Chiman Ram Gurgeso Khodhar
10. Uto Chhajari
11. Gokal Chand Baranthiye
12. Suratram Baid
13. Ratiram Guraso Baid
14. Sivdan Kiumara Hirawat
15. Kusatchand Parakh
16. Kalu Hirawt Maharajaro
17. Dolo Hadato Baid
18. Khemasi Khusalo Parakh
19. Hajarimal Kothari
20. Punalal Parakh
21. Muharo Parakh
22. Khemo Parakh
23. Juharo Dugar
24. Hudanram Parakh
25. Pratapo Modat
26. Chhago Surana
27. Amal Bhantiye
28. Santokchand Harkho Kothari
29. Gulabo Kothari
30. Tarachand Mandan Parakh
31. Chunnilal Kothari
32. Kheevo Sidhi
33. Chudechand Labhchand Kothari
34. Khubchand Banthiye
35. Jeevan Kothari
36. Bhenuk Veeratho Banthiye
37. Lachhiram Lunapo
38. Movatram Banthiye
39. Kalu Hirawatchand Mandara
40. Bheri Kago
41. Bhagvano Kothari
42. Bhero Vonoyo Rajgarhiyo
43. Daulatram Hirawat
44. Ravo Manadara.
45. Ruplal Mitaro
46. Udhar Jali Sidhi
47. Sitaram Pediwal
48. Gunosdas Mitari
49. Tokraj Manada
50. Lalo Kago
51. Madhopi Rani
52. Dalukano Mitari
53. Salo chand Kago
54. Guleso Sukhini
55. Nanag Kothari
56. Veeradho Holodi
57. Gangaram Mitari
58. Shahvo Mangalo Sathado
59. Dudo Holado
60. Jeevan Bihadi

61. Rupo Modi
62. Seko Radi
63. Padama Manada
64. Duro Tapdiyo
65. Bhopo Lakhotiyo
66. Rupo Kago
67. Bhivoki Radi
68. Salgo Manglo Madado
69. Cheno Chivwano Behadi
70. Heero Mitari
71. Hadat Mitari
72. Jetram Hilodi
73. Jugal Manada
74. Gafursi Bihodi
75. Ramratan Kago
76. Gunesi Manado
77. Kanol Khotiyo
78. Ramatan Manado
79. Ramratan Mitari
80. Aso Surako
81. Tanu Hanato Goyandak
82. Dhano Lumpo
83. Bhikhojo Bihana
84. Hero Mitari
85. Hadato Mitari
86. Bhopo Goyandako
87. Harsukhdas Dhoniko
88. Ramkisandas Saikh Sarraf
89. Khetoraman Napoli
90. Rupram Teevadelwal
91. Sivanaryan Dudhwewale
92. Sivanarayan Vajoriyo
93. Ramdev Bhojatvachag Lunpo
94. Narso Davalewali
95. Lakhno Pasari
96. Gumosi Kesariwal
97. Khewasi Sarawagi
98. Minu Raivalo
99. Makhan Lilo
100. Chetan Bajaj
101. Ramjo Bajaj
102. Tiloki Singhaniyo
103. Chandarbhan Baghlo
104. Dalsukh Rainwalo
105. Manganiram Singhaniyo
106. Lakhman Kandoi
107. Motiram Kaseri
108. Ravat Goyandako
109. Sivana Kandoi
110. Dalothu Vajpo
111. Gunosi Chaudhari
112. Hori Goyandako
113. Hajari Kandoi
114. Sivnath Goyandakho
115. Phulo Gheeso Bajaj
116. Murali Bagaiyo
117. Ramsukh Kejariwal
118. Ramsukh Kejariwal
119. Chimano Kripal
120. Mohi Pankarkhuro
121. Harmukh Bhagirathro
122. Jugalhev Devalo
123. Sanehiram Bhagirathro
124. Lakhman Potdar
125. Heermal Kasturmal
126. Salgo Bhagirathro
127. Amarchand Lohiyo
128. Harsukh Bajaj
129. Gunaso Goyandako
130. Murali Bajaj
131. Sambhu Bhut
132. Dalshukh Bajaj
133. Veeru Khemako
134. Kalu Kesou
135. Narain Lunapo
136. Moti Mirajo Baghalo
137. Chuno Sarawaji
138. Ramnarayan Potdar
139. Sarugurdipal Modi
140. Gurdipal Lunapo

141. Manakram Hardipal
142. Bheryo Kandoi
143. Sivbagas Utapevaj
144. Ramratan Prathi Sarafo
145. Mahchand Ghanghuko
146. Rakho Sarawargi
147. Ramrath Bajaj
148. Hiro potdar
149. Rampratap Bhagirathro
150. Gomadovas Bajaj
151. Vakhta Varsivanath Bajaj
152. Veekraj Kheton
153. Sivram Deepak Tai
154. Ramnarain Durgadut Potdar
155. Pikar Mahariwal
156. Kano Bhigirathro
157. Iramu Kalu Lohiyo
158. Varmal Taiwalo
159. Kuloharsukh Taiwalo
160. Sitaram Sarawagi
161. Kheto Chunni Khemako
162. Lali Agrawal
163. Tarachand Baghala
164. Gorakhram Nanagram Khemka
165. Bhumi Khameka
166. Ghuja Khemako
167. Manako Bajaj
168. Sarusalu Chaudhari
169. Sukhram Sarfu
170. Khusalolaho
171. Pali Potadar
172. Netsigaru Bajaj
173. Darsotamdas Khemako
174. Matiram Goyandako
175. Taro Sarawagi
176. Khalo Gopi Potdar
177. Taro Bajaj
178. Gorakhram Khemako
179. Neto Goyandako
180. Girdhari Sarraf
181. Chetochuno Mankvero
182. Khalisram Sarraf
183. Ratu Jaluko
184. Hardapal Bajaj
185. Harsamal Lohiyo
186. Tolo Sarawaji
189. Chuno Lohiyo
190. Jethmal Lohiyo
191. Khusaliram Ramgarhiyo
192. Puno Kejariwal
193. Bhagatu Kandoi
194. Makhan Potdar
195. Hirori Khetwalo
196. Ramnarayan Khemako
197. Sanchar Sarapo
198. Raghunath Chaudhari
199. Puno Sarraf
200. Gorakho Goyandkho
201. Ramkisandas Potdar
202. Vainsukhdas Lohiyo
203. Lalo Sarawagi
204. Kano Jalon
205. Hukumchand Lohiyo
206. Gomanchand Sarawagi
207. Gangaram Himmeto Sarraf
208. Kuto Vahra Khemako
209. Veeko Sarwagi
210. Gangaram Sarraf
211. Ghagchand Mamraj
212. Salago Bajaj
213. Khalu Hardevo Mankavero
214. Jugato Khemako
215. Ramdayal Harmukh Jaluko
216. Raghunath Chamadiye
217. Machand Ramratan
218. Rambhagat Potdar
219. Vilasi Sarawagi
220. Norang Kunthiye

221. Sevaram Bhani Kesan
222. Khalu Jaluko
223. Ramnathji Khandelwal
224. Jogiram Dharam Khemko
225. Mahesan Goyandako
226. Kalu Lohiyo
227. Puran Dudhwala
228. Vanraj Chimanram Baghla
229. Pochar Bagadiye
230. Chuno Chamadiyo
231. Sivadipal Khemako
232. Sukho Jalan
233. Guvarimal Sivaram
234. Chuni Khemko
235. Macho Ramgharhiye
236. Jokhiram Sarawagi
237. Hemo Jasrasariye
238. Harji Bhartiye
239. Rupovipa Liwali
240. Sivaji Gurudayal Lohiyo
241. Udho Potdar
242. Baldev Sarwagi
243. Khusalo Jaluko
244. Madho Lohiyo
245. Kalu Kandoi
246. Pano Kasaro

CHAPTER 8

Trading Junctions of Marwar: A Study of Pali and Nagaur

The archival material relating to the trade routes and transportation cover a long period from seventeenth century to the early twentieth century. These records were compiled from various categories of rural-urban and commercial papers from western Rajasthan which provide valuable information related to different commodities, taxes, markets, trade and commerce,[1] etc. To evaluate the position of Pali and Nagaur, we have employed these contemporary sources such as *parwanas* (*sanad parwana bahis* and *khas rukka parwana bahis*),[2] and *hakikat bahis*.[3] They furnish us an insight into the rural-urban commercial life, specially the functioning of the market, money-lending transactions and inter-regional trade of the state of Rajasthan as well as the external trades linked with urban-trading centres of western and other parts of India. Besides, these documents contain evidence on market rates of commercial goods and taxes, trade routes, business centres, means of transport, trade fairs, etc. These sources can be of help in studying the emergence of Pali and Nagaur as centres of trade and commerce during eighteenth-nineteenth century Rajasthan.

Trade is one of the indices for the measurement of the development of any small area, town, state or even a country, either today or any time in the past history of the world. The central power of the region also plays a role in this kind of phenomenon. In this regard one can see the history of Mughals after the death of Aurangzeb in 1707. According to R.P. Vyas[4] the death of Aurangzeb, the mighty Mughal emperor, brought down the entire superstructure of the empire to a crumbling stage, reducing the imperial Mughals to nothing more than a *nominis umbra*. According to Sunita

Zaidi, during the eighteenth century, the various princely states of Rajputana experienced considerable political instability and insecurity. This found reflection in de-urbanization and decay of some significant towns and cities in north-western India.[5] This process of decay was interrupted in the second half of the eighteenth and the first half of the nineteenth century, when regional powers began to carve out new states. In case of Rajasthan our records provide immense information about a large number of towns which emerged and flourished in eighteenth and early nineteenth centuries,[6] and started to decline in the second half of the nineteenth century.

I

Pali was generally considered as an antique city while inscriptions dated back to the eleventh century suggest that this town was known as Pallika and Palli.[7] It is located around 70 km south-east of Jodhpur and situated on the right bank of Bandi River.[8] According to Sunita Zaidi, there are two etymological possibilities: One, the name of Pali might have been derived from the Sanskrit word *palaka* (meaning to guard, to defend, to protect, or to govern), since the place remained in constant threat of pillaging activities of certain tribes of surrounding regions. It is probable that the town had a defence function and that is why the name Pali (meaning to guard or to defend) might have been given to the place. Two, in Sanskrit, the word Pali means boundary, limit, margin, and edge and since it is on a border, it might have been given this appellation.[9] This town had great influence of the Brahmins[10] who were holding grants given by the Paramara and Parihar Rajputs before the advent of the Rathors and Rao Siha who became its master. The Paliwal Brahmins appear to have derived their name from this town.[11] Prior to coming of the railways, it was a very important trade emporium, where goods from China and the Middle East were exchanged. Pali was even the centre for the eastern and western regions where the productions of India including Kashmir and China were interchanged with those from Europe, Africa, Persia and Arabia.[12] Later the place became known for dyeing of woollen, silk and cotton cloths.[13] The water of the Bandi River is supposed to have some peculiar chemical qualities which give a certain degree of permanency and fastness to the colours used by the dyers.[14] It is very interesting to note that this town being a centre of trade and commerce in the past, attracted people from different parts of India in general and Rajasthan in particular who came and settled here and hence there are various *mohallas* made which is known after the settlers like the Gujarati Bas, etc.[15] R.P. Vyas provides a list of their settlements such as Jodhpuria Bas, Ajmeria Bas, Sojati Bas, etc.

Pali appears to have witnessed a rich building construction work. There are several temples, some are very old, namely Somnath and Naulakha. Naulakha is a Jain temple and noteworthy for its size and elaborate carving while the Somnath temple is a beautiful structure remarkable for its exquisite mouldings. It contains an inscription of AD 1153 mentioning the name of Kumarapala of Gujarat to whom its construction is attributed. Naulakha bears many inscriptions indicating the repair carried out from time to time; the earliest inscription is of eleventh century.[16] It is also interesting to note that near Pali town, a village Choteela is locally very popular for a fair held here in the memory of Dhulesa Pir.[17] It remained a place of pilgrimage for the Jains. According to James Tod,

> Pali was entre-pot for the eastern and western regions, where products of Malwa, Kashmir and China were inter-exchanged for those of Europe, Africa, Persia and Arabia. The *caravans* from the port of Cutch and Gujarat brought Elephant's teeth, copper, dates, gum arabic, borax, coconuts, broad cloths, silks, sandalwood, camphor, dyes, drugs, sulphuret of arsenic, spices, coffee etc. In exchange they carried chintz, dry fruits, *jeerah*, asafoetida (*heeng*) from Multan, sugar and opium from Kota and Malwa and silk, fine cloths, potash, shawls, dyed blankets, arms and salt all locally manufactured from Pali.[18]

The route of the *caravans* from Cutch and Gujarat to Pali passed through Sanchor, Bhinmal and Jalor.[19] Tod praised this town as an emporium of Rajasthan.[20] Tod estimates the commercial duties of Pali yielded around Rs. 75,000 annually to the exchequer.[21]

The information about the businessmen is available in abundance in the *khas-rukka-parwana bahis*, and other sources of Marwar which enable us to estimate the volume of trade including the organization of trading activities. It appears that trade and commerce was organized both at individual and the family level. Numerous firms were active there namely; Akhai Chand Kesari Chand, Shah Nanu Ram Ram Gopal, Mohan Das Khatri, Tej Bhan Multani, Seth Abhai Chand Luniya, Seth Ram Das Lakchhman Das, Shah Jiwan Das, Seth Jaskaran Man Das Bikaneriya, and Seth Khusal Chand. In fact, these were noted business firms of Pali who were extensively engaged both in the internal and external trade.[22] A piece of evidence shows that Khema of Pali established his business at Burhanpur.[23] Besides, commercial activities, religion also provided a boost to Pali. Its geographical location proved an additional advantage to the town, as it was situated on the route leading to the famous pilgrimage centre of Dwarka on the western coast of Gujarat.[24] It served as a halting place for the pilgrims. Thus, commerce and religion together enhanced the significance of the town.[25]

On the basis of the records, the trade connections of different regions with Pali are being divided here into three categories for easy understanding. These important routes that passed through Pali are given below:

(A) Internal Trade Routes (see Map 8.1)

1. Bikaner to Pali	Bikaner-Nagaur-Jodhpur-Pali[26]
2. Bikaner to Udaipur	Bikaner-Nagaur-Pali-Desuri-Udaipur
3. Rajgarh to Pali	Rajgarh-Churu-Nawalgarh-Didwana-Nagaur-Pali[27]
4. Jhunjhunu to Pali	Jhunjhunu-Fatehpur-Ladnu-Didwana-Nagaur-Pali[28]

(B) External Trade Routes (see Map 8.2)

1. Agra to Ahmadabad and Surat	Agra-Fatehpur Sikri-Hindaun-Lalsot-Mozamabad-Bander Sindree-Ajmer-Pali-Sirohi-Palanpur-Ahmadabad-Surat[29]
2. Malwa to China	Malwa-Pali-China[30]

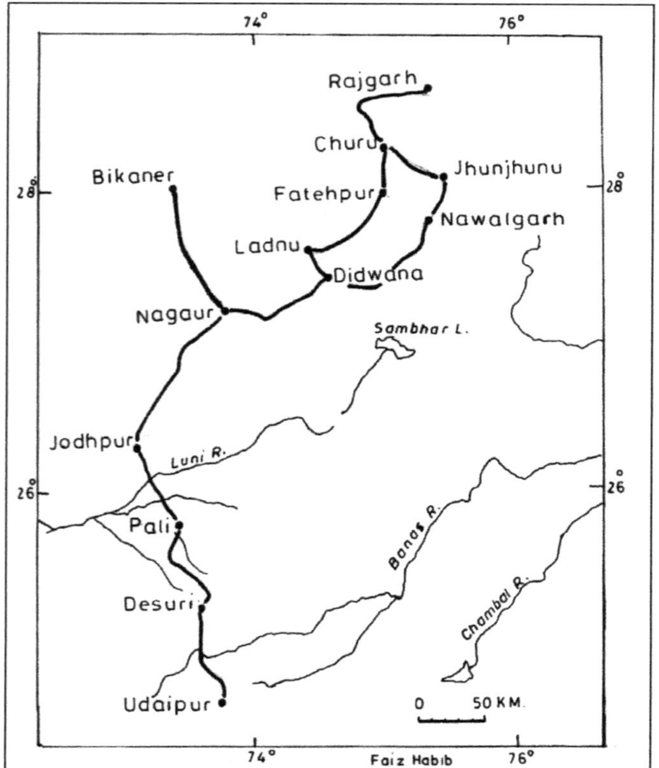

Map 8.1: Internal Trade Routes

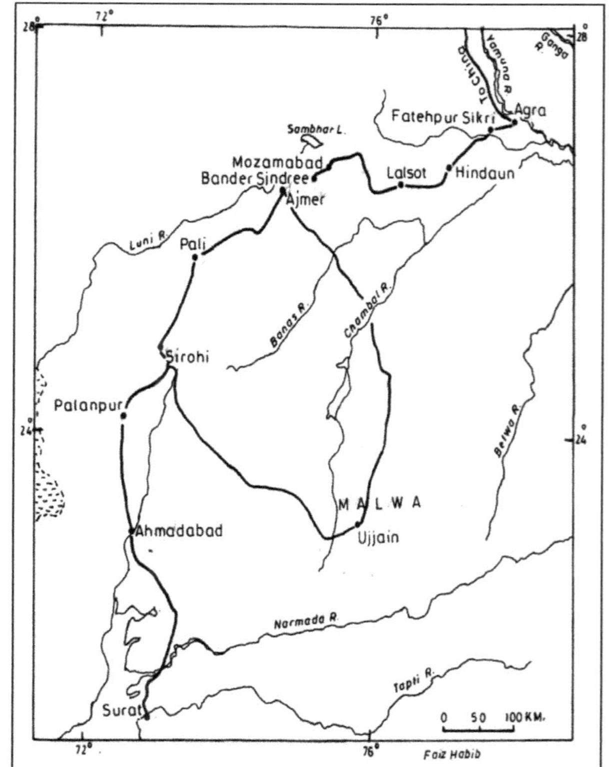

Map 8.2: External Trade Routes

(C) Routes Passing through Pali Based on C.K.M. Walter (see Map 8.3)

1. Ajmer to Ahmadabad	Ajmer-Bar-Chandwal-Sojhat-Jadhan-Pali-Gundoj-Dhola-Sanderao-Nar Nadi-Doli-Sarvarhi-Pachpadra-Jasol-Ahmadabad[31]
2. Jodhpur to Udaipur	Jodhpur-Mogra-Rohat-Pali-Busi-Jiwand-Desuri-Jilwara-Udaipur
3. Jodhpur to Mount Abu	Jodhpur-Mogra-Rohat-Pali-Gundoj-Dhola-Sanderao-Mount Abu
4. Jodhpur to Ajmer	Jodhpur-Bisalpur-Bogal-Jhak-Balunda-Lambian-Kurkhi-Govindgarh-Pushkar-Ajmer

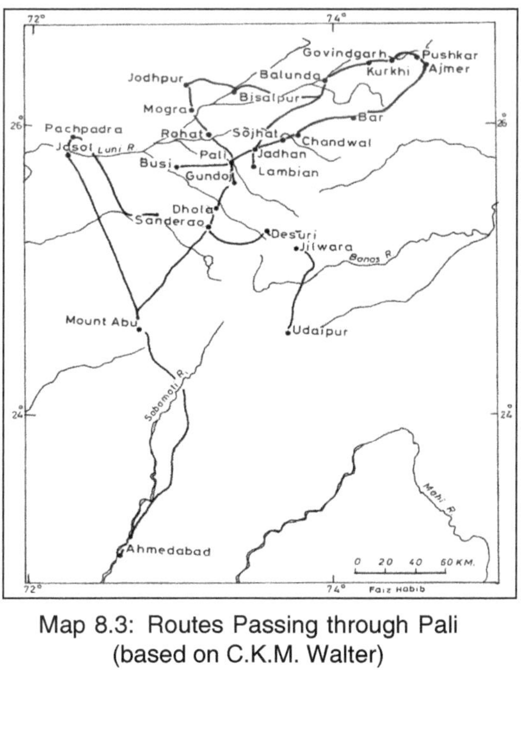

Map 8.3: Routes Passing through Pali (based on C.K.M. Walter)

Table 8.1 shows the goods and commodities exported from Pali and imported in Pali.

TABLE 8.1: COMMODITIES/GOODS FROM PALI TO OTHER REGIONS AND VICE VERSA

Name of Commodity	From	To	Remarks
FROM PALI TO OTHER REGIONS (EXPORT ITEMS)			
Salt	Pali	Other places	Chief article of export from Marwar (principal sources of salt in Marwar were Sambhar, Pachpadra, Phalodi and Didwana)
Woollens	Pali	Other places	It was exported not only within India but also to England and the USA)
Course cotton cloths	Pali	Other places	Made in Pali town
Coarse paper	Pali	Other places	Made in Pali town
Lois (blankets)	Pali	Other places	Cost ranged between Rs. 4 and 60 per pair
Scarfs and Turbans	Pali	For locals	Produced only for local consumption and not for export
FROM OTHER REGIONS TO PALI (IMPORT ITEMS)			
Mehandi	Sojhat	Pali	
Methi (fenugreek)	Sojhat	Pali	
Zeera (cumin seed)	Merta	Pali	
Saji (soda)	Bahawalpur	Pali	
Opium[32]	Kota	Pali	Malwa opium was also reaching Pali for export abroad
Chintz	Kota	Pali	
Sugar	Jaipur	Pali	
Various types of cloths	Jaipur	Pali	
Swords	Bhuj	Pali	
Horses	Bhuj	Pali	
Gur (sugar cane)	Bareli, Hatharas, Mewar	Pali	

contd.

TABLE 8.1 contd.

Name of Commodity	From	To	Remarks
Rice	Chandausi and Sindh	Pali	
Kerosene oil	Bombay	Pali	
Ivory	Bombay	Pali	
Tobacco	Panipat, Malwa, Nadia	Pali	
Chintzes (glazed cotton cloth)	Multan	Pali	
Wood (for household furniture)	Multan	Pali	
Mahua flowers	Sirohi	Pali	
Wheat	Punjab	Pali	

The above table evidently indicates that the exports of home production were of two staple articles, viz. salt and woollens and we may add coarse cotton cloth and rough paper made in the town of Pali.[33] Blankets made here were popular throughout the country with its price ranging between Rs. 4 and 60 per pair. The people of this town also made scarfs and turbans of the same material but only for local consumption and not for export. It is interesting to note that salt was the chief article of export from Marwar. According to R.P. Vyas, the revenue arising there was around equal to half of the land revenue of the state.[34] The principal sources of salt in Marwar were Sambhar, Pachpadra, Phalodi and Didwana.[35]

Pali known as an important place for dyeing and printing of cotton cloth was also famous for its ivory carvings especially toys and bangles, matchlocks, swords and other related implements. It was also famous for making iron boxes, and tin boxes which resembled those manufactured in Europe.[36]

Table 8.2 prepared to show the amount of export from Pali to other places.

Table 8.2 shows that *khand* was being sent from Pali to Pokaran Idar and Jodhpur as amount of 10 camel (loaded), 51 and 30 *mann* respectively. Maximum amount of 400 *mann loha* (iron) was ex-

TABLE 8.2: AMOUNT OF EXPORT FROM PALI TO OTHER PLACES

Goods	Amounts	From	To
Khand (sugar)	51 *mann*	Pali	Idar
Singhara (water-chestnut)	12 *mann*	Pali	Jodhpur
Kudhav of Iron	04 *nug* (item)	Pali	Jodhpur
Loha (iron)	400 *mann*	Pali	Nagaur
Khand (sugar)	30 *mann*	Pali	Jodhpur
Gur	09 *mann*	Pali	Jodhpur
Narial (coconut)	02 *mann*	Pali	Jodhpur
Khand (sugar)	10 *Oont*/Camel (loaded)	Pali	Pokran
Kishmish (dried grape)	0.25 *mann*	Pali	Jodhpur

ported to Nagaur. Other amounts were being exported, 12 *mann singhara*, 4 *nag kudhav*, 9 *mann gur*, 2 *mann narial* and 0.25 *mann kishmish* from Pali to Jodhpur. This information is shown the significance of Pali as an important export centre in Rajasthan.

The significance of camels for carrying goods particularly in desert Rajasthan is well known. Pali was the centre for purchasing and selling camels of Marwar which were known for their endurance. A good camel used for commercial loading could be purchased for about Rs. 60. The goods passing through Pali were being carried on by these beasts, except salt and coconut.[37]

Table 8.1 also shows regarding the import items from the different areas of the country and abroad as well. Pali got opium[38] and chintz from Kota, sugar and various types of cloths from Jaipur and swords and horses from Bhuj.[39] Besides these articles Pali imported *gur* from Bareli, Hathras and Mewar, rice from Chandausi and Sindh, kerosene oil and ivory from Bombay, tobacco from Panipat, Malwa and Nadia, *mahua* flowers from Sirohi and wheat from Punjab.[40]

Various articles were imported in Pali. These included elephant tusk, rhinoceros hides, copper, tin, pewter, dates (dried and moist *kharaks* and *pindkhijur*) of which there had been an immense consumption in Rajputana, gum arabic, borax, coconut, broad cloths, striped silk (*putung*), dyes, particularly crimson colour, drugs (especially, oxides of arsenic and quick silver), spices, sandalwood, camphor, tea, green glass, etc., from western coast of the country.

Bahawalpur was supplier of soda (*sajji*), the dyes called *aal* and *munjeet*, matchlocks, dried fruits, asafoetida, Multan chintz and wood for household furniture to the town.[41]

Pali, during sixteenth-seventeenth century was under the *jagir* of Rathor chiefs of Jodhpur. This town flourished while the period was running as one of relative political tranquillity. The Table 8.3[42] suggests that the town was growing in its income.

Table 8.3 evidently shows that the revenue collection fell remarkably in the years 1658 and 1660 (see Graph 8.1). It is possible that in these years there was some natural calamity.

It is noticeable that from the last quarter of the seventeenth century at least two factors played a significant role; one the political feud between the Mughals and the Rathors of Jodhpur, and two, the decay of Mughal power in the eighteenth century and reformation and reorganization of the Marwar State. This became the cause of internecine wars between the subordinate *sardars* and the Marwar State. The region of Marwar as a whole including Pali came under tremendous pressure due to frequent raids of Marathas and Pindaris during the said periods.[43] But this would not reverse or stop the growth of Pali. It continued to grow particularly in the eighteenth and early nineteenth centuries. During the second half of the eighteenth century, the revenue figures of the commercial

TABLE 8.3: REVENUE OF THE PALI *PARGANA* YEAR-WISE (1595-1770)

Year	Revenue in Rupees	Remarks
1595	6,250	Based on *Ain-i-Akbari*
1654	13,978	*Marwar-ra-pargana-ri-vigat*
1655	13,440	
1656	12,355	
1657	12,148	
1658	4,993	
1659	18,361	
1660	9,538	
1661	22,902	
1662	16,823	
1770	16,661	

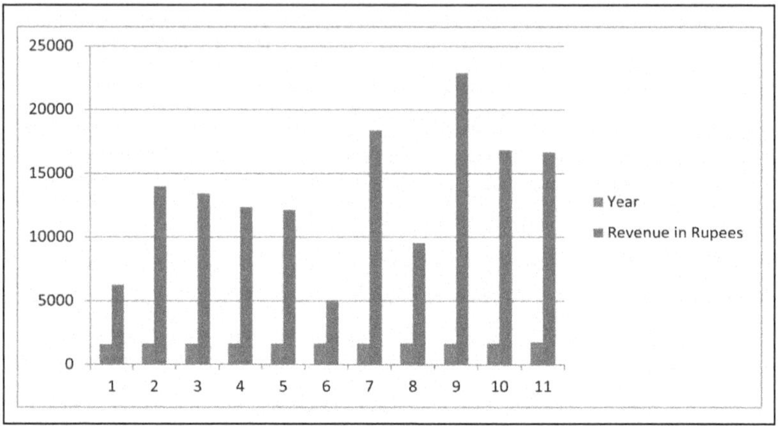

Graph 8.1: Revenue of the Pali *Pargana* Year-wise, 1595-1770 (based on Table 8.3)

taxes were four times more than the land revenue, i.e. *mal hasil.* The land revenue figures rupees 16,661, *annas* 12, and *paisa* 3[44] for the year 1770 remained more or less static for several years, but the amount collected from taxes like *mapa* (it was levied on the sale and purchase of commodities in the permanent and weekly markets of a town, and during the course of fairs), *rahdari* (it was realized in the form of transit duty from the traders carrying goods through the territory of a ruler), *sair-mela* (fair) and *hundawana* (a commission *hundi*), etc., were rupees 67,213, *annas* 2, and *paisa* 3. These figures clearly suggest the increasing significance of Pali as a commercial town.[45] The increasing commercial significance and the boom in the money market economy in Pali helped merchants a great deal. In 1788, Pali opened its own mint.[46] The commercial significance of Pali expanded beyond India to include other regions of the world.

II

Nagaur is the chief town of the same name in Jodhpur division of Rajasthan and lies in the latitude 27°12'N and longitude 73°44'E.[47] It was a place of great antiquity,[48] and being situated in the centre of Rajasthan; it shares its border with several other districts of the state. On the north it is bound by Bikaner and Churu, on the east by Sikar and Jaipur, on the south by Ajmer and Pali and on the west by Jodhpur.[49] It is also known in history as an important centre of Jainism[50] and Sufism.[51] After the defeat of Prithviraj III in 1192 by Mohammad Ghori, it passed into the hands of Muslim rulers, who governed this place through a number of Turkish governors from AD 1195 onwards.[52] According to Isami's *Futuh-us-Salatin,* Qazi Hamiduddin Nagori was appointed as *qazi* (judge) of Nagaur, after the Second Battle of Tarain (1192). Nagaur also served as a mint town under the Muslim Sultans of Delhi.[53] According to the different sources, minting of gold,[54] silver, and copper were much more familiar in the period of Sultan Shamsuddin Iltutmish,[55] Ghiyasuddin Balban[56] and Mughal emperor Akbar.[57] Firoz Khan son of Shams Khan Dandani, the founder of Khanzada dynasty of Nagaur, was also involved in minting the *tanka* coin at Nagaur in AD 1433.[58] It shows the importance of Nagaur in medieval Rajasthan.

Nagaur was one of the important trading centres of Rajasthan since early medieval period. Involvement of traders in transportation of goods between Nagaur and Multan is well known and they were involved as mediators between Bahauddin Zakaria Suhrawardi of Multan and Shaikh Hamiduddin Chishti of Nagaur to transmit their letters to each other.[59] Besides this, numerous routes passed through this desert town.[60] The important routes passing through Nagaur is shown below:

(A) External Trade Routes (Based on Epigraphic and Persian Sources)

1. Nagaur to Multan[61]	This route frequently used by a trader (Map 8.4). [Multan to Nagaur via Bikaner-eighteenth century]
2. Delhi to Malwa[62]	Gwalior and Nagaur were connected this route (Map 8.5)
3. Agra to Nagaur[63]	Agra-Tonk-Toda[64]-Nagaur (Map 8.6)
4. Mewat to Bikaner[65]	Mewat Region-Nagaur-Bikaner (Map 8.7)

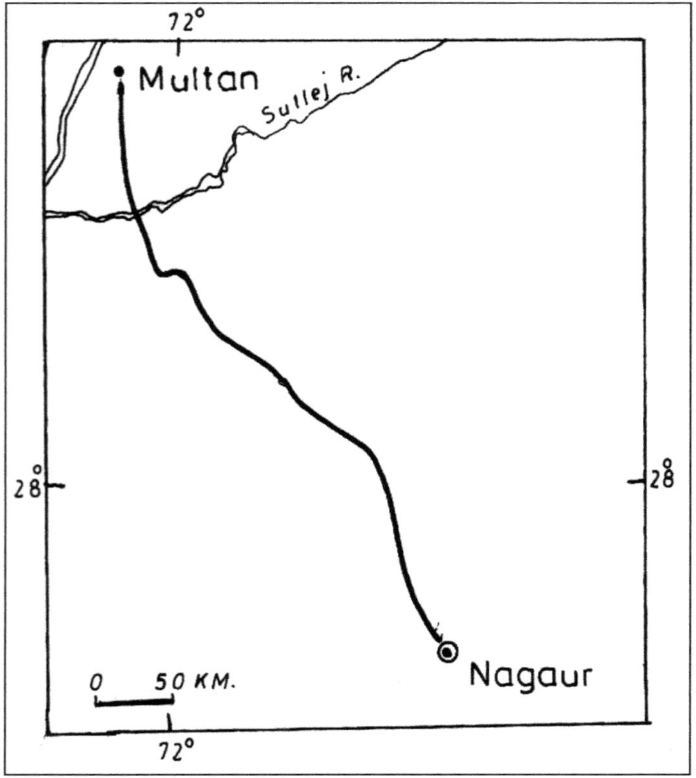

Map 8.4: Nagaur to Multan

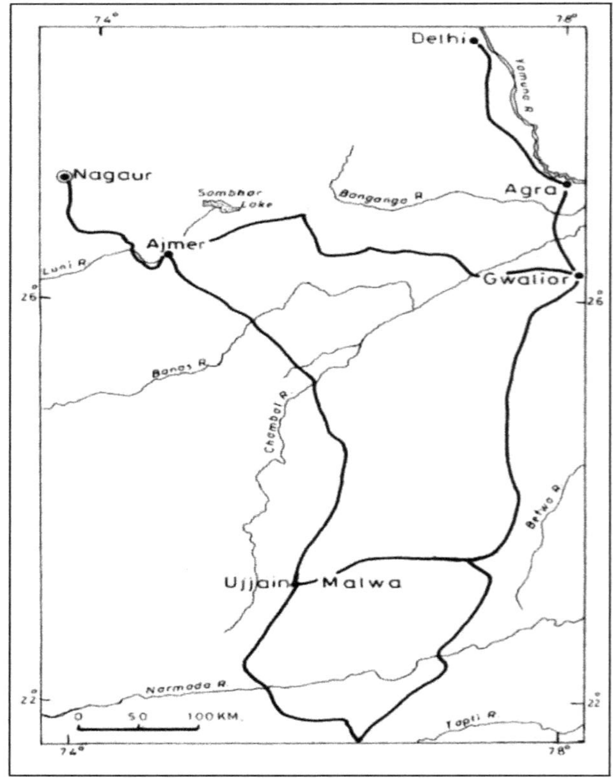

Map 8.5: Delhi to Malwa

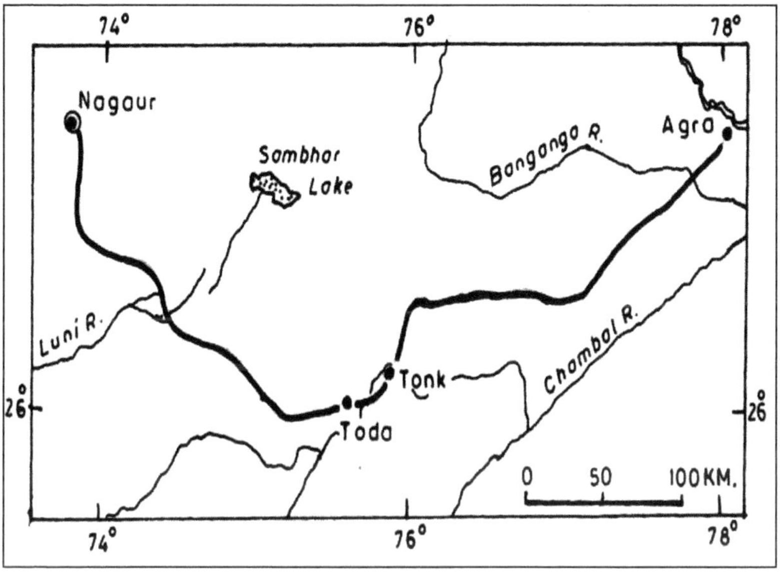

Map 8.6: Agra to Nagaur

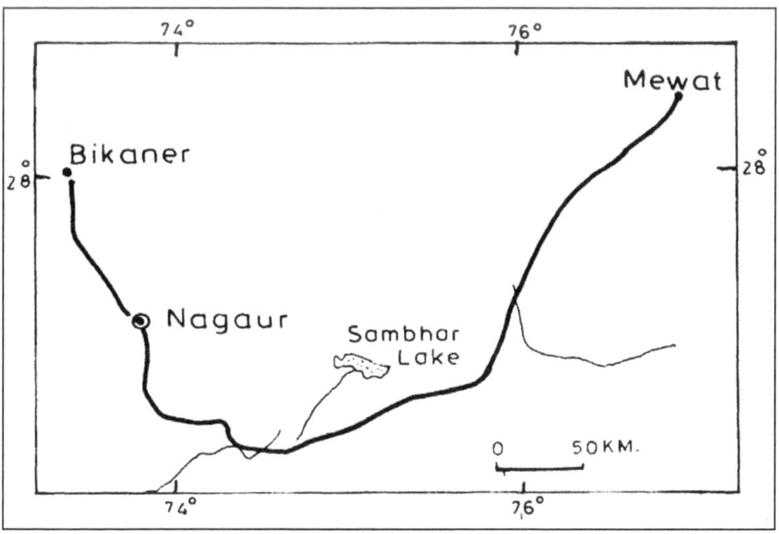

Map 8.7: Mewat to Bikaner

(B) External Trade Routes (Based on Persian, Rajasthani and other Sources)

1. Multan to Jodhpur[66]	Multan-Bahawalpur-Pugal-Bikaner-Nagaur-Jodhpur (Map 8.8)
2. Jodhpur to Kashmir[67]	Jodhpur-Nagaur-Hardesar-Nohar-Sirsa-Bhatinda-Amritsar-Kashmir (Map 8.8)
3. Bikaner to Deccan[68]	Bikaner-Nagaur-Merta-Bundi-Kota-Jhalara Patan-Ujjain-Deccan (Map 8.9)
4. Delhi to Ahmadabad/ Delhi-Gujarat[69]	Narayana-Narhad-Reni-Nagaur-Ajmer-Ahmadabad/ Gujarat (Map 8.10)
5. Agra to Ahmadabad/ Gujarat[70]	Agra-Nagaur-Ahmadabad/ Gujarat (Map 8.10)
6. Ajmer to Ahmadabad[71]	Nagaur was connected to Ahmadabad through this route (Map 8.10)
7. Nagaur to Ayodhya[72]	Nagaur-Ajmer-Ayodhya (Map 8.11)
8. Ajmer to Jodhpur[73]	Ajmer-Nagaur-Bikaner-Jodhpur (Map 8.11)

(C) Internal Trade Routes (Based on Archival Sources: *Sanad Parwana Bahi*)

Sanad Parwana Bahi provides information on the internal trade routes, connected to the important towns of Rajasthan with each other. The routes were highly beneficial to the traders, *banjaras*, and modes of transport were available. The important internal routes (Map 8.12) mentioned as below:

1. Nagaur to Pugal	Nagaur-Bikaner-Pugal[74]
2. Kota to Nagaur	Kota-Bundi-Deoli-Ajmer-Merta-Nagaur[75]

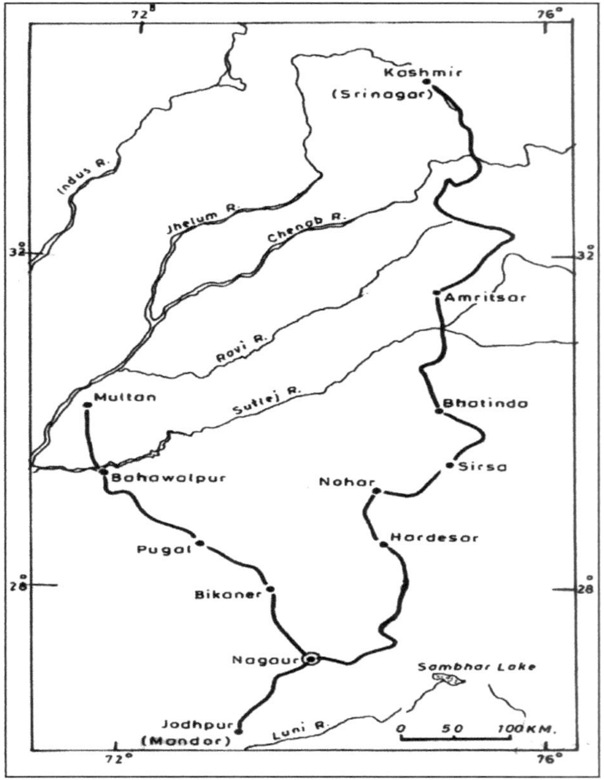

Map 8.8: Multan to Jodhpur

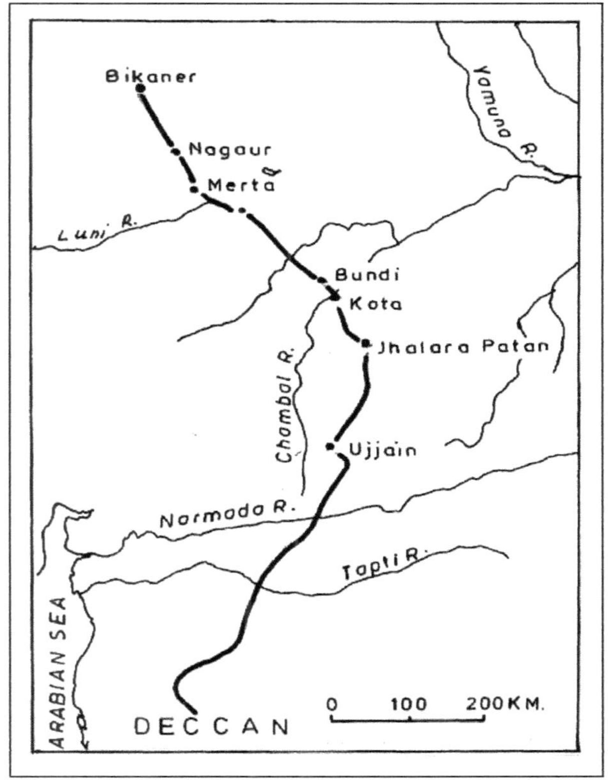

Map 8.9: Bikaner to Deccan

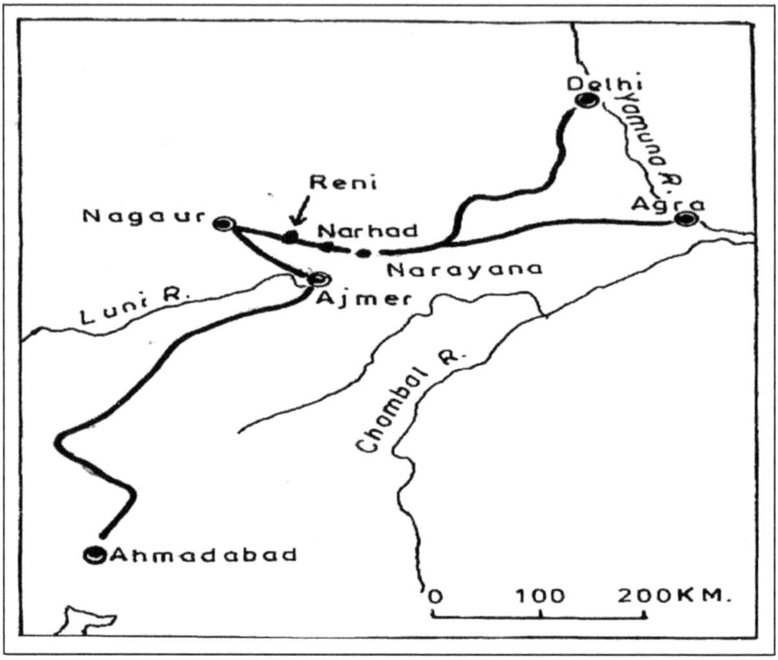

Map 8.10: Delhi to Ahmadabad

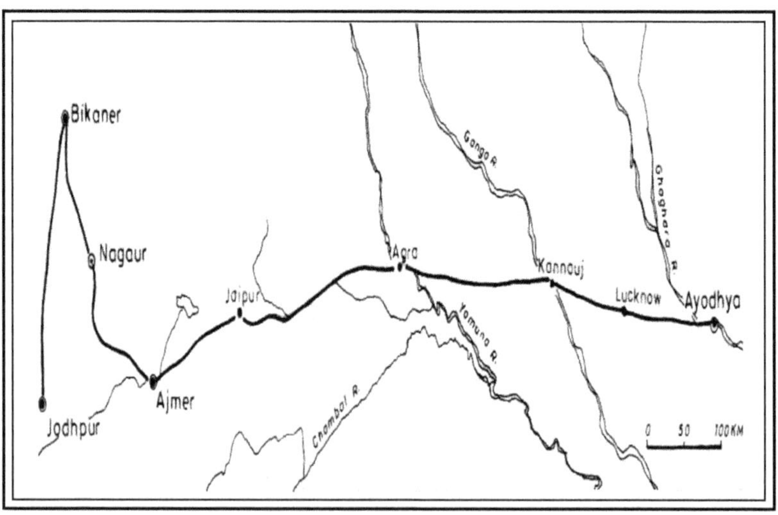

Map 8.11: Nagaur to Ayodhya

3.	Bikaner to Jaipur	Bikaner-Nagaur-Rupnagar-Jaipur[76]
4.	Bikaner to (Jodhpur)	Bikaner-Nagaur-Khiwasar-Jodhpur (Mandor)[77]
5.	Bikaner to Pali	Bikaner-Nagaur-Jodhpur-Pali[78]
6.	Bikaner to Udaipur	Bikaner-Nagaur-Pali-Desuri-Udaipur[79]
7.	Rajgarh to Pali	Rajgarh-Churu-Nawalgarh-Didwana-Nagaur-Pali[80]
8.	Jaisalmer to Jaipur	Jaisalmer-Pokaran-Phalodi-Nagaur-Rupnagar-Jaipur[81]
9.	Jhunjhunu to Pali	Jhunjhunu-Fatehpur-Ladnun-Didwana-Nagaur-Pali[82]
10.	Ajmer to Anupgarh	Ajmer-Merta-Nagaur-Bikaner-Mahajan-Anupgarh[83]

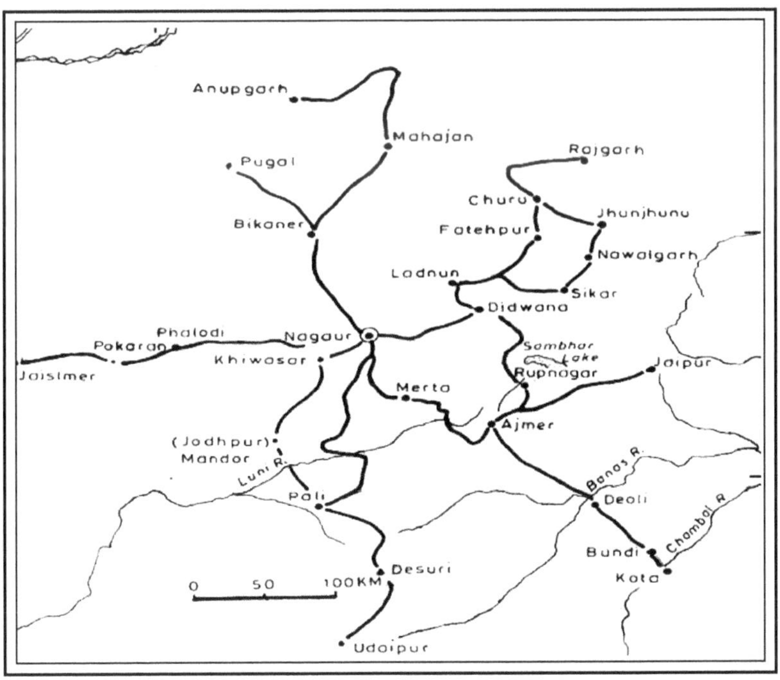

Map 8.12: Internal Trade Routes

TABLE 8.4: COMMODITIES/GOODS FROM NAGAUR TO OTHER REGIONS AND VICE VERSA

Name of Commodity	From	To	Remarks
FROM NAGAUR TO OTHER REGION (EXPORT ITEMS)			
Wool	Nagaur	Nohar, Bikaner and Churu	Other export items from Nagaur to Bikaner were iron, lead, cloth (*kori* cloth), mica, indigo, *kasumba*, chilly, borax, zinc, coconuts, vermilion, catechu
Silk	Nagaur	Nohar	
Bullocks	Nagaur	Multan, Sindh	It was also being sent to many places of Rajputana (Rajasthan)
Iron	Nagaur	Multan	
Blankets	Nagaur	Jodhpur	Other export items from Nagaur to Jodhpur were iron goods, copper and brass utensils and ivory toys.
FROM OTHER REGIONS TO NAGAUR (IMPORT ITEMS)			
Lead	Pali	Nagaur	Other import items to Nagaur from Pali were flax and iron
Pashmina	Kashmir	Nagaur	
Sindha salt	Bikaner	Nagaur	Other imports to Nagaur from Bikaner were woollen cloth salum, lac, dry fruits, dry ginger, etc.
Woollen cloths, alum, sindha/ sendha salt, lac, asafoetida, dry fruits, harde, nutmeg, fullers' earth, dry ginger, aniseed	North Region via Bikaner	Nagaur	

Table 8.4, clearly indicates that Nagaur was an important trade centre in Marwar. The caravans from one place to another were passing through this town, and therefore, considered as the nodal

centre of Rajasthan for trade. According to the *Sawa-mandi-sadar-Bahi* of Bikaner, there is a reference of export of 30 bullocks from Nagaur to Multan,[84] because Nagauri bullocks had had earned good reputation and therefore always remained in great demand in Multan, Sindh and other principalities of Rajputana. Besides, Nagaur was a centre of woollen and cotton cloth industry.[85] Various types of woollen cloths were being produced here[86] and the wool was mostly exported to Bikaner and Nohar, and transmitting further in the north.[87]

This area is rich in minerals such as red stone, salt, mica and gypsum and the state earned considerable revenue from it.[88] It was a centre of the manufacture of a large number of goods such as ivory toys, utensils of iron, copper, brass, etc.[89] These items were in great demand all over Rajputana.

There is adequate information in the eighteenth-century documents about the local and outside traders, who were engaged in internal and external trades, their daily activities and their names and residences (permanent and non-permanent). It is mentioned that Navneet Roy, Messrs Sahib Ray, Thakur Das Bhiwani, Bhawani Das Meghani were the prominent traders who were living in Nagaur. Similarly, Shah Ram Nagauri, and Akhai Ram were well reputed local traders with their trading activities.[90]

Table 8.4 shows that a large number of goods were reached at *Mandi* Nagaur from northern region through Bikaner. These items were woollen cloths, alum, sindha/sendha salt, lac, asafoetida, dry fruits, harde, nutmeg, fullers' earth, dry ginger, aniseed. Some items, viz., lead, iron and flax had been imported by Nagaur from Pali while pashmina from Kashmir. It is interesting to note that Nagaur not only imported goods but a large number of items were exported, namely copper and brass utensils, blankets, iron goods, ivory toys to Jodhpur; silk and wool to Nohar; iron, lead, cloth (*kori*-cloths), mica, indigo, *kasumba*, chilly, borax, zinc, coconut, vermilion, catechu, etc., to Bikaner.[91]

The information on trade, commerce and trade routes demonstrates the commercial links of Nagaur with various towns and cities of Rajasthan, and other neighbouring regions like Multan in west, Kashmir in north, Delhi and Agra in north-east, and Gujarat,

Malwa, Deccan in south. This brought the city into prominence in the trading world. Similarly, Pali had flourished in the eighteenth century as an important trading and commercial centre and as Nagaur; it was connected to many urban centres of Rajasthan and other neighbouring regions served as a trading junction and consequently attracted a large number of professional workers, traders and artisans resulting in augmentation in population. Also trade routes were helpful in the growth of both internal and external trade of Rajasthan since early medieval time and which continued in later period too. It was because of these routes that the traders could frequently move with their goods not only within the boundary of Rajasthan, but other parts of India as well with agility.

On the basis of the foregoing study, we can say that because of the royal patronage and the ardent interest shown by the rulers of Marwar, the trade and commerce in the region was in flourishing condition till the end of the eighteenth century. But during nineteenth century the prosperity of Pali gradually started to decline due to many causes. Prominent among them were the imperial interest and the economic policy adopted by the British in this part of the century. Besides this, insecurity of land routes, excessive and oppressive duties imposed on merchandise by the State of Marwar, passing of rail routes through Marwar Junction bypassing Pali on one side and the salt agreements between the British government and the State of Marwar reduced the commercial prominence of Pali. The development of Ajmer as a trading centre also minimized the importance of Pali as a commercial mart. Besides these, Sunita Zaidi has pointed out many other reasons for the decline of Pali.[92] One of them was the continuous financial deterioration of the state and the coercive methods of exacting money from the *mahajans,* which forced many of them to migrate to different commercial markets especially the British regions. The lucrative benefit of the British India attracted traders from the princely states and resultantly decline in population in these areas. Pali gradually lost its former grandeur as a centre of trade and commerce in late nineteenth century, which found reflection in de-urbanization.

NOTES

1. *Sanad Parwana Bahis, Khas Rukka Parwana Bahis, Haqiqat Bahis* of different years are preserved at Rajasthan State Archives, Bikaner.
2. *Parwana* is the letter of instructions issued by Maharaja to his senior officials or traders. [In *sanad parwana bahi*, the copies of the *parwanas* sent by the ruler of Jodhpur to the village officials are preserved. They provide information on different type of taxes and cesses, rate of land revenue (*bhog*) demand and various methods of revenue assessment such as *batai* and *zabti*. Besides, the duties and functions of the *pargana* officials are mentioned in these *bahis*. The *khas-rukka parwana-bahis* contain the *rukkas* sent by the Jodhpur rulers to *jagirdars* or *pattayats*. They provide information about those village/*qasbas* which are granted in *sasan* to the Brahmins and Charans. These grants were given to them in the form of land which was free from all obligations. The grant holders were entitled to collect land revenue and other cesses in their territories.]
3. *Haqiqat bahis* are available in the Rajasthan State Archives, Bikaner.
4. R.P. Vyas, 'Trade Centres of Marwar and Linked Trade Routes During 18th Century AD', published in *Shodh-Patrika*, ed. Dev Kothari, July-December 1995, Udaipur, pp. 45-56.
5. Sunita Zaidi, 'State and Cities in Rajasthan: Pali between the 17th and 19th Centuries', in *Contributions to Indian Social Sciences*, April-June 2010, pp. 68-79. See quoted number of names who worked on this topic are: C.D. Deshpande, 'Cities and Towns of Bombay Provinces: Aspects of Urban Geography', *Indian Geographical Journal*, vol. XVI, no. 3, 1941, p. 281; A.H. Dani, *Dacca: A Record of Changing Future*, Dacca, 1957; Ashin Das Gupta, *Indian Merchant and the Decline of Surat (1700-1750)*, Manohar, New Delhi, 1994; Lakshmi Subramanian, *Indigenous Capital and Imperial Expansion: Bombay, Surat and the West Coast*, Oxford University Press, New Delhi, 1996; B.G. Gokhale, *Poona in the Eighteenth Century: An Urban History*, Oxford University Press, New Delhi, 1988.
6. *Arhsatta* for Amber; *Toji-do-varkhi-baje-talke* for Kota; *Sava bahi* for Bikaner, *Sanad parwana bahi* for Marwar.
7. Zaidi, 'State and Cities in Rajasthan: Pali between the 17th and 19th Centuries', op. cit., pp. 68-79. Cf. Satya Prakash Jain, III, p. 430, Nahar Jain Inscription, nos. 809, 813, 814 and 815, Calcutta, 1918-29.
8. *Rajasthan District Gazetteers*, Pali, ed. K.K. Sehgal, Government of Rajasthan, Jaipur, 1976, p. 471.
9. Zaidi, 'State and Cities in Rajasthan: Pali between the 17th and 19th Centuries', op. cit., p. 70.

10. *Rajasthan District Gazetteers*, Pali, op. cit., p. 471. Cf. K.D. Erskine, *Rajputana Gazetteer*, Gurgaon, 1992, p. 211.
11. *Rajasthan District Gazetteers*, Pali, op. cit., p. 471.
12. G.S.L. Devra, 'A Study of the Trade: Relations between Rajasthan and Sindh-Multan (1650-1800 AD)', a chapter in his edited book entitled *Socio-Economic History of Rajasthan*, Shri Jagdish Singh Gahlot Research Institute, Jodhpur, 1980, p. 43.
13. *Rajasthan District Gazetteers*, Pali, op. cit., p. 471.
14. Ibid.
15. Ibid.
16. Ibid., p. 472.
17. Ibid., p. 473.
18. James Tod, *Annals and Antiquity of Rajasthan*, vol. II, Humphrey Milford, Oxford University Press, London, 1920, pp. 1127-8.
19. Ibid., p.128.
20. Devra, 'A Study of the Trade: Relations between Rajasthan and Sindh-Multan (1650-1800 AD)', op. cit., p. 43.
21. James Tod, *Annals and Antiquity of Rajasthan*, vol. I, Humphrey Milford, Oxford University Press, London, 1920, p. 554.
22. *Khas-rukka-rarwana-rahi*, no.1, VS 1825/AD 1768, VS 1846/AD 1789, VS 1847/AD 1790, Jodhpur records. Also these kinds of records are available in Rajasthan State Archives, Bikaner.
23. *Haqiqat bahi*, VS 1824/AD 1767.
24. Zaidi, 'State and Cities in Rajasthan: Pali between the 17th and 19th Centuries', op. cit., p. 70.
25. Ibid.
26. *Byav-ri-bahi*, no. 158, VS 1827/AD 1770, RSA, Bikaner.
27. *Kagad-ri-bahi*, no. 6, VS 1839/AD 1782, RSA, Bikaner.
28. *Sanad-arwana-bahi*, no. 9, VS 1826/AD 1769, Jodhpur Records. Also these kinds of records are available in Rajasthan State Archives, Bikaner.
29. De Laet, *De Imperio Magni Mogolis*, English translation, J.S. Hoyland, Bombay, 1928, pp. 64-6. (As quoted by B.L. Gupta, *Trade and Commerce in Rajasthan During 18th Century*, op. cit., p. 134.)
30. Lt. Alexander Burns, F. Department Secret Cons., 14 October 1830, nos. 3-8. (Pali was the route through which the Malwa opium was exported to China and the Western Asia.)
31. This route was being frequently used and trafficked by camels and track was appropriate for way of carts.
32. Burns, F. Department Secret Cons., 14 October 1830, nos. 3-8, op. cit.

33. Vyas, 'Trade Centres of Marwar and Linked Trade Routes during 18th Century AD', op. cit., p. 49. (Also see Table.)
34. Ibid., p. 49.
35. The bullocks of Marwar, particularly those of Nagaur had been famous throughout the western side of India. They were kept chiefly for the purpose of traffic between Kutch and Marwar and for bringing the salt from its sources like Pachpadra, Sambhar, etc., to Pali, the main market place of Marwar. Thousands of bullocks forming a caravan could be seen who were passing the roads daily. These were generally owned or escorted by Charans or Bhats, locally known as *Baldia Bhats*.
36. Vyas, 'Trade Centres of Marwar and Linked Trade Routes During 18th Century AD', op. cit., pp. 45-56. Cf. Tod, *Annals and Antiquities*, vol. II, pp. 126-7.
37. Burns, op. cit., no. 7.
38. Pali was situated on the route through which the Malwa opium was exported to China and the Western Asia.
39. Tod, op. cit., vol. I, pp. 553-4. Sugar was imported from Bareli, Kanpur, Chandausi and Muzaffarnagar via Jaipur.
40. *Imperial Gazetteer*, vol. III A, 1903, p. 119.
41. Vyas, 'Trade Centres of Marwar and Linked Trade Routes during 18th Century AD', op. cit., p. 51.
42. This figure is collected by Sunita Zaidi from *Ain-i-Akbari* and *Marwar-ra-pargana-ri-Vigat*. See her article, 'State and Cities in Rajasthan: Pali between the 17th and 19th Centuries', op. cit., p. 71.
43. Zaidi, ibid., p. 71.
44. Ibid. [At that time the currency was in terms of rupees, *annas*, and *paisa*; twelve *paisa* would make an *anna*, and sixteen *annas* a rupee.]
45. G.D. Sharma, 'Urban Economy in Western India', in Indu Banga, ed., *The City in India*, Manohar, Delhi, 2015, p. 105 (1st pub. 1991).
46. B.N. Reu, *Marwar Ka Itihas* (Hindi), part II, Jodhpur Archaeological Department, Jodhpur, 1940, p. 641.
47. *Rajasthan District Gazetteers*, Nagaur, ed. K.K. Sehgal, Government of Rajasthan, Jaipur, 1975, pp. 456-7.
48. K.C. Jain, *Ancient Cities and Towns of Rajasthan*, Motilal Banarsidass, Delhi, 1972, p. 242. (Nagaur was known by various names such as Nagapura, Nagapattana, Ahipura, and Bhujanganagara.)
49. *Rajasthan District Gazetteers*, Nagaur, op. cit., p. 1.
50. K.C. Jain, 'Jaina Sources for the History of Nagaur', in *Nagaur ka Rajnitic aur Sanskritic Vaibhav*, ed. D.B. Ksheersagar and Naval Krishna, Maharaja Mansingh Pustak Prakash, Mehrangarh, Jodhpur, 1998, p. 128.

51. Many Persian source such as; *Sarur-us-Sudur; Ain-i-Akbari,* etc. For details see M.H. Siddiqui, *Madhya Kaleen Nagaur ka Itihas* (Hindi), Maharaja Mansingh Pushtak Prakash, Mehrangarh, Jodhpur, 2001.
52. Jain, *Ancient Cities and Towns of Rajasthan,* op. cit., p. 242
53. Ibid.
54. Its weight was 70.6 *grain* (1 *grain* = 0.0648 or 1.5 *ratti*).
55. Advard Thomas, 'The Chronicles of the Pathan Kings of Delhi', p. 78. A.B.M. Habibullah, *The Foundation of Muslim Rule in India,* 290. (Also see an article of M.H. Siddiqui, 'Madhya Kaleen Nagaur ke Pramukh Shrot (AD 1260-1752)', in *Nagaur ka Rajnitic aur Sanskritic Vaibhav*', ed. D.B. Ksheersagar and Naval Krishna, Maharaja Mansingh Pushtak Prakash, Mehrangarh, Jodhpur, 1998, pp. 6-13.)
56. Shoshani Museum of Lahore still has some of the coins which were minted by Balban at Nagaur (M.A. Chuqtai, 'Nagaur a Forgotten Kingdom', *Bulletin of the Deccan College Research Institute,* Poona, part 2, nos. 1-2, November 1940), p. 167.
57. Abul Fazl, *Ain-i-Akbari,* part I, pp. 32-3. English translation by H. Blockman. (Nagaur made a *sarkar* by Emperor Akbar, while total *sarkars* were seven under the *suba* of Ajmer.) The different types of copper coins of Akbar were minted in Nagaur such as *dam adhela* (half of *dam*), *pawala* (one-fourth of *dam*), and *damadi* (one-eighth of *dam*).
58. Nizamuddin Ahmad, *Tabqat-i-Akbari,* pp. 201-2. Farishta, *Tarikh-i-Farishta,* p. 32.
59. K.A. Nizami, *Some Aspects of Religion and Politics in India during the 13th Century,* Oxford University Press, New Delhi, 1961, p. 180 and comment no. 4. [A trader of Nagaur carried mustard (*sarso*) from Nagaur and sold it to Multan and further carried cotton from Multan and sold to Nagaur.] G.S.L. Devra, explained in details in one of his articles entitled 'A Study of the Trade Relations between Rajasthan and Sindh-Multan (1650-1800 AD)', in *Socio-Economic History of Rajasthan,* ed. G.S.L. Devra, op. cit., pp. 36-50.
60. Yahya-bin-Ahmad, *Tarikh-i-Mubarakshahi,* pp. 34, 166, 193, 217. G.N. Sharma, *Rajasthan Studies,* Lakshmi Narain Agarwal, Educational Publisher, Agra, 1970, p. 163. G.N. Sharma, *Social Life in Medieval Rajasthan,* L.N. Agarwal, Agra, 1968, p. 323. [Many more routes were extremely important both concerning battles and trading point of views were also passing through Nagaur. A route from Delhi to Malwa was attached with Gwalior and Nagaur.]
61. Nizami, *Some Aspects of Religion and Politics in India,* op. cit.
62. Yahya-bin-Ahmad, *Tarikh-i-Mubarakshahi,* op. cit.
63. Ibid., pp. 192-3.

64. Toda is presently located 63 miles away in the south-west of Jaipur on latitude 26°4' and longitude 75°39′. In *Arhsatta,* it is mentioned as Toda Bhim under Rajputana Principality. Akbar also visited Toda, when he undertook his journey from Agra to Ajmer (see an article of Jibraeil, 'Contribution of Sufis in the Growth of Urban Centres in Rajasthan During the 18th Century', in *Sufi Movement in Rajasthan,* ed. S.M. Azizuddin Hussain, Idara-i-Adabiyat-i Dilli, Delhi, 2007, pp. 62-75. Cf. Abul Fazl, *Akbarnama,* translated into English by H. Beveridge, vol. II, rpt., Delhi, 1993, pp. 510-11.
65. *Tarikh-i-Farishta,* pp. 199-201. [In the sixteenth and seventeenth centuries trade through the desert routes was also running well. Emperor Akbar issued a *farman* to Rai Singh, then the king of the Bikaner State, not to realize the customary dues from the traders who were passing through the routes lying in the territory of the Bikaner State, except the little money which was required for the administration and safety of the routes. See Devra, 'A Study of the Trade Relations between Rajasthan and Sindh-Multan (1650-1800 AD)', op. cit., p. 37. Cf. Emperor Akbar's *farman* to Rai Singh, D/7th Urdi Bihist, 37, 12th Rajab-ul-Murajjab 990 AH, Lalgarh Palace, Bikaner.]
66. *Zakat/jagat bahi,* no. 81, VS 1807/AD 1750, RSA, Bikaner.
67. *Sanad-parwana-bahi,* no. 25, VS 1838/AD 1781, f. 77, Record of Jodhpur.
68. Ibid., f. 238, Record of Jodhpur [In the author's study, Ajmer was on the way of this route (Nagaur-Ajmer) and comes after Merta, but scholars did not plot it in their attempted.]
69. Dasrath Sharma, *Rajasthan through the Ages,* part 1, Rajasthan State Archives, Bikaner, 1966, pp. 491-2 and 740.
70. *Akbarnama,* part 2, pp. 535-50.
71. Siddiqui, op. cit., pp. 257.
72. Sharma, *Rajasthan Studies,* op. cit., p. 164. G.N. Sharma, *Social Life in Medieval Rajasthan,* op. cit., p. 324. Also see *Kharita* of different years, RSA, Bikaner.
73. Abul Fazl, *Akbarnama,* translated into English by H. Beveridge, vol. II, op. cit., pp. 372-3.
74. *Sava-mandi-sadar-bahi,* no. 11, VS 1822/AD 1765, RSA, Bikaner. B.L. Gupta also mentioned in details about the internal trade routes of Rajasthan in his book *Trade and Commerce in Rajasthan,* op. cit.
75. *Sanad-parwana-bahi,* no. 21, VS 1835/AD 1778, f. 239, Jodhpur Records.
76. Ibid., no. 19, VS 1834/AD 1777, Jodhpur Records.
77. Ibid., no. 8, AD 1768, Jodhpur Records. Also See *Zakat/jagat bahi* of Bikaner, no. 7, VS 1806/AD 1749.
78. *Byav-ri-bahi,* no.158, VS 1827/AD 1770, RSA,Bikaner.

79. *Sanad-parwana-bahi*, no. 8, AD 1768, Jodhpur Records.
80. *Kagad-ri-bahi*, no. 6, AD 1782, RSA, Bikaner.
81. *Sanad-parwana-bahi*, no. 13, VS 1830/AD 1773, f. 58, Jodhpur Records.
82. Ibid., no. 9, AD 1769, Jodhpur Records.
83. *Byav-ri-bahi*, no.158, VS 1827/AD 1770, RSA, Bikaner.
84. *Sawa-mandi-sadar-Bahi*, no. 4, VS 1807-10/AD 1750-3, RSA, Bikaner. [A good pair of Bullocks would some times fetch over Rs. 200 but the average price was Rs. 150.]
85. Munhot Nainsi, *Marwar-ra-pargana-ri-Vigat*, part 2, p. 424.
86. Naqvi, *Urbanisation and Urban Centres Under the Great Mughals*, op. cit., p. 51.
87. Vyas, 'Trade Centres of Marwar and Linked Trade Routes During 18th Century AD', op. cit., p. 52.
88. *Vigat* II, 423-4. *Imperial Gazetteer, Provincial Series, Rajputana*, p. 184. [As quoted by Vyas, 'Trade Centres of Marwar and Linked Trade Routes During 18th Century AD, op. cit., pp. 52-3; Gupta, *Trade and Commerce in Rajasthan*, op. cit., p. 113.]
89. Ibid.
90. *Sanad-parwana-bahi*, no. 21, VS 1835/AD 1778, Jodhpur Records.
91. Vyas, 'Trade Centres of Marwar and Linked Trade Routes During 18th Century AD', op. cit., p. 53.
92. For details see, Sunita Zaidi, 'State and Cities in Rajasthan: Pali between the 17th and 19th Centuries', op. cit., p. 70. Cf. G.N. Sharma, *Social Life in Medieval Rajasthan*, op. cit., p. 341. [The diminishing financial condition of the state forced it to demand a huge sum arbitrarily from the *mahajans* and *seths*. A report by Trevelyan to Colebrook mentioned a case of 9 August 1828 in which the *kotwal* (police chief) of Jodhpur demanded Rs. 20,000 from the *mahajans* who in protest closed their shops.]

CHAPTER 9

Population Composition of Marwar between 1803 and 1843

James Tod came to Marwar only once in the time of Maharaja Man Singh in 1820. He had specific interest in demography, and therefore, estimated the population of Marwar. First of all he recorded the geographical expanse of the area. According to him, the extreme breadth of Marwar lies between two points in the parallel of the capital, namely, Girabs, west and Shamgarh, on the Aravalli range, east. This line measures 270 British miles. The greatest length, from the Sirohi frontier to the northern boundary, was about 220 miles.[1] According to him, the south-east is a fertile tract[2] which contains 80 *souls* (individuals) in a square mile, while he assigns 30 individuals to the area located in the north-east.[3] The desert, an infertile area, contains only 10 families in a square mile.[4] For this region, he estimated the population in round figures at about two million (20,00,000) persons.[5] He also parenthetically gives the total population of the town of Jodhpur at about 80,000.[6]

An attempt has been made in this chapter to analyse the information on urban population and its caste composition and professional groups contained in Tod. The study is divided into four parts. The first part deals with Tod's information about the number of houses. The second part covers comparison of the worked-out population of 1820s with the census of 1891. The third part is an analysis of Tod's data on professional groups of the town of Jalor and the fourth part is the comparison of data of professional groups of Jalor with that of the census of 1931.

I

The study of the size and composition of urban population in the pre-census period is a subject of great interest, but the necessary data are hard to obtain. We have some evidence which can help us to estimate the population of towns of Marwar during the first half of the nineteenth century. B.L. Bhadani has applied a method to work out the population for the second half of the seventeenth century. He has used the number of houses to estimate the population of some towns of Marwar for the 1660s. He estimated the population of few towns and villages on the basis of two types of information, first, the number of ploughs for a number of villages, and second, the total numbers of houses count in almost all *pargana* headquarters.[7] S.P. Gupta has also calculated the population of more or less the same *pargana* headquarters.[8]

Following the same methodology, I venture to attempt to estimate the population of some of the towns of Marwar on the basis of the house-count contained in Tod. It appears that his count of houses was either communicated to him by some officials in the government or obtained through the official records. The data on urban houses provided by him enables us to estimate the urban population of the period of the 1820s which coincides with the reign of Maharaja Man Singh. The details of towns with their number of houses are given in Table 9.1.

The total number of houses in the fourteen towns of Marwar comes to 40,242. If we multiply this figure by 5 persons per house, the rate given by Tod himself, we would get a total population in round numbers as 2,01,210 (40,242 × 5) for the 14 towns,[9] while Jodhpur alone had a population of 80,000.[10] Adding this to the total comes to 2,81,210. Breakup of the population of different towns is set given in the Table 9.2.

Table 9.2 clearly shows the population of individual towns whose sum total comes to 2,81,210 including Jodhpur. Of these, the town of Merta is dominant with a population of 100,000, followed by Jodhpur (80,000), Pali (50,000), Jalor (15,085), Pipar and Bhinmal (7,500 each), Bharunda and Barmer (6,000 each), Sanchor (3,750), Morsin, Bhadrajan and Kotra (2,500 each), Shiv (1,500), Indawar (1,000), and Nandala (625).

TABLE 9.1: NUMBER OF HOUSES IN DIFFERENT TOWNS OF MARWAR REGION IN 1820S AS GIVEN BY JAMES TOD

Name of the town	No. of houses	Remarks
Pali[11]	10,000	
Merta[12]	20,000	
Pipar[13]	1,500	
Jalor[14]	3,017	
Bhinmal[15]	1,500	
Indawar[16]	200	
Nandala[17]	125	
Morsin[18]	500	
Sanchor[19]	750	½ of Bhinmal*
Bhadrajan[20]	500	
Shiv[21]	300	
Kotra[22]	500	
Bharunda[23]	1,200	
Barmer[24]	1,200	
Jodhpur[25]**	NA	
Total	40,242	40,242 × 5⁺ = 2,01,210

Notes: *According to Tod, the number of houses of Sanchor was half of Bhinmal.
**The number of houses of Jodhpur is not mentioned by Tod, but its total population is given as 80,000.
⁺Tod assumes the conventional ratee of 5 persons in a house.

TABLE 9.2: WORKED-OUT POPULATION OF DIFFERENT TOWNS OF MARWAR REGION IN THE 1820S

Name of the town	No. of houses	Population (no. of houses × 5*)
Pali	10,000	50,000
Merta	20,000	100,000
Pipar	1,500	7,500
Jalor	3,017	15,085
Bhinmal	1,500	7,500
Indawar	200	1,000
Nandala	125	625
Morsin	500	2,500
Sanchor	750	3,750
Bhadrajan	500	2,500

contd.

TABLE 9.2 contd.

Name of the town	No. of houses	Population (no. of houses × 5*)
Shiv	300	1,500
Kotra	500	2,500
Bharunda	1,200	6,000
Barmer	1,200	6,000
Jodhpur**	NA	80,000
Total	40,242	2,81,210

Notes: * Tod assumed the conventional figure 5 persons per house.
** Total population of Jodhpur was 80,000.

II

In this part we have taken the number of houses in towns along with their worked-out population for the 1820s and the population of the same towns in 1891 (Table 9.3 and Graph 9.1).

TABLE 9.3: COMPARISON OF POPULATION OF DIFFERENT TOWNS OF MARWAR REGION (1820s WITH 1891)

Name of the town	No. of houses	Population (no. of houses × 5)[26]	Population 1891
Pali	10,000	50,000	17,156[27]
Merta	20,000	1,00,000	7,142[28]
Pipar	1,500	7,500	8,153[29]
Jalor	3,017	15,085	9,657[30]
Bhinmal	1,500	7,500	5,736[31]
Indawar	200	1,000	1,063[32]
Nandala	125	625	310[33]
Morsin	500	2,500	2,500[34]
Sanchor	750	3,750	2,635[35]
Bhadrajan	500	2,500	1,837[36]
Shiv	300	1,500	901[37]
Kotra	500	2,500	1,279[38]
Bharunda	1,200	6,000	1,584[39]
Barmer	1,200	6,000	5,610[40]
Jodhpur	NA	80,000	61,759[41]
Total	40,242	2,81,210	1,27,322

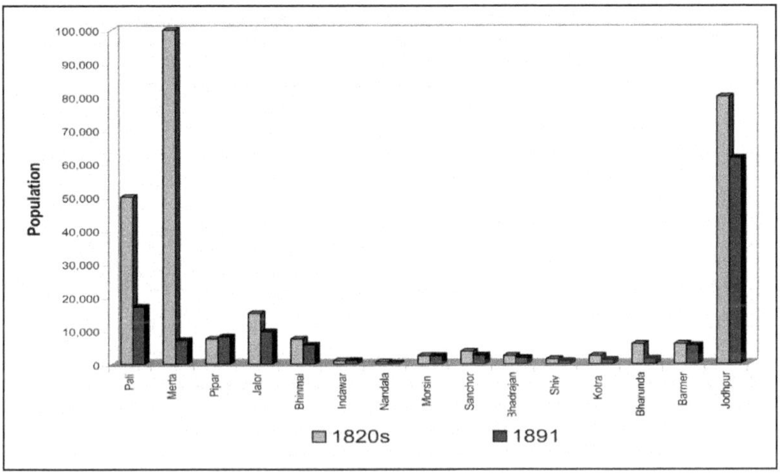

Graph 9.1: A Comparison of Population of Towns of Marwar (1820s with 1891)

Table 9.3 clearly shows decline in population in all the individual towns except two and the total population of the towns in 1820s comes to 2,81,210, which is higher than the population of 1891, which comes to 1,27,322 (see Graph 9.2). Thus the study shows a 55 per cent decline in population which is quite interesting. The question that arises here is whether the decline in the last decade of the nineteenth century can be linked to the de-urbanization caused by the influx of British goods into the region.

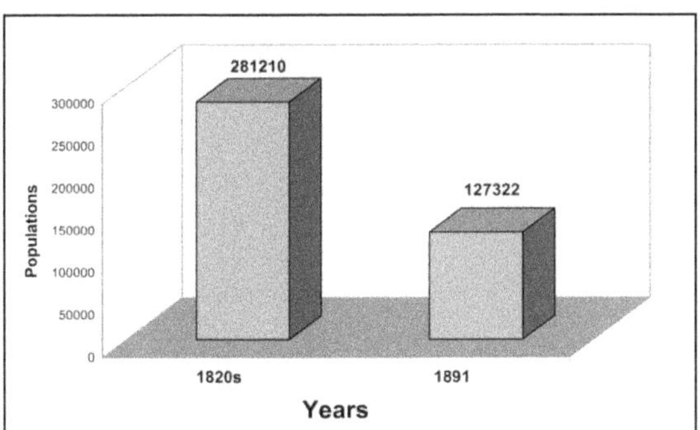

Graph 9.2: A Comparison of Total Population of Fifteen Towns of Marwar (1820s with 1891)

Though we do not have direct evidence on this phenomenon but the total disappearence of calico printers (*chhinpas*) and weavers (*julahas*) in 1931 (see Table 9.4) confirms the influence of some alien factors. But before reaching any final conclusion one should certainly look for more direct data bearing on this phenomenon.

III

James Tod further provides caste and profession-wise breakup of the houses of the town of Jalor[42] which are put in the Table 9.4.

The total population of 21 castes/professional groups comes to 14,305. Of these, bankers, merchants and shopkeepers occupy

TABLE 9.4: WORKED-OUT CASTE/PROFESSION-WISE POPULATION OF JALOR TOWN IN 1820s

Name of Caste/Profession	No. of houses	Population (No. of houses × 5)[43]
Malis (gardeners)	140	700
Telis (ghanchi, oilmen)	100	500
Kumbhars (potters)	60	300
Thatheras (braziers)	30	150
Chhinpas (calico printers)	20	100
Bankers/Merchants/Shopkeepers	1,156	5,780
Musalmans	936	4,680
Khatiks	20	100
Nais (barbers)	16	80
Kalals (wine distillers)	20	100
Julahas (weavers)	100	500
Silk weavers	15	75
Yatis (Jain priests)	2	10
Brahmins	100	500
Gujars	40	200
Rajputs	5	25
Minas	60	300
Bhils	15	75
Sweetmeat sellers	8	40
Lohar (iron smith and carpenters)	14	70
Churiwal (bangle makers)	4	20
Total	2,861	14,305

the first place in terms of the number of houses (1,156) with their population at 5,780.[44] Such a large concentration of bankers and merchants indicates the importance of the town as a trading centre.

IV

The caste-wise houses of the town of Jalor of 1820s could be compared with that of 1931 (see Graph 9.3). Both the figures are given in Table 9.5.

TABLE 9.5: COMPARISON OF POPULATION OF DIFFERENT CASTES/PROFESSIONAL GROUPS IN JALOR TOWN: 1820s WITH 1931

Name of Caste/Profession	No. of houses	Population (no. of houses × 5) (1820s)	Population 1931
Malis (gardeners)	140	700	34.36
Telis (ghanchi, oilmen)	100	500	DA*
Kumbhars (potters)	60	300	8,273
Thatheras (braziers)	30	150	DA
Chhinpas (calico printers)	20	100	DA
Bankers/Merchants/Shopkeepers[45]	1,156	5,780	17,131
Musalmans[46]	936	4,680	2,066
Khatiks	20	100	38
Nais (barbers)	16	80	1,685
Kalals (wine distillers)	20	100	DA
Julahas (weavers)	100	500	DA
Silk weavers	15	75	DA
Yatis (Jain priests)	2	10	DA
Brahmins	100	500	3,441
Gujars	40	200	112
Rajputs[47]	5	25	14,988
Minas	60	300	7,022
Bhils	15	75	6,751
Sweetmeat sellers	8	40	DA
Lohar (ironsmith and carpenters)	14	70	1,337
Churiwal (bangle makers)	4	20	DA
Total	2,861	14,305	66,280

Note: *DA stands for Disappeared.

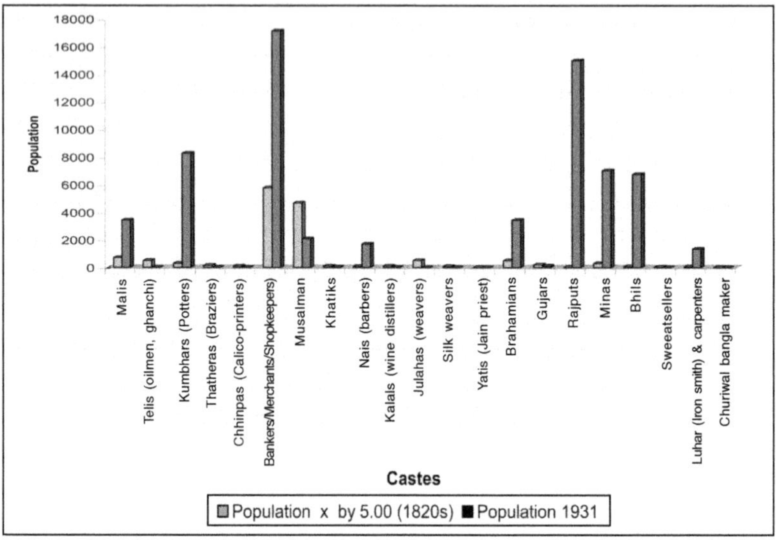

Graph 9.3: A Comparison of Caste Population of *Qasba* Jalor in Marwar Region (1820s with 1931)

According to James Tod, the total number of castes and professional groups of Jalor town was 21, with their total number of houses at 2,861 and their population at 66,280.[48] When we compare these data with that of 1931,[49] we get infor-mation only about twelve castes, while the rest have either changed their professions or migrated from Jalor to other places. The disappeared professional groups are generally textile workers such as; Julahas (weavers), Chhinpas (calico printers), silk-weavers including others such as Telis, Thatheras, Kalals (wine distillers) and Churiwalas (bangle makers), etc.[50]

Table 9.5 also shows that few of the castes have increased in numbers remarkably, while others either decreased or remain static. The population of Kumbhars (300), Nais (80), Brahmins (500), Minas (300), Bhils (75) and Lohars (70) has increased and is 8,273, 1,685, 3,441, 7,022, 6,751 and 1,337 respectively. The number of Muslims declined from 4,680 to 2,066. But there is little confusion about the population of Rajputs, because their population in 1931 is quite high which was mentioned as 14,988, but in Tod's time their numbers of houses were only five with a population 25. There are two strong possibilities; first, either Tod must have counted only Rajput cultivators and left out the areas of the Rajput *bhumias* who were controlling large areas in Jalor or second, they might have purchased the land from the cultivators.

The decline of textile workers such as: Chhinpas (calico printers), Julahas (weavers) and silk-weavers indicate the decline of the industry in the last quarter of the nineteenth century.

NOTES

1. James Tod, *Annals and Antiquities of Rajasthan*, vol. II, Humphrey Milford, Oxford University Press, London, 1920, p. 1104.
2. In this tract the following districts fall: Didwana, Nagaur, Merta, Jodhpur, Pali, Sojhat, Godwar, Siwana, Jalor, Bhinmal and Sanchor. Cf. Tod, ibid.
3. The places of this tract were Nagaur, Phalodi, Pokaran, etc. Cf. Tod, ibid.
4. The places of this portion were Gugadeo-Ka-Thal, a desert of Guga, Shiv, Bharmer, Kotra and Chhotan. Cf. Tod, ibid.
5. Tod, vol. II, ibid., pp. 1104-5.
6. Ibid., p. 821.
7. B.L. Bhadani, *Peasants, Artisans and Entrepreneurs: Economy of Marwar in the 17th Century*, Rawat Publications, Jaipur, 1999, pp. 20-31. S.P. Gupta, 'Evidence for Urban Population and its Composition from 17th to 18th Century Rajasthan', *PIHC,* Calicut, 1976, pp. 179-80.
8. Gupta, 'Evidence for Urban Population and its Composition from 17th to 18th Century Rajasthan', ibid., pp. 179-80.
9. Tod assumed the conventional figure as 5.
10. Tod, op. cit., vol. II, p. 821.
11. Ibid., p. 811.
12. Ibid., pp. 855-6
13. Ibid., p. 851.
14. Tod, vol. III, pp. 1266-8.
15. Ibid., p. 1269.
16. Tod, op. cit., vol. II, p. 854.
17. Ibid., p. 850.
18. Tod, op. cit., vol. III, p. 1269.
19. Ibid.
20. Ibid.
21. Ibid., p. 1272.
22. Ibid.

23. Tod, op. cit., vol. II, p. 853.
24. Tod, op. cit., vol. III, pp. 1272-3.
25. Tod, op. cit., vol. II, p. 821.
26. Population obtained after multiplying by assumed conventional rate 5 persons per house.
27. *Mardum Shumari Raj Marwar*, vol. II, 1892, p. 290.
28. Ibid., p. 133.
29. Ibid., p. 253.
30. Ibid., p. 148.
31. *Census of India*, 1931, op. cit., p. 10.
32. *Mardum Shumari*, op. cit., p. 109.
33. Ibid., p. 2.
34. Ibid., p. 233.
35. Ibid., p. 235.
36. Ibid., p. 157.
37. Ibid., p. 327.
38. Ibid., p. 323.
39. Ibid., p. 98.
40. *Census of India*, 1931, op. cit., p.10.
41. *Mardum Shumari*, op. cit., p. 1. (Before James Tod, a Maratha document also records the number of houses for Jodhpur which were 45,000 in 1785. We can obtain the total population of the city of Jodhpur, multiplying it by 5 persons per house. Thus, the total population comes to 2,25,000 (45,000 × 5) which was quite higher than Tod's figures. This shows that the decline of the town had been started in early phase of the British rule. See *Parampara* 2, ed. Narayan Singh Bhati, Chaupasani, Jodhpur. (This figure was recorded after an earthquake in Jodhpur city.)
42. Tod, op. cit., vol. III, pp. 1267-8.
43. Population of different caste and professional groups.
44. Tod, op. cit., vol. III, pp. 1267-8.
45. Merchants/bankers/shopkeepers, considered as mahajan in the *Census of India*, 1931.
46. Musalmans constitutes Fakirs 59, Jogis 66, Kaimkhanis 12, Pathans 158, and Shaikhs 1771.
47. James Tod mentions the total number of houses of Rajputs as 5. While in another source, the Rajputs formed one-eleventh of the population. See, Padamja Sharma, *Maharaja Man Singh of Jodhpur and His Times*, Agra, 1972, p. 244.
48. Tod, op. cit., vol. III, pp. 1267-8.
49. *Census of India*, 1931, op. cit., pp. 10-15.
50. Tod, op. cit., vol. III, pp. 1267-8.

CHAPTER 10

Tod's Estimation of Population of Some Urban Centres of Rajasthan

James Tod had a fascination for demography. He made attempts to work out the population of the area about which he was writing. In his pursuit, he always tried to collect data helpful in the calculation of the population of that area. He had collected data of number of houses, tax collection and other kinds of miscellaneous information. This shows his deep interest in the estimation of population. The data collected of town population is extremely useful because it belongs to the pre-census period.

In this chapter an attempt has been made to have a close look at the nature and character of the data preserved in his *Annals and Antiquities,*[1] which provides direct as well as indirect evidence on town population for the 1820s.[2] For this, we have taken almost all those towns for which he had collected data. These are Jaisalmer, Bikaner, Udaipur, Bhilwara, Pur, Mandal and Gosunda and few other small towns of Rajasthan.[3] He records the number of houses for almost all the towns and calculated their population by applying a certain ratio. Tod assumed the conventional figure of 5 persons per house for the states of Jaisalmer (*qasba* headquarter), Bikaner and Mewar while 4 persons for the rest of the small towns of Jaisalmer. The study is divided into three Sections. Section I deals with the towns of Jaisalmer and their population. Section II covers the towns of Bikaner and Section III the towns of Mewar.

I. JAISALMER

The estimation of the population of the towns of Jaisalmer is based on the number of houses and inhabitants collected in 1815[4] by Tod,[5] which are given in Table 10.1(a) and 10.1(b).

TABLE 10.1(a): TOWNS OF JAISALMER (AD 1815)

Town	No. of houses	No. of inhabitants
Jaisalmer	7,000	35,000*
Bikampur	500	2,000
Sirara	300	1,200
Nachna	400	1,600
Katori	300	1,200
Kaba	300	1,200
Kuldharo	200	800
Satla	300	1,200
Jinjiniali	300	1,200
Devi-Kot	200	800
Bhap	200	800
Balana	150	600
Saliasa	100	400
Baru	200	800
Chaun	200	800
Loharki	150	600
Naontala	150	600
Lahti	300	1,200
Dangari	150	600
Bijorai	200	800
Mandai	200	800
Ramgarh	200	800
Birsalpur	200	800
Girajsar	180	600
Total	12,350	56,400

Note: * The assumed conventional figure 5 persons per house for Jaisalmer, while for the rest of the towns is 4.

From [Table 10.1(a)], it becomes clear that the towns located in the desert of Jaisalmer area were twenty-four[6] in number and their total number of houses comes to 12,350. Further he gives population of each town whose total comes to 56,400.[7] For estimation of their population, he applies different ratio for Jaisalmer and other towns. For the former, he obtains the population by multiplying the number of houses by 5, while the ratio of 1:4

is applied for the rest. The higher ratio was applied to Jaisalmer because of its status as a capital headquarters. Holding this position, it contains the highest population of 35,000 while the lowest inhabitants 400 belonged to Saliasa town.[8]

The comparison of population obtained by James Tod for various towns and the corresponding towns of 1891 would be interesting. This would show the change in the population during the period of eighty years (see Graph 10.1).

We have prepared another table [Table 10.1(b)] stating the population in 1815 and the population of the same towns in 1891. The census of 1891 does not provide data for 24 towns, but only for Jaisalmer.[9] The probable reason is that the census of 1891 records the population of only those towns which contained 5,000 or more inhabitants, while Tod had mentioned the population of all those places which were called *qasbas.*

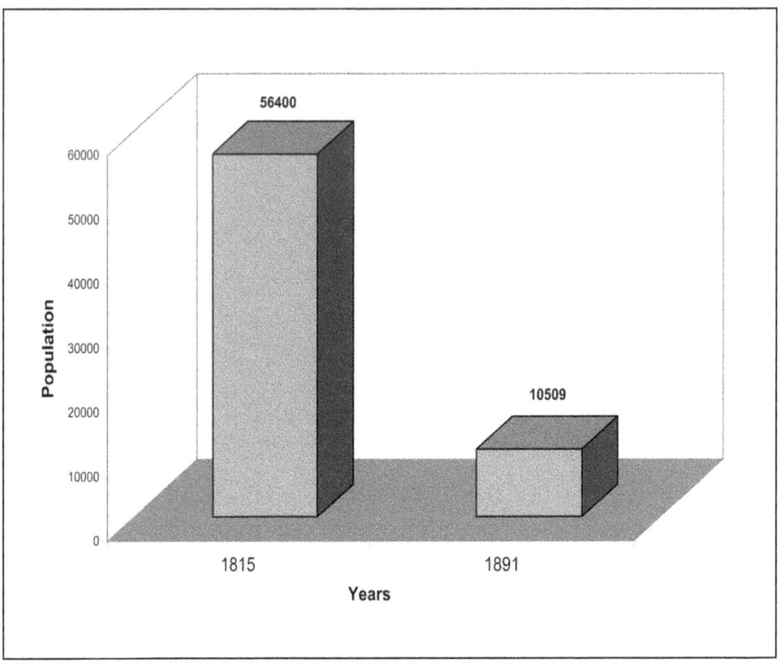

Graph 10.1: A Comparison of Population of Towns of Jaisalmer (1815 with 1891)

TABLE 10.1(b): A COMPARISON OF POPULATION OF THE TOWNS OF JAISALMER: 1815 WITH 1891

Town	Inhabitants in 1815	Inhabitants in 1891
Jaisalmer	35,000	10,509
Bikampur	2,000	NA*
Sirara	1,200	NA
Nachna	1,600	NA
Katori	1,200	NA
Kaba	1,200	NA
Kuldharo	800	NA
Satla	1,200	NA
Jinjiniali	1,200	NA
Devi-Kot	800	NA
Bhap	800	NA
Balana	600	NA
Saliasa	400	NA
Baru	800	NA
Chaun	800	NA
Loharki	600	NA
Naontala	600	NA
Lahti	1,200	NA
Dangari	600	NA
Bijorai	800	NA
Mandai	800	NA
Ramgarh	800	NA
Birsalpur	800	NA
Girajsar	600	NA
Total	56,400	10,509

Note: * NA stands for not available.

Two things emerge from the above comparison: first, all the *qasbas* lost their status in next eighty years and second, the trend of decline in urban population is visible in the case of Jaisalmer (35,000 to 10,509) (see Graph 10.2). The decline was more than three times which a clear case of de-urbanization is. The effect of the British imports could be seen even in the deep desert of Jaisalmer.

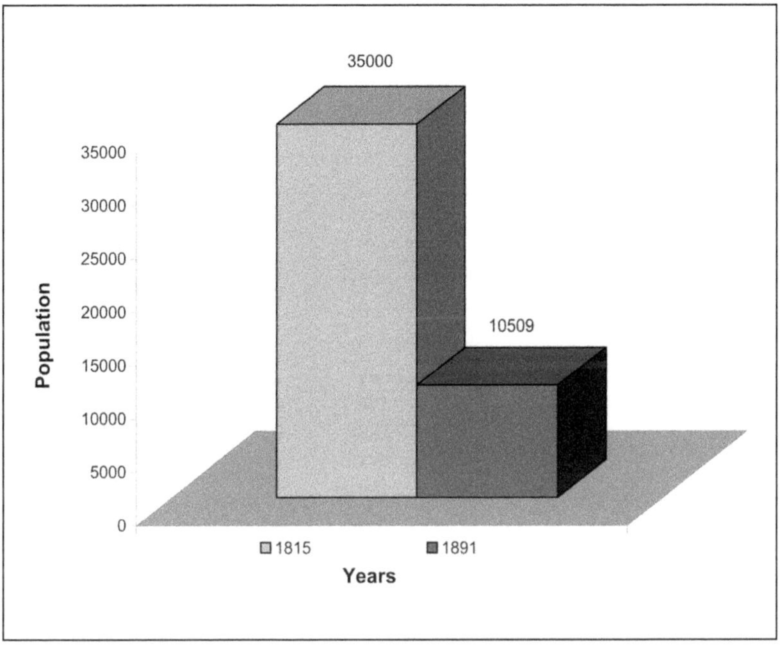

Graph 10.2: A Comparison of Population of Jaisalmer (Town only) (1815 with 1891)

II. BIKANER

The evidence furnished by Tod about the state of Bikaner is of two kinds: first, the number of houses of the towns[10] and second, the number of houses for all the villages.[11] In the second kind of information he categorizes villages into four groups, probably according to their respective sizes and assigned different number of houses to each group. Thus, he worked-out the total number of houses for all 1,200 villages in the state.[12] His assumption about the different group of villages is put in the Table 10.2.

The information of house-count of towns furnished by James Tod is used for estimation of the urban population. By multiplying the number of houses by 5 (as assumed by Tod himself) we can obtain a figure for practically the entire town's population in the 1820s. The worked out population is set out in Table 10.2(a), (b), (c) and (d).

After obtaining the population of towns for 1820s, we can make a comparison of the population of the same towns in 1891,[13] which could indicate the changes between seven decades.

TABLE 10.2(a): TOWNS OF BIKANER (AD 1820s)

Name of Town[14]	Number of houses	Inhabitants = (no. of houses × 5)
Bikaner	12,000	60,000
Nohar	2,500	12,500
Bahaduran	2,500	12,500
Reni	1,500	7,500
Rajgarh	3,000	15,000
Churu	3,000	15,000
Mahajan	800	4,000
Jethpur	1,000	5,000
Bidasar	500	2,500
Ratangarh	1,000	5,000
Deshnokh	1,000	5,000
Sinthal	50	250
Total	28,850	1,44,250

TABLE 10.2(b): A COMPARISON OF THE POPULATION OF THE TOWNS OF BIKANER: 1820s WITH 1891

Name of Town	Inhabitants in 1820s	Inhabitants in 1891
Bikaner	60,000	50,513
Nohar	12,500	5,655
Bahaduran	12,500	NA
Reni	7,500	6,553
Rajgarh	15,000	4,677
Churu	15,000	14,014
Mahajan	4,000	NA
Jethpur	5,000	NA
Bidasar	2,500	4,392
Ratangarh	5,000	10,536
Deshnokh	5,000	NA
Sinthal	250	NA
Total	1,44,250	96,340

TABLE 10.2(c): VILLAGES OF BIKANER (AD 1820s)

Number of Villages and Houses	Total no. of houses[16]	Inhabitants = (no. of houses × 5)
100 villages each having 200 houses	20,000	1,00,000
100 villages each having 150 houses	15,000	75,000
200 villages each having 100 houses	20,000	1,00,000
800 villages each having 30 each	24,000	1,20,000
Total	79,000	3,95,000

TABLE 10.2(d): URBAN-RURAL RATIO: 1820s WITH 1931

Bikaner	Population			
	1820s		1931	
	No. of inhabitants	%	No. of inhabitants	%
Urban	1,44,250	26.75	2,15,205	22.99
Rural	3,95,000	73.25	7,21,013	77.01
Total	5,39,250	100	9,36,218	100

It appears from the above table that of 12 towns in 1820s, five had either disappeared or lost the designation of town by 1891.[15] Of remaining seven towns, five show decline in population while two show increase. Overall, there was also decline in absolute number in seven towns[17] (1,44,250 to 96,340) (see Graph 10.3).

The second category of information belongs to the rural population where Tod offers number of houses for different categories of villages.

As mentioned above [Table 10.2(c)] he assigns specific number of houses to four groups of villages, according to their varied sizes, ranging from 30 to 200 houses to each village.[18] Thus, he gives the total number of houses as 79,000.[19] Then, he multiplies number of houses by 5 persons, thereby obtaining the rural population, which comes to 3,95,000.[20]

Now we have totalled the rural population [(shows in Table 10.2(c)]

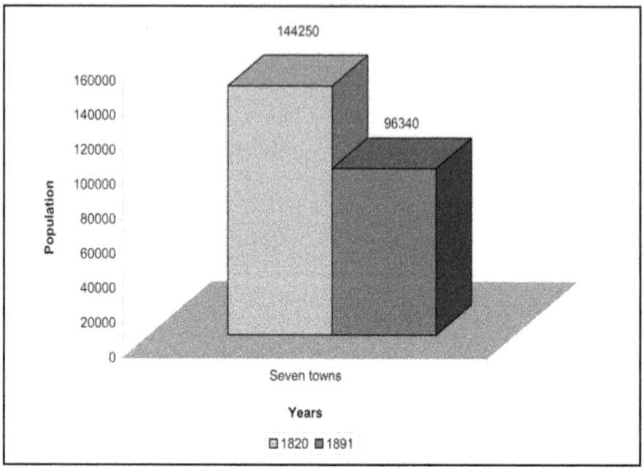

Graph 10.3: A Comparison of Population of Towns of Bikaner (1820 with 1891)

and urban population [(in Table 10.2(a)] to obtain the whole population of the state of Bikaner in the table of Urban-Rural Ratio [(Table 10.2(d)]. Along with it, we have also put the urban and rural population of 1931.[21] Then, we have worked-out the rural and urban ratio for both the periods [(Table 10.2(d)]. This shows that the urban ratio to that of the total population in 1820s was about 27 per cent, while in 1931 it was 23 per cent, which clearly shows the decline of 4 per cent in urban population in the past one hundred years (see Graph 10.4).

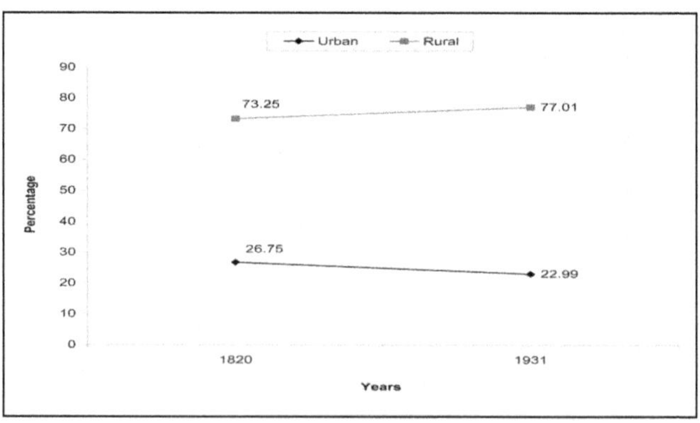

Graph 10.4: A Comparison of Population of Urban-Rural Ratio in Bikaner (1820s with 1931)

III. MEWAR

The information of James Tod about Mewar is very scanty.[22] He records the number of houses for Udaipur, Bhilwara, Pur, Mandal and Gosunda.[23] By mentioning population of two years, i.e. 1818 and 1822,[24] he intended to make a comparison of population on the eve of the treaty between Mewar and the British (1818) and change in the population after four years in 1822. So he has mentioned the house-count for both the years in Table 10.3(a).

Table 10.3(a) shows that the number of houses of five towns of Mewar (Udaipur,[25] Bhilwara,[26] Pur, Mandal and Gosunda) comes to 3,840 in 1818 and increased to 14,650 in 1822 which means an increase of 58.46 per cent. James Tod wanted to show that the urban population of the towns increased after the treaty with the British. This means that the British relations were beneficial for the Sisodia state.

Further we have prepared Table 10.3(b) to compare the population of 1822 with that of 1891. From this table, it is quite clear that the total population of five towns in 1822 was 73,250.[27] While it declined to 63,836[28] in 1891 (see Graph 10.5). Thus, this decline of about 13 per cent in population was most likely the result of the British influence.

James Tod also collected some strong references without the number of houses of some towns such as Jaipur[29] (with 1,85,670 persons). Hanumangarh[30] (800 inhabited houses/4,000 persons). Garot[31] (1,200 houses/6,000 persons) and Jhalarapatam[32] (6,000 dwellings with a population of at least 25,000-30,000 persons).

TABLE 10.3(a): TOWNS OF MEWAR (1818 AND 1822)

Town[33]	No. of houses in 1818	No. of houses in 1822
Udaipur	3,500	10,000
Bhilwara	NA	2,700
Pur	200	1,200
Mandal	80	400
Gosunda	60	350
Total	3,840	14,650

TABLE 10.3(b): POPULATION: COMPARISON OF TOWNS OF MEWAR (1822 WITH 1891)

Town[34]	No. of houses in 1822	Population in 1822 (no. of houses in 1822 × 5)	Population of 1891
Udaipur	10,000	50,000	46,693
Bhilwara	2,700	13,500	10,343
Pur	1,200	6,000	6,800
Mandal	400	2,000	NA*
Gosunda	350	1,750	NA
Total	14,650	73,250	63,836

Note: *NA: Not available.

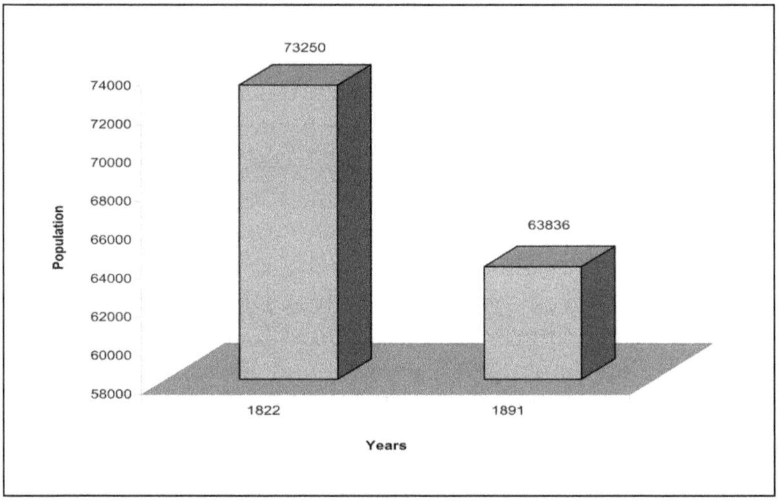

Graph 10.5: A Comparison of Population of Towns of Mewar (1822 with 1891)

Overall, James Tod's data for the pre-census period is extremely useful as it enables us to make a comparative study with that of 1891 and 1931. The result drawn from this comparison broadly corresponds with the theory of de-urbanization in India. The data collected by Tod for the towns of Mewar exclusively for two years, i.e. 1818 and 1822, just to show the increase in the urban population, particularly after the British treaty with the Sisodia state, require further investigation. But one thing is certain that the period of four years is too short to judge the British impact on Mewar.

NOTES

1. James Tod, *Annals and Antiquities of Rajashtan*, vols. I, II and III, Humphrey Milford, Oxford University Press, London, 1920. Also his *Travells in Western India,* Oriental Publishers, Delhi, 1971.
2. Ibid.
3. Ibid.
4. Ibid., vol. II, pp. 1244-5. James Tod visited Jaisalmer in 1815.
5. Ibid., p. 1245.
6. Ibid.
7. James Tod assumes the conventional figure to estimate the populations of towns. For Jaisalmer town, it was 5, while for the rest this number was 4 persons per house.
8. Tod, op. cit., vol. II, p. 1245.
9. B.L. Cole, *Census of India, 1931, Rajputana Agency, Report and Tables,* vol. XXVII, rpt., Manohar, Delhi, 1992, p. 12 (chapter of Towns Classified by Population).
10. Tod, vol. II, p. 1147.
11. Ibid., vol. II, p. 1147. [According to James Tod, total of 5,39,250 persons (urban + rural), giving an average of 25 to the square mile], which cannot think exaggerated and making the desert regions depending on Bikaner equal in the density of population, the highlands of Scotland. Of these population, full ¾ are the aboriginal Jats, the rest are their conquerors, descendants of Bika, including the Saraswat Brahmins, Charans, Bards and a few of the best classes, whose numbers conjointly are not one tenth (1/10) of the Rajput).
12. Tod., vol. II, p. 1147.
13. *Census of India,* 1931, op. cit., pp. 10-14.
14. Tod., vol. II, p. 1147.
15. *Census of India,* 1931, op. cit.
16. Tod., vol. II, p. 1147.
17. Ibid.
18. Ibid.
19. Ibid.

20. Ibid.
21. Ibid.
22. Ibid., vol. I, p. 585.
23. Ibid.
24. Ibid.
25. Ibid.
26. Ibid., vol. I, p. 585. [According to James Tod, Udaipur, which formerly reckoned 50,000 houses within the walls had now about 3,000 occupied, the rest were in ruins, the rafters being taken for firewood.]
27. Tod, vol. I, p. 562. [Bhilwara was the commercial hub of Rajputana which ten years before (prior 1822 when Tod reached the place) contained 6,473 families should not a vestige of existence. Bhilwara rapidly rose from its ruins, and in a few months contained 1,200 houses, half of which were occupied by foreign merchants. In 1822, Bhilwara contained nearly 3,000 dwellings which were chiefly inhabited by merchants, bankers, and artisans.]
28. Tod, vol. I, p. 585. (No. of houses of 1,822 multiplied by assumed conventional figure 5.)
29. *Census of India*, 1931, op. cit., pp. 10-14.
30. Tod., op. cit., vol. III, p. 1428.
31. Ibid., pp. 1726-7.
32. Ibid., pp. 1771-2.
33. Ibid., pp. 1782-3.
34. Ibid., vol. I, p. 585.

CHAPTER 11

Conclusion

In our study of the *Economy and Demographic Profile of Urban Rajasthan* during eighteenth-nineteenth centuries we have used a number of archival sources such as *arhsattas, yaddastis, chittis, dastur-ul-amals, amal-dasturs, arzdashts, nirkh-bazars, takhminas, khasras, toji-do-varkhi-baje-talke, taqsims, sava bahis, zakat/jagat bahis, kagad bahis, rukka parwana bahis,* etc.[1]

The study of the size and composition of population in the pre-census period is an interesting but challenging exercise, which is attracting the attention of urban historians and economists alike. Direct data on population count before 1881 are elusive. Therefore, scholars have adopted different methods to estimate the population of that period. Pioneer among them is Moreland.[2] His methods were refined by Irfan Habib[3] and later on Shireen Moosvi.[4] S.P. Gupta[5] and B.L. Bhadani[6] worked out the urban population of Marwar on the basis of house count. Besides urban population, Bhadani has worked out the rural population on the basis of plough count and thus come out with the total population of Marwar in the second half of the seventeenth-century Marwar. The researches by the above scholars prove that the different kinds of data on taxes, military strength, house-plough count and agricultural productivity can be used to arrive at population estimates.

To estimate the population of different urban centres of Rajasthan during eighteenth-nineteenth centuries we have used house-count as well as two different kinds of taxes, *kholari* and *dhuan.*[7] *Kholari* is a house tax on professional groups who were engaged in production in village or town, while *dhuan* tax was collected from each house inhabited by members of various castes or groups in rural as well as urban areas. Both these taxes imply the counting of houses of a locality which can be used to estimate the population of different urban centres. By multiplying the number of houses by 5 (the conventional figure for each household)[8] we can obtain a figure for practically the entire population of the town.

As has been mentioned earlier in this study, there were a large number of towns and cities in different Rajput principalities of Rajasthan during eighteenth-nineteenth centuries. We get information about more than 290 towns scattered all over Rajasthan.[9]

After studying the archival and other private documents we can make a number of inferences about the urban centres of Rajasthan and their populations during eighteenth-nineteenth centuries. Some of these are as follows:

The higher receipts from *sair-jihat* (non-agrarian taxes) from many areas of Rajasthan, such as Shekhawati region and Sanganer town, show that these areas were developing as the agrarian marts earned the status of the *qasba*. Besides, the enormous availability of *mal-o-jihat* (agricultural tax) from the same areas shows that most of these *qasbas* may be designated as semi-urban centres. The preference of peasants for cash crops in these areas also indicates their emergence as open commercial marts and acquiring the status of *qasbas*. The *pargana* headquarters were primarily emerging as agrarian open markets. Subsequently these were acquiring the status of *qasbas*.[10]

Many of these developing towns and cities were simultaneously getting industrialized. Enormous availability of cotton and revenue income from indigo in Sanganer, and the cultivation of commercial crops related to textile in Sangod and Mangrol shows potentialities of the development of textile industry in these areas. The large number of *chhinpas* living in Sanganer and the revenue collected from *chhapa* also shows that the dyeing and textile industries were in a flourishing condition in Rajasthan in eighteenth-nineteenth centuries.[11]

However, things started changing in the last quarter of the nineteenth century. Approximately six textile groups and other professional classes disappeared from *qasba* Sangod and Mangrol in the census of 1931.[12] Same was the case in *qasba* Churu located in the middle of the desert. Here, also we have the names of at least six textile castes which completely disappeared in the same period.[13] The same trend is visible in *qasba* Jalor.[14] So this phenomenon could be seen in every corner of Rajasthan. The prices of British yarn and cloths either reduced or declined many folds. In the meantime the increases demand for British goods in India had at adverse impact on the indigenous products. Besides, British cloths gradually generated larger demand and this affected the demand for locally produced cloths.[15] There is interesting information on trade and commerce in Rajasthan for which we have at least two commercial centres of Marwar for a sample study.[16] One was Pali, a commercial mart and exchange centre during eighteenth and early nineteenth centuries but in the second half of the nineteenth century the prosperity of Pali gradually started to decline due to several causes. Prominent among them were the imperial interest and the economic policy adopted by the British in this part of the century. Besides this, insecurity of land routes, excessive and oppressive duties imposed on merchandise by the state of Marwar, passing of rail routes through Marwar Junction by passing Pali on one side and the salt agreements between the British government and the State of Marwar reduced the commercial prominence of Pali. The development of Ajmer as a trading centre also minimized the importance of Pali as a commercial mart. Besides these, it is also pointed out as another reason for the decline of Pali, was the conti-nuous financial deterioration of the state and the coercive methods of extracting money from the *mahajans,* which forced many of them to migrate to different commercial markets especially during the British regions.[17] The lucrative benefit of British India attracted traders from the princely states and resultantly decline in population in these areas. Pali gradually lost its former grandeur as a centre of trade and commerce in late nineteenth century, which found reflection in de-urbanization.[18] Another town, Nagaur was a nodal cenre for trade and was connected to many trading centres of Rajasthan, India and abroad.[19] This *qasba* was not only known for its commercial importance but also for its two shrines, i.e. shrine of Shaikh Hamiduddin Nagauri and Bare Peer Ki Dargah.[20]

There was also a clearly perceptible decline in the population of many towns of Rajasthan in the last quarter of the nineteenth century, which points to the process of de-industrialization and de-urbanization. For example, the population of Marwar region declined from 2,81,210 to 1,27,322 between 1820s and 1891.[21] All the *qasbas* of Jaisalmer lost their status and the population of Jaisalmer itself got reduced to a third (from 35,000 to 10,509) during the same period.[22] Out of the twelve towns of Bikaner in 1820s, five had either disappeared or lost the designation of a 'town' in 1891.[23]

Overall, the result drawn from the comparison of population as calculated by us for the years 1731, 1741, 1751, 1786, 1815, 1820s, 1842, and 1850 with that of census 1891 and 1931, broadly corresponds with the theory of de-urbanization and de-industrialization in India. Thus, Rajasthan could not be counted as an exception.

NOTES

1. See Chapter 1.
2. The pioneer attempt was made many decades ago by W.H. Moreland, *India at the Death of Akbar*, Low Price Publications, Delhi, 1962 (rpt. 1990).
3. *The Cambridge Economic History of India*, vol. I: *c. 1200-c. 1750*, ed. Tapan Raychaudhuri and Irfan Habib, Cambridge University Press, Cambridge, 1982 (rpt. 2004).
4. Shireen Moosvi, 'Production Consumption and Population in Akbar's Time', *IESHR*, vol. X, no. 2, 1973, pp. 181-95.
5. S.P. Gupta, 'Evidence for Urban Population and its Composition from the 17th-18th Century Rajasthan', *Proceedings of Indian History Congress* (hereafter *PIHC*), Calicut, 1976, pp. 179-80.
6. B.L. Bhadani, *Peasants, Artisans and Entrepreneurs: Economy of Marwar in the 17th Century*, Rawat Publication, Jaipur, 1999, pp. 20-33. Also his article 'Population of Marwar in the Second Half of the 17th Century', *IESHR*, vol. XIV, no. 4, pp. 415-27.
7. See Chapters 6 and 7.
8. This method for estimation of population was adopted by James Tod, S.P. Gupta, B.L. Bhadani and M.S. Ranawat.
9. See Chapter 3.

10. See Chapters 4 and 5.
11. See Chapters 5 and 6.
12. See Chapter 6.
13. See Chapter 7.
14. See Chapter 8.
15. See Chapters 6 and 7.
16. See Chapter 8
17. Ibid. Cf. Sunita Zaidi, 'State and Cities in Rajasthan: Pali between the 17th and 19th Centuries', in *IASSI: Contributions to Indian Social Sciences*, April-June 2010, p. 70. Cf. G.N. Sharma, *Social Life in Medieval Rajasthan*, p. 341. [The diminishing financial condition of the state forced it to demand a huge some arbitrarily from the *mahajans* and *seths*. A report by Trevelyan to Colebrook mentioned a case of 9 August 1828 in which the *kotwal* of Jodhpur demanded Rs. 20,000 from the *mahajans* who in protest closed their shops.]
18. Ibid.
19. Ibid.
20. Ibid. Cf. Jibraeil, 'Contribution of Sufis in the Growth of Urban Centres in Rajasthan During the Eighteenth Century', in a seminar proceeding entitled *Sufi Movement in Rajasthan*, ed. S.M. Azizuddin Husain, Idarah-i-Adabiyat-i-Dilli, Delhi, 2007, pp. 62-75. Another article of Jibraeil, '*Qasba* Nagaur: A Centre of Cultural Heritage of Medieval Rajasthan', in *Essays in Indian History and Culture*, ed. Ishrat Hussain Ansari, Idarah-i Adabiyat-i-Dilli, Delhi, 2013, pp. 92-122.
21. See Chapter 9.
22. See Chapter 10.
23. Ibid.

Bibliography

ARCHIVAL SOURCES

Rajasthani

JAIPUR (AMBER)

(A) *Arhsattas* (Jaipur)

1. *Arhsatta Pargana*, Ajabgarh, vs 1783, 1787, 1788.
2. *Arhsatta Pargana*, Amarsar, vs 1768, 1781, 1830.
3. *Arhsatta Pargana*, Alwar, vs 1810 and 1818.
4. *Arhsatta Pargana*, Antela, vs 1790.
5. *Arhsatta Pargana*, Amber, vs 1853, 1862, 1883.
6. *Arhsatta Pargana*, Ujeerpur, vs 1807, 1808.
7. *Arhsatta Pargana*, Udaipur/Udai, vs 1766.
8. *Arhsatta Pargana*, Kathumbar, vs 1773 and 1774.
9. *Arhsatta Pargana*, Kama, vs 1825 and 1830.
10. *Arhsatta Pargana*, Kalakh, vs 1801.
11. *Arhsatta Pargana*, Kuwavo, vs 1768 and 1769.
12. *Arhsatta Pargana*, Kotla, vs 1770.
13. *Arhsatta Pargana*, Khandela, vs 1862.
14. *Arhsatta Pargana*, Kotputli, vs 1826, 1827.
15. *Arhsatta Pargana*, Khandari, vs 1808, 1820, 1823.
16. *Arhsatta Pargana*, Khoh, vs 1773.
17. *Arhsatta Pargana*, Khohari, vs 1808, 1809, 1810.
18. *Arhsatta Pargana*, Udaigeer, vs 1775 and 1821.
19. *Arhsatta Pargana*, Gajee ka Thana, vs 1808, 1816, 1821.
20. *Arhsatta Pargana*, Gaori, vs 1816, 1818, 1821.
21. *Arhsatta Pargana*, Geejgarh, vs 1800, 1801, 1827.
22. *Arhsatta Pargana*, Chandvaji, vs 1780 and 1840.
23. *Arhsatta Pargana*, Chaksu, vs 1771 and 1831.
24. *Arhsatta Pargana*, Chal Kalyan, vs 1795 and 1827.
25. *Arhsatta Pargana*, Chhani/Chari, vs 1791 and 1815.
26. *Arhsatta Pargana*, Jalalpur, vs 1791 and 1897.
27. *Arhsatta Pargana*, Jobner, vs 1800 and 1807.
28. *Arhsatta Pargana*, Jaitpur, vs 1798 and 1799.

29. *Arhsatta Pargana*, Tonk, vs 1807, 1809, 1820.
30. *Arhsatta Pargana*, Toda Bheem, vs 1807 and 1845.
31. *Arhsatta Pargana*, Toda Raisinghpura, vs 1815 and 1857.
32. *Arhsatta Pargana*, Didwana, vs 1765 and 1777.
33. *Arhsatta Pargana*, Torawati, vs 1864 and 1875.
34. *Arhsatta Pargana*, Thana va Boli, vs 1783 and 1785.
35. *Arhsatta Pargana*, Dausa, vs 1808, 1812, 1842.
36. *Arhsatta Pargana*, Naraina, vs 1768 and 1819.
37. *Arhsatta Pargana*, Narayanpur, vs 1827.
38. *Arhsatta Pargana*, Narnol, vs 1811 and 1837.
39. *Arhsatta Pargana*, Niwai, vs 1821 and 1827.
40. *Arhsatta Pargana*, Nehar, vs 1722.
41. *Arhsatta Pargana*, Nainwa, vs 1818.
42. *Arhsatta Pargana*, Nohari, vs 1721.
43. *Arhsatta Pargana*, Pahari, vs 1773 and 1884.
44. *Arhsatta Pargana*, Prayagpura, vs 1784 and 1841.
45. *Arhsatta Pargana*, Patari, vs 1791 and 1818.
46. *Arhsatta Pargana*, Pawata, vs 1793 and 1824.
47. *Arhsatta Pargana*, Pindayan, vs 1722 and 1830.
48. *Arhsatta Pargana*, Punkhar, vs 1797 and 1810.
49. *Arhsatta Pargana*, Phagi, vs 1794 an 1854.
50. *Arhsatta Pargana*, Banawar, vs 1748 and 1770.
51. *Arhsatta Pargana*, Bahatri/Baswa, vs 1721 and 1829.
52. *Arhsatta Pargana*, Baspur, vs 1828 and 1836.
53. *Arhsatta Pargana*, Bairat, vs 1781, 1808, 1813.
54. *Arhsatta Pargana*, Bhagotgarh, vs 1819 and 1835.
55. *Arhsatta Pargana*, Bhadlav, vs 1784 and 1809.
56. *Arhsatta Pargana*, Bhangarh, vs 1769.
57. *Arhsatta Pargana*, Bhinai, vs 1769 and 1793.
58. *Arhsatta Pargana*, Bhusavar, vs 1751 and 1759.
59. *Arhsatta Pargana*, Manoharpur, vs 1765 and 1840.
60. *Arhsatta Pargana*, Malarna, vs 1721, 1824, 1845.
61. *Arhsatta Pargana*, Malpura, vs 1770 and 1841.
62. *Arhsatta Pargana*, Mojabad, vs 1721 and 1845.
63. *Arhsatta Pargana*, Mojpur, vs 1747 and 1774.
64. *Arhsatta Pargana*, Mahwa, vs 1844 and 1862.
65. *Arhsatta Pargana*, Mundawar, vs 1721 and 1770.
66. *Arhsatta Pargana*, Ramgarh, vs 1804, 1815, 1828.
67. *Arhsatta Pargana*, Rampura, vs 1772 and 1820.
68. *Arhsatta Pargana*, Rewari, vs 1722.

69. *Arhsatta Pargana*, Lawari, VS 1790.
70. *Arhsatta Pargana*, Lalgarh, VS 1767 and 1841.
71. *Arhsatta Pargana*, Lalsot, VS 1743 and 1841.
72. *Arhsatta Pargana*, Liwali, VS 1846.
73. *Arhsatta Pargana*, Baval, VS 1721.
74. *Arhsatta Pargana*, Sawai Jaipur, VS 1790, 1828, 1830.
75. *Arhsatta Pargana*, Sawai Madhopur, VS 1826 and 1861.
76. *Arhsatta Pargana*, Sahar, VS 1746 and 1770.
77. *Arhsatta Pargana*, Salavad, VS 1768 and 1841.
78. *Arhsatta Qasba*, Sanganer, vs 1765, 1767, 1768, 1769, 1772, 1773, 1775, 1780, 1781, 1785, 1786, 1787, 1788, 1789, 1790, 1792, 1793, 1804, 1805, 1808, 1812, 1813, 1816, 1817, 1818, 1820, 1821, 1823, 1824, 1825, 1827, 1828, 1829, 1830, 1843.
79. *Arhsatta Pargana*, Sambhar, VS 1768,1834, 1852.
80. *Arhsatta Pargana*, Shahipur, VS 1763 and 1838.
81. *Arhsatta Pargana*, Sikrai, VS 1810 and 1835.
81. *Arhsatta Pargana*, Siroj Bhaisala, VS 1788.
82. *Arhsatta Pargana*, Serpur, VS 1790 and 1820.
83. *Arhsatta Pargana*, Shri Madhopur, VS 1824, 1833, 1837.
84. *Arhsatta Pargana*, Bayana, VS 1790.
85. *Arhsatta Pargana*, Jhak, VS 1777.
86. *Arhsatta Pargana*, Hastera, VS 1769 and 1779.
87. *Arhsatta Pargana*, Hasanpur, VS 1770.
88. *Arhsatta Pargana*, Hindon, VS 1769, 1819, 1832, 1852

(B) *Yaddasht* or *Yadidashti* (Jaipur)
1. *Yadidashti Haqiqat Hal, Pargana* Chal Kalyan, VS 1722.
2. *Yadidashti Hal, Pargana*, Bawal, VS 1723.
3. *Yadidashti Pattadar* Mina, VS 1721.
4. *Yadidashti Haqiqat, Dehai, Pargana*, Pahari, VS 1746.
5. *Yadidashti Hal, Bail Pargana* Niwai, VS 1766.
6. *Yadidashti Haqiqat Hal, Bail Pargana, Zubani, Patel, Patwari*, Bayana, Chatsu Babat, VS 1723.
7. *Yadidashti Nazar Bhent, Tika, Sriji, Pargana* Toda Bhim, VS 1802.

(C) *Jamaandis* (Jaipur)
1. *Pargana* Kotla, VS 1720.
2. *Pargana* Mathuraji, VS 1780.
3. *Pargana* Malarna, VS 1720
4. *Pargana* Phagi, VS 1755.

5. *Pargana* Chal Kalyan, vs 1722.
6. *Pargana* Udai, vs 1722.
7. *Pargana* Kotputli, vs 1722.
8. *Pargana* Nainwah, vs 1720.
9. *Pargana* Dausa, vs 1720.
10. *Pargana* Mundawar, vs 1746.
11. *Qasba* Nainwah, vs 1717.
12. *Qasba* Mauzabad, vs 1722.
13. *Qasba* Liwali, vs 1721.
14. Village Akora (Kotla), vs 1720.

(D) *Dastur-ul-Amal* and *Amal Dastur* (Jaipur)

1. *Dastur-ul-Amal Pargana*, Amrsar, vs 1783.
2. *Dastur-ul-Amal Pargana*, Udai, vs 1722.
3. *Dastur-ul-Amal Pargana*, Khohri, vs 1760.
4. *Dastur-ul-Amal Pargana*, Bhairano, vs 1780.
5. *Dastur-ul-Amal Pargana*, Jhak, vs 1798.
6. *Dastur-ul-Amal Pargana*, Toda Thek, vs 1798.
7. *Dastur-ul-Amal Pargana*, Antela Bhabro, vs 1798.
8. *Dastur-ul-Amal Pargana*, Malpura, vs 1798.
9. *Dastur-ul-Amal Pargana*, Harsana, vs 1798.
10. *Dastur-ul-Amal Mal-o-Jihat, Wa Sair-Jihat Pargana*, Diwana, vs 1798.
11. *Dastur-Rahdari Pargana*, Malpura, vs 1798.
12. *Amal Dastur Pargana*, Baroda, vs 1798.

(E) *Nirkh Bazar* (Jaipur)

1. Niwai, vs 1800 and 1807.
2. Udai, vs 1799 and 1805.
3. *Qasba* Chatsu, vs 1788 and 1807.
4. Bahatri, vs 1799.
5. Toda Bhim, vs 1795 and 1797.
6. Tonk, vs 1797.
7. *Qasba* Dausa, vs 1796.
8. Geejgarh, vs 1798.
9. Hindaun, vs 1800-1807.
10. *Qasba* Lalsot, vs 1801 and 1804.
11. Phagi, vs 1805, 1807.
12. Rini, vs 1799.
13. Naraina, vs 1804 and 1807.
14. *Qasba* Malarna, vs 1806 and 1808.

15. *Qasba* Amber, vs 1797.
16. *Qasba* Sanganer, vs 1787-1843.
17. Rampura, vs 1805.
18. Bairat, vs 1781.
19. *Qasba* Manoharpur, vs 1798.
20. *Qasba* Khatu, vs 1793.
21. Gazi Ka Thana, vs 1793.
22. Mauzabad, vs 1793.
23. Khohri, vs 1793.
24. Punkhar, vs 1793.
25. Amarsar, vs 1793.
26. Lalgarh, vs 1793.
27. Ajabgarh, vs 1793.
28. Pragpur, vs 1793.
29. Wazipur, vs 1793.
30. Chandawaji

(F) *Khasra* Documents (Jaipur)

1. *Khasra Qasba*, Amber, vs 1736.
2. *Khasra Mauza*, Aniyala, *Pargana* Malarna, vs 1767.
3. *Khasra Balai*, Maunza Meragher *Pargana* Tonk, vs 1713.
4. *Khasra Mauza Hirapuro*, Sakh Unhalu, Tappa Khoh, Sawai Jaipur.
5. *Khasra Jamabandi*, Fasal Kharif *Pargana* Chatsu.

(G) *Taqsim* (Jaipur)

1. *Taqsim Dahsala Pargana,* Dausa, vs 1787 and 1798.
2. *Taqsim Dahsala Pargana*, Punkhar, vs 1789 and 1798.
3. *Taqsim Dahsala Pargana*, Geejgarh, vs 1787 and 1798.
4. *Taqsim Dahsala Pargana*, Udai, vs 1791 and 1800.
5. *Taqsim Dahsala Pargana,* Amarsar, vs 1758 and 1767.
6. *Taqsim Pargana,* Didwana.
7. *Taqsim Dahsala Tappa Jhak Pargana*, Phagi, vs 1773 and 1782.

KOTA (HADAUTI)

(A) *Toji-do-Varkhi Parchajat Baje-Talke* (Kota)

1. *Toji-do-Varkhi-Parchajat-Baje-Talke, Qasba,* Sangod, vs 1798 and 1808.
2. *Toji-do-Varkhi-Parchajat-Baje-Talke, Qasba,* Mangrol, vs 1788 and 1843.
3. *Toji-do-Varkhi-Parchajat-Baje-Talke, Qasba,* Kaithun, vs 1807.
4. *Toji-do-Varkhi-Parchajat-Baje-Talke, Qasba,* Barod, vs 1821.

5. *Toji-do-Varkhi-Parchajat-Baje-Talke, Qasba,* Baran, vs 1792.
6. *Toji-do-Varkhi-Parchajat-Baje-Talke, Qasba,* Nandgaoun, vs 1776.
7. *Toji-do-Varkhi-Parchajat-Baje-Talke,* vs 1861.
8. *Toji-do-Varkhi-Parchajat-Baje-Talke,* vs 1853.
9. *Toji-do-Varkhi-Parchajat-Baje-Talke,* vs 1867.
10. *Toji-do-Varkhi-Parchajat-Baje-Talke,* vs 1867.

(B) *Jamabandis* (Kota)

1. *Pargana* Nandgaon, B. No. 37/2, vs 1779.
2. *Mauza Udhanu,* B. No. 47, vs 1790.
3. *Pargana* Bersana, B. No. 51/1, vs 1798.
4. *Jamabandi,* Kota, B. No. 51, vs 1849.
5. *Jamabandi,* Kota, B. No. 66, vs 1852.
6. *Jamabandi,* Kota, B. No. 61, vs 1853.
7. *Jamabandi,* Kota, B. No. 63, vs 1854.
8. *Katata Mall Hasil,* B. No. 68, vs 1856.
9. *Katata Maal Hasil,* B. No. 69, vs 1856.

(C) *Talik Bahis* (Kota)

1. *Pargana* of Raipur, Patan, Urmal and Gagraon, Basta No. 3, Bh. No. 3, vs 1853.
2. *Pargana* Manohar Thana and Tappa Nandgaon, Basta No. 3/1, Bh. No. 3 vs 1861.
3. *Pargana* Barod etc., Basta No. 3/2, Bh. No. 3, vs 1861.
4. *Khata Talik,* Basta No. 17, Bh. No. 3, vs 1864.
5. *Jagir Jatiwar,* Muqata, Basta No. 25, Bh. No. 5, vs 1860-1900.
6. *Talik Parganawar,* Basta No. 21, Bh. No. 5, vs 1858.

(D) *Taqsim* (Kota)

1. *Taqsim Parganawar,* Basta No. 2, Bh. No. 6, vs 1784 and 1799.
2. *Taqsim Parganawar* , Basta No. 4, Bh. No. 6, vs 1825 and 1831.
3. *Taqsim Parganawar,* Basta No. 7, Bh. No. 6, vs 1834 and 1835.
4. *Taqsim Parganawar,* Basta No. 3/4, Bh. No. 6 (Sangod, Mangrol, Barod, Nandgaon, Basthunivs 1800 and 1824.
5. *Taqsim Pargana,* Basta No. 3/3, Bh. No. 6, Kujod, Mangrol, vs 1803 and 1823.
6. *Taqsim Parganawar,* Basta No. 6, Bh. No. 6, vs 1833.
7. *Taqsim Pargana,* Basta No. 7/1, Bh. No. 6, *Madhkargarh,* Golna, Basthuni, Barod, vs 1834.
8. *Taqsim,* Basta No. 8/1, Bh. No. 6, *Parganawar,* Sangod, vs 1836.

9. *Taqsim*, Basta No. 22/2, Bh. No. 6, *Parganawar*, Chipa Barod, vs 1859-1861.
10. *Taqsim Parganawar* (approximately all the *Qasbas* of Kota).

BIKANER

(A) *Sava Bahi* (Bikaner)
1. *Sava Bahi,* Rini, vs 1815, 1825, 1835, 1845, 1855.
2. *Sava Bahi,* Rajgarh, vs 1831, 1841, 1851, 1861, 1871.
3. *Sava Bahi*, Nohar, vs 1871, 1881.
4. *Sava Bahi*, Bhadra, vs 1876, 1885, 1904.
5. *Sava Bahi*, Tibi, vs 1921, 1918, 1914.
6. *Sava Bahi*, Hanumangarh, vs 1908, 1916, 1931.
7. *Sava Bahi*, Suratgarh, vs 1921, 1931, 1941.
8. *Sava Bahi*, Anoopgarh, vs 1912, 1921, 1931.
9. *Sava Bahi*, Chhapar, vs 1921, 1931, 1941.
10. *Sava Bahi*, Sardarshar, vs 1921, 1931, 1941.
11. *Sava Bahi*, Ratangarh, vs 1911, 1921, 1931.
12. *Sava Bahi*, Ratan Nagar, vs 1921, 1931, 941.
13. *Sava Bahi*, Rajaldesar, vs 1929, 1933, 1947.
14. *Sava Bahi*, Surpura, vs 1951 and 1955.
15. *Sava Bahi*, Bhinasar, vs 1931 and 1945.
16. *Sava Bahi*, Sardargarh, vs 1921, 1931, 1941.
17. *Sava Bahi*, Sujangarh, vs 1931, 1941, 1951.
18. *Sava Bahi*, Shri Dungargarh, vs 1939 and 1941.
19. *Sava Bahi*, Churu, vs 1879, 1880, 1899, 1907, 1911, 1918, 1928, 1929

(B) *Hasil Bahi* (Bikaner)
1. *Dhawa ri Chire ri Bahi*, vs 1989.
2. *Bahi Dhuwa ri Ginati ri Jama Bahi*, vs 1948.
3. *Khalsa ri Gawa ri Bahi*, vs 1768.
4. *Khalsa ra Gawa Vigat*, vs 1755.
5. *Bahi Reni ri Gawan ri Dhuwe ri*, vs 1952.
6. *Puniye ri Pargana ri*, vs 1884.
7. *Hasal ri Bahi*, vs 1822.
8. *Korna, Dhuraj, Jakheero Charasehat ri Bahi*, vs 1823.
9. *Puniya ri Pargama ro Khato*, vs 1824.
10. *Khalsa Gawan ri Hasal Bhanch, Bhog, Kunte ri Bahi*, vs 1825.
11. *Khalsa ri Goon ri Hasal ri Bahi*, vs 1838.

12. *Khalsa Gawa ri Hasil Banch ri Bahi*, VS 1895.
13. *Khalsa Gawa ri Hasil Banch ri Bahi*, VS 1896.
14. *Khalsa Gawa ri Bahi*, VS 1897.

(C) *Lekha va Jama Kharach Bahi* (Bikaner)

1. *Bhog Tatha Kothari ri Dhan ri Lekha ri Bahi*, VS 1941.
2. *Rokar Nara ri Bahi*, VS 1941.
3. *Pargana ri Jama Kharch ri Bahi*, VS 1750.
4. *Phalodi Pargana ri Jama Kharch ri Bahi*, VS 1751.
5. *Qasba Reni ri Jama Kharch ri Bahi*, VS 1753.
6. *Rokar Bahi Jama Kharch*, VS 1796.
7. *Puniya ri Sivaran Pargana ri Lekha Bahi*, VS 1809.
8. *Sujangarh ri Fauj ri Jama Kharch*, VS 1886.

(D) *Kagad Bahis* (Bikaner)

1. *Kagad ri Bahi*, VS 1811 and 1831.
2. *Kagad ri Bahi*, VS 1838 and 1840.
3. *Kagad ri Bahi*, VS 1839 and 1861.
4. *Kagad ri Bahi*, VS 1863 and 1898.
5. *Kagad ri Bahi, Bikaner*, VS 1899 and 1900.

(E) *Jagaat Bahis* (Bikaner)

1. *Jagaat Bahi, Bikaner*, VS 1800 and 1805.
2. *Nohar ri Thane ri Jama Kharch ri Bahi*, VS 1814.
3. *Rajgarh ri Jagaat Bahi*, VS 1831.
4. *Suratgarh Tehsil ri Jagaat Bahi*, VS 1831.
5. *Churu ri Jagaat ri Bahi*, VS 1832.
6. *Nohar ri Vano ri Jagaat Bahi*, VS 1832.
7. *Shri Loonkaransar ri Jagaat Bahi*, VS 1844.
8. *Magra ri Kheri Pati ri Jagaat Bahi*, VS 1858.
9. *Shri Ratangarh ri Dukano va Guwaro ri*, VS 1860.
10. *Rini ri Mandi ro Savo*, VS 1872.
11. *Bahi Sujangarh ri Mandi ri Jaggat ri*, VS 1890.

(F) *Kamthana Bahis* (Bikaner)

1. *Kamthana ri Bahi*, VS 1727.
2. *Kamthana ri Bahi*, VS 1808 and 1814.
3. *Shri Ratangarh ri Kot navo Karayo tero khato*, VS 1877.
4. *Pokher ri Chithi ri Nakal Bahi*, VS 1899

JODHPUR (MARWAR)

(A) *Jodhpur Bahiyat* (Jodhpur)
1. *Khazana Ki Jama Kharch Ki Bahi*, Basta No. 1, vs 1910.
2. *Phalodi Ke Aagar va Nava Ke Sambandh Ki Bahi*, Basta No. 4, vs 1821.
3. *Takhtgarh Va Jodhpurgarh Ke Sambandh I Bahi*, Basta No. 11, vs 1826.
4. *Bahi Mal Parwana, Kacheri, Chotara Taksal, Muljamaan Aadi ke Sambendh Ki Bahi*, Basta No. 14, vs 1830 and 1840.
5. *Parbatsar Ke Sair Tatha Jamabandhi Ki Bahi*, Basta No. 23.
6. *Jodhpur Ke Kacheri Tatha Jama Kharch Ka Maaswara*, Basta No. 25, vs 1834.
7. *Pargana Pachpadara Ke Kacheri Ke Jama Kharch Ka Maaswara*, Basta No. 26, vs 1834.
8. *Pargana Merta Ke Kacheri Ke Mahinadaro Ki*, Basta No. 31, vs 1835.
9. *Bahi Parwana Jalor Ke Sambandh Ke va Daroga Daftar ke Baare Me.*

(B) *Khazana Bahis* (Jodhpur)
1. *Khanaza Bahi*, Basta No. 1, vs 1940 and 1951.
2. *Khanaza Bahi*, Basta No. 2, vs 1952 and 1954.
3. *Khanaza Bahi*, vs 1955 and 1957.

(C) *Patta Bahis* (Jodhpur)
1. *Patta Bahi*, Basta No. 1, vs 1764 and 1770.
2. *Patta Bahi*, Basta No. 2, vs 1774 and 1791.
3. *Patta Bahi*, Basta No. 3, vs 1822 and 1840.
4. *Patta Bahi*, Basta No. 5, vs 1841 and 1847
5. *Patta Bahi*, Basta No. 6, vs 1848 and 1850.

(D) *Haqiqat Khata Bahis* (Jodhpur)
1. *Khapwar Khata Bahi*, Basta No. 16, vs 1930 and 1935
2. *Khapwar Khata Bahi*, Basta No. 18, vs 1953 and 1967

(E) *Sanad Parwana Bahis* (Jodhpur)
1. *Sanad Parwana Bahi*, Basta No. 1, vs 1821.
2. *Sanad Parwana Bahi*, Basta No. 14, vs 1831.
3. *Sanad Parwana Bahi*, Basta No. 30, vs 1841.
4. *Sanad Parwana Bahi*, Basta No. 46, vs 1851.
5. *Sanad Parwana Bahi*, Basta No. 58, vs 1861.
6. *Sanad Parwana Bahi*, Basta No. 66, vs 1871.
7. *Sanad Parwana Bahi*, Basta No. 76, vs 1881

8. *Sanad Parwana Bahi*, Basta No. 89, VS 1891
9. *Sanad Parwana Bahi*, Basta No. 134, VS 1901.
10. *Sanad Parwana Bahi*, Basta No. 122, VS 1911.

PERSIAN SOURCES

1. Abul Fazl, *Ain-i-Akbari*, 2 vols., ed. Blochmann, Bib. Ind., Calcutta, 1867.
2. Abul Fazl, *Akbarnama*, 3 vols., Asiatic Society, Calcutta, 1873-87, 1897-1921.
3. *Hardayal Singh Mathur Collection* (Photocopy of Persian Documents) Department of History, AMU, Aligarh. (Original in RSA, Bikaner.)
4. *Jama Dami* table of *suba* Ajmer, M.S. Royal Asiatic Society, London, Pers. 173 (rotograph in the Department of History, AMU, Aligarh).
5. *Waqai-i-Sarkar Ranthambhor wa Ajmer*, AD 1678-80, Asafiya Library, Hyderabad, transcript in the Department of History, AMU, Aligarh (2 vols).

PUBLISHED SOURCES

(a) *Rajasthani*

1. *Bankidas-ri-Khyat*, ed. Narottam Das Swami, Rajasthan Oriental Research Institute, Jaipur, 1956.
2. S. Dayal Das, *Dayaldas-r-Khyat*, part II, ed. Dashrath Sharma, Dina Nath Khatri and Jaswant Singh, Anoop Sanskrit Library, Bikaner, 1948.
3. Shyamal Das, *Vir Vinod*, 2nd rpt., Motilal Banarsidass, Delhi, 1986.

(b) *Private Collections*

1. *Poddar Collection*, Granth No. 928, Nagar Shree Churu.
2. *Kaviraj Collection*, Natnagar Shodh Sansthan, Sitamau.
3. *Khajanchi Collection*, Rajasthan Oriental Collection, Bikaner.
4. *Pareek Collection*, Bharatiya Vidya Mandir, Shodh Pratishthan, Bikaner.
5. *Phutkar Khyat*, Granth No. 79, MS Kaviraj Collection, NSS, Sitamau.
6. *Poddar Collection*, Nagar Shree Churu.
7. *Qanungo Bahi*, Jalor.
8. Preserved at *Rajasthan Shodh Sansthan*, Chaupasani, Jodhpur.

(c) *Administrative Reports and Lists*

1. Descriptive List of *Arzdasht*, Rajasthan State Archives (RSA), Bikaner.
2. Descriptive List of the *Farman and Nishan*, RSA, Bikaner.
3. Descriptive List of *Vakils Report*, 2 vols., RSA, Bikaner, 1967.

4. Hardayal Singh, *Report Majmui Halat-wa-Intizam, Marwar*, Jodhpur, 1885.
5. Administrative Reports 1889-90, Jodhpur.
6. Jodhpur Administrative Report, 1883-4, Jodhpur.
7. Report on Administration of the Marwar State, 1895-6, Jodhpur, 1896.
8. Report on the Administration of Jodhpur State, 1885-6, Jodhpur.
9. Settlement Report, 1923 (typescript).
10. Settlement Report: Rent-Rate Report of *Pargana* Neta, Parbatsar and Sambhar, Mehkama Khas, Government of Jodhpur, RSA, Bikaner.

(d) *Gazetteers*

1. K.D. Erskine, *Rajputana Gazetteers*. The W.R.S. Residency and Bikaner Agency, vol. III A, 1901 and III, 1908, Allahabad.
2. *Rajasthan District Gazetteers*, of different districts: Jaipur, Bikaner, Jaisalmer, Jodhpur, Kota, Churu, Udaipur, Jalor.
3. *Rajputana Gazetteers* (relevant volumes).
4. W.W. Hunter, *The Imperial Gazetteer of India* (Rajputana), Oxford, 1921.

European Travellers

1. Francois Bernier, *Travels in the Mughal Empire*, English tr., ed. A. Constable and V.A. Smith, Low Price Publication, Delhi (1st pub. 1934).
2. James Tod, *Annals and Antiquities of Rajasthan*, vols. I, II and III, Humphrey Milford, Oxford University Press, London, 1920.
3. James Tod, *Travels in Western India*, Oriental Publishers, Delhi, 1971.
4. Jean Baptists Tavernier, *Travels in India, 1640-67*, Macmillan and Co., London, 1889.
5. Mountstuart Elphinstone, *Account of the Kingdom of Caubul (Kabul)*, Richard Bentley, London, 1939.
6. Manucci, *Storio do-Mogor,* Temple Press, Culcutta, 1966, rpt.

Census/Atlas/Survey

1. *Agricultural Statistics of Marwar: World Agricultural Census, 1929-30* (typescript), Mehkamakhas, Government of Jodhpur.
2. Ashish Bose, *India's Urban Population, 1991, Census Data, State, Districts, Cities and Towns*, Wheeler Publications, New Delhi, 1st edn., 1994.
3. Ashok Mitra and Ram Prakash Sachdeva, *Population and Area of Cities, Towns and Urban Agglomeration (1872-1971)*, Allied, Bombay, 1980.

4. B.L. Cole, *Census of India 1931 (Rajputana Agency), Population Agency Reports*, Manohar, New Delhi, 1992.
5. *Census Atlas*, 1961, vol. XIV, Rajasthan, part IX A.
6. *Census Atlas: Census of India*, 1961, XIV, Rajasthan, part IX A, 1967.
7. *Census Cattle (1929-44)*, Commercial Intelligence Deptt. India, 1930 (typescript), Mehkamakhas, Government of Jodhpur, RSA, Bikaner.
8. *Census of India 1961*, vol. XIV, *Rajasthan*, part IX-A & IX-B, *Census Atlas*, Superintendent of Census Operations, Rajasthan, 1967.
9. C.A. Gait, *Census of India*, 1911, vol. I, part II, 1st edn., 1931, Calcutta, Superintendent Government of India, rpt., Manohar, Delhi, 1987.
10. *Census of India: Marwar*, 1931, Jodhpur.
11. *Census of Marwar and Mallani*, 1891, Jodhpur.
12. G.A. Grierson, *Linguistic Survey of India*, vol. IX, Low Price Publication, Delhi, 1916 (rpt. 1990).
13. Irfan Habib, *An Atlas of the Mughal Empire*, Oxford University Press, Delhi, 1982.
14. J.H. Hutton, *Census of India*, 1931, vol. I (published in three volumes), Gian Publishing House, Delhi (1st rpt. in India in 1989).
15. *National Atlas of India*, Jaipur, Plate No. 113, 1951 (Population), 1960.
16. *Report Mardum Sumari, Riyasat* Jodhpur, 1901.
17. *Report Mardumsumari Raj Marwar*, 1891, part 3 (2 vols.), part I, 1895 and part II, 1896, Jodhpur.
18. *The Geological Survey of India*, vol. XXXVIII, 1908.
19. *The Wealth of India*, Council of Scientific and Industrial Research, New Delhi, 1971.
20. *World Agricultural Census: Statistics of Marwar*, 1929-30 (typescript), RSA, Bikaner.

SECONDARY WORK

(a) *Books*

1. A.J. Qaisar and Som Prakash Verma, eds., *Art and Culture*, Abhinav Publishers, Jaipur, 1993.
2. Ashin Das Gupta, *Indian Merchant and the Decline of Surat (1700-1750)*, Manohar, Delhi, 1994.
3. B.C. Mehta, *Regional Population Growth: A Case Study of Rajasthan*, Research Book, Jaipur, 1978.
4. B.L. Bhadani, *Peasants, Artisans and Entrepreneurs: Economy of Marwar in the 17th Century*, Rawat Publication, Jaipur, 1999.

5. B.L. Gupta: *Trade and Commerce in Rajasthan during the 18th Century*, Jaipur Publishing House, Jaipur, 1987.
6. B.N. Reu, *Marwar Ka Itihas* (Hindi), part II, Jodhpur Archaeological Department, Jodhpur, 1940.
7. Bajrang Lal Lohiya, ed., *Rajasthan-ki-Jatiyan*, Calcutta, 1954.
8. C.A. Bayly, *Indian Society and Making of the British Empire*, The New Cambridge History of India, Cambridge, 1998.
9. C.A. Bayly, *Rulers, Townsmen and Bazars, North Indian Society in the Age of British Expansion 1770-1870*, Cambridge University Press, New Delhi, 1983.
10. D.B. Ksheersagar and Naval Krishna, eds., *Nagaur Ka Rajnitik Evam Sanskritik Vaibhav*, Maharaja Mansingh Pustak Prakash, Mehrangarh, Jodhpur, 1998, p. 128.
11. Dashrath Sharma, *Lecture on Rajput History*, Motilal Banarsidass, Delhi, 1970.
12. Dashrath Sharma, *Rajasthan Through the Ages*, vols. I and II, Rajasthan State Archives, Bikaner, 1966.
13. Dilbagh Singh, *State Landlords and Peasants: Rajasthan in the 18th Century*, Manohar, Delhi, 1990.
14. G.D. Sharma, *Rajput Polity*, Manohar, Delhi, 1977.
15. G.H. Ojha, *Rajputana Ka Itihas*, Vyas and Sons, Ajmer, 1936.
16. G.N. Sharma, *Rajasthan through the Ages*, vol. II (*1300-1761*), Rajasthan State Archives, Bikaner, 1990.
17. G.N. Sharma, *Social Life in Medieval Rajasthan* (*1500-1800*), L.N. Agarwal, Agra, 1968.
18. G.S.L. Devra, *Rajasthan Ki Prashashnik Vyavastha* (*1564-1818* AD), Dharati Prakashan, Bikaner, 1981.
19. Girija Shankar Sharma, *Sources on Social and Economic History of Rajasthan (17th-20th Centuries)*, Vikash Prakashan, Bikaner, 2005.
20. Govind Agrawal, *Churu Mandal ka Shodhpurna Itihas*, Lok Sanskriti Sodh Sansthan, Churu, 1974.
21. Gulab Kothari, *Colourful Textiles of Rajasthan*, Jaipur Printers, Jaipur, 1995.
22. H.K. Naqvi, *Mughal Hindustan: Cities and Industries 1556-1803*, Karachi, 1958.
23. H.K. Naqvi, *Urban Centres and Industries in Upper India (1556-1803)*, Asia Publishing House, Bombay, 1968.
24. H.K. Naqvi, *Urbanization and Urban Centres under the Great Mughals*, Indian Institute of Advanced Study, Simla, 1972.
25. Harphul Singh Arya, *Shekhawati Ke Thikano Ka Itihas Evam Yogdan*, Panchsheel Prakashan, Jaipur, 1987.

26. Hari Vallabh Maheshwari Jaisal, *Jaisalmer Rajya Ka Madhya Kalin Itihas*, Rajasthani Granthagar, Jodhpur, 1997.
27. Irfan Habib, *The Agrarian System of Mughal India*, 2nd rev. edn., Oxford University Press, Delhi, 1999.
28. Jagdish Singh Gahlot, *Marwar Raj Ka Ithihas*, 2nd edn., Hindi Sahitya Mandir, Jodhpur, 1925.
29. John Irvin and Margret Hall, *Indian Painted and Printed Fabrics,* vol. I, Calico Museum, Ahmadabad, 1971.
30. John Irvin and P.R. Schwartz, *Studies in Indo-European Textiles History*, Calico Museum of Textile, Ahmadabad, 1966.
31. K.C. Jain, *Ancient Cities and Towns of Rajasthan,* Motilal Banarsidass, Delhi, 1972.
32. Kaluram Sharma, *Unnisavi Shadi Ke Rajasthan Ka Samajik Evam Arthik Jivan*, Rajasthan Granth Akadami, Jaipur, 1974.
33. K.S. Lal, *Growth of Muslim Population in Medieval India (AD 1000-1800)*, Research Publication, Delhi, 1973.
34. K.S. Singh, *People of India, Rajasthan,* part I, vol. XXXVIII, Anthropological Survey of India, Popular Prakashan, Mumbai, 1998.
35. K.S. Singh, *People of India: India's Communities (H-M)*, National Series, vol. V, Anthropological Survey of India, Oxford University Press, Delhi, 1998.
36. K.T.S. Saravo, *Urban Centres and Urbanization as Reflected in the Pali, Vinaya and Sutta Pitaka*, Vidyanidhi, Delhi, 1990.
37. Kailashnath Vyas, *Rajasthan Ki Jatiyon Ka Samajik Evam Arthik Jeevan*, (Hindi), Jagdish Singh Gahlot Shodh Sanshthan, Jodhpur, 1995.
38. Lakshmi Subramanian, *Indigenous Capital and Imperial Expansion: Bombay, Surat and the West Coast*, Oxford University Press, New Delhi, 1996.
39. M.L. Sharma, *Kota Rajya Ka Itihas* (Hindi), vols. I, II, Rajasthani Granthagar, Jodhpur, 2008 (Sanshodhit Sanskaran, ed. Jagat Narain).
40. M.P. Singh, *Town, Market, Mint and Port in the Mughal Empire 1556-1707*, Adam Publication, Delhi, 1985.
41. M.S. Jain, *Rajasthan Through the Ages (A Comprehensive History of Rajasthan 1761-1949)*, vol. III, Rajasthan State Archives, Bikaner, 1996.
42. Madhu Tandon Sethia, *Rajput Polity Warriors, Peasants and Merchants (1700-1800)*, Rawat Publication, Jaipur, 2003.
43. Manohar Singh Ranawat, *Itihaskar Muhnot Nainsi Aur Uske Itihas Granth*, Rajasthani Granthagar, Jodhpur, 1984.
44. Masanori Sato and B.L. Bhadani, *Economy and Polity of Rajasthan: Study of Kota and Marwar (17th-19th Centuries),* Publication Scheme, Jaipur, 1997.

45. Nand Kishor Sharma, *Jaisalmer Ka Rajnaitik Itihas*, Simant Prakashan, Jaisalmer, 1993.
46. Nand Kishor Sharma, *Jaisalmer Ka Samajik Evam Sanskritik Itihas*, Simant Prakashan, Jaisalmer, 1993.
47. Nirmala M. Upadhyay, *The Administration of Jodhpur State (1800-1947 AD)*, International Publication, Jodhpur, 1973.
48. O.P. Kachhawaha, *Famines in Rajasthan*, Hindi Sahitya Mandir, Jodhpur, 1985.
49. Pandit Vishveshwarnath Reu, *Marwar Ka Itihas* (vols. I: 1938 and II: 1940), Jodhpur Archaeological Department, Jodhpur, 1938.
50. R.C. Sharma, *Settlement Geography of the Indian Desert*, Kumar Brothers, New Delhi, 1972.
51. Ramprasad Dadheech, *Maharaja Man Singh Vyaktitva Evam Krititva* (Hindi), Chaupasani, Jodhpur, 1972.
52. R.K. Saxena, *Peasant and the State*, Panchsheel Prakashan, Jaipur, 1999.
53. R.L. Singh, *India, A Regional Geography*, National Geographical Society of India, rpt., Varanasi, 1987.
54. R.N. Prasad, *Raja Man Singh of Amber*, World Publication, Calcutta, 1966, pp.106-19.
55. R.S. Mathur, *Relations of the Hadas with the Mughals*, Delhi, 1986.
56. Raghunath Singh Kali Pahari, *Shekhwati Pradesh Ka Rajnitik Itihas*, Tha. Mallusingh Smriti Granthagar, Jhunjhunu, 1998.
57. S. Nurul Hasan, *The Thoughts on Agrarian Relations in Mughal India*, Peoples Publication House, Delhi, 1973 (rpt. 1990).
58. S. Subramaniyan, ed., *Money and the Markets in India*, Oxford University Press, Delhi, 1994.
59. S.P. Gupta and S.H. Khan, *Mughal Documents: Taqsim, c. 1649-c. 1800,* Publication Scheme, Jaipur, 1996.
60. S.P. Gupta, *Agrarian System of Eastern Rajasthan,* Manohar, Delhi, 1986.
61. Shireen Moosvi, *The Economy of the Mughal Empire,* Oxford University Press, Delhi, 1987 (rpt. 2015).
62. Sumbul Halim Khan, *Art and Craft Workshops under the Mughals: A Study of Jaipur Karkhanas,* Primus Books, Delhi, 2015.
63. Tapan Raychaudhuri and Irfan Habib, eds., *The Cambridge Economic History of India,* vol. I: *c. 1200-c. 1750*, 1982 (rpt. 2004).
64. Thakur Desraj, *Jat Itihas* (Hindi), Maharaja Surajmal Smarak Shiksha Sansthan, Delhi, 2002.
65. Udaivir Sharma, *Shekhawati Ka Itihas*, Unique Traders, Jaipur, 1984.
66. V.C. Mishra, *Geography of Rajasthan,* National Book Trust, Delhi, 1967.

67. Vijay K. Thakur, *Towns in Pre-Modern India*, Janaki Prakashan, Patna, 1994.
68. W.H. Moreland, *India at the Death of Akbar*, Low Price Publications, Delhi, 1962 (rpt. 1990).

(b) *Articles*

1. Ashok V. Desai, 'Population and Standard of Living in Akbar's Time', *IESHR*, vol. IX, no. 1.
2. B.L. Bhadani, 'Economic Conditions in *Pargana* Merta (Rajasthan)', *PIHC*, 1975.
3. B.L. Bhadani, 'Revenue Estimation and Realization in the Mughal Empire: A Case Study of Marwar', *Islamic Culture*, vol. XIV, no. 1, January 1990.
4. B.L. Bhadani, 'Land Tax and Trade in Agricultural Produce in 16th Century Western Rajasthan', *IESHR*, vol. XXIX, no. 2, April-June 1972.
5. B.L. Bhadani, 'Population of Marwar in the Second Half of the 17th Century', *IESHR*, vol. XVI, October-December 1979.
6. B.L. Sharma, 'Rekh in Rajasthan', *JRIHR*, July-September 1969.
7. Bipin Chandra, 'Reinterpretation of Nineteenth Century Indian Economic History', *IESHR*, vol. V, no. 1, 1968.
8. C.D. Deshpande, 'Cities and Towns of Bombay Provinces: Aspects of Urban Geography', *Indian Geographical Journal*, vol. XVI, no. 3, 1941.
9. Dilbagh Singh, 'The Role of Mahajans in the Rural Economy in Eastern Rajasthan during the 18th Century', *Social Scientist*, no. 22, May 1974.
10. Dilbagh Singh, 'Nature and Incidence of Taxes Levied on Inland Trade in Eastern Rajasthan during the 17th-18th Centuries', *PIHC*, Bhubaneswar, 1977.
11. Dilbagh Singh, 'The Pattern of Agricultural Production in the *Qasbas* of Chatsu and Malarna (*c.* 1709-1770)', *PIHC*, 1975.
12. Gianchand Sharma, 'Taxation in 18th Century Rajashtan', *Shodhak*, vol. 6, no. 17, Udaipur, 1977.
13. G.D. Sharma, 'Agricultural Taxes in Marwar', *PRHC*, vol. VII, Pali, 1974.
14. G.S.L. Devra, 'Nature of Incidence of *Rokad-Rakam* (Non-Agricultural Taxes) in the Land Revenue System of Bikaner State (1650-1750)', *PIHC*, 1976.
15. G.S.L. Devra, 'A Study of the Trade Relation between Rajasthan and Sindh/ Multan (1650-1800)', *PIHC*, 1978; and in G.S.L. Devra, ed., *Socio-*

Economic History of Rajasthan, Shri Jagdish Singh Gahlot Research Institute, Jodhpur, 1980.

16. Indu Banga, 'Agrarian Roots of Urbanization: The Case of Medieval Batala', *PIHC*, 1981.
17. Irfan Habib: *A Note on Population* (cyclostyled).
18. Irfan Habib, 'The Peasant in Indian History', *PIHC*, Kurukshetra, 1982.
19. Madhavi Bajekal, 'The State and the Rural Grain Market in Eighteenth Century, Eastern Rajasthan', in *Merchant, Markets and the State in Early Modern India*, ed. Sanjay Subramariyam, Delhi, 1990.
20. Madhavi Bajekal, 'Agricultural Production and the Peasant Economy of Eastern Rajasthan in the Eighteenth Century' (cyclostyle).
21. Masanori Sato, 'The Mughal Impact on the Political and Social Institutions of the Rajputs', *Acta Aciatica*, Tokyo, no. 48, 1985.
22. N. Benjamin, 'The Population of Rajputana in the 1850: A Note', *PRHC*, vol. VII, Jodhpur, February 1974.
23. R.P. Vyas, 'Trade Centres of Marwar and Linked Trade Routes During 18th Century AD', published in *Shodh Patrika*, ed. Dev Kothari, July-December 1995, Udaipur.
24. Satish Chandra, 'Some Aspects of the Growth of a Money Economy in India during the 17th Century', *IESHR*, vol. III, no. 4, 1966.
25. Satish Chandra, 'Some Aspects of Indian Village Society in Northern India during the 18th Century', *PIHR*, 1974.
26. S. Chandra, 'The 18th Century in India: Its Economy and the Role of Marathas, the Jats, the Sikhs and the Afghans', Calcutta, 1991 (cyclo-style).
27. S.N. Hasan, K.N. Hasan and S.P. Gupta, 'The Pattern of Agricultural Production in the Territories of Amber (*c*. 1650-1700)', *PIHC*, 1966.
28. S. Nurul Hasan and S.P. Gupta, 'Prices of Food Grain in the Territories of Amber', *PIHC* (Patiala), 1967, part I, Patna, 1968.
29. S.P. Gupta, 'The System of Rural Taxation', *PIHC*, 1972.
30. S.P. Gupta, 'New Evidence on Agrarian and Rural Taxation in Eastern Rajasthan', *PIHC*, 1975.
31. S.P. Gupta, 'Methods of Revenue Assessment and Realization in Eastern Rajasthan', *PRHC*, 1975.
32. S.P. Gupta, 'Evidence for Urban Population and Its Composition from the 17th-18th Century, Rajasthan', *PIHC*, Calcutta, 1976.
33. Shireen Moosvi, 'Production, Consumption and Population in Akbars Time', *IESHR*, vol. X, no. 2, 1973.
34. Sunita Zaidi, 'State and Cities in Rajasthan: Pali between the 17th and 19th Centuries', in *Contributions to Indian Social Sciences*, April-June 2010.

35. Tapan Raychaudhuri, 'A Reinterpretation of Nineteenth Century Indian Economic History', *IESHR*, vol. V, no. 1, 1968.

(c) *Journals* (following journals of different years of relevant articles have been used and cited in this book)

1. *Acta Asiatica*
2. *Indian Economic and Social History Review*
3. *Indian Geographical Journal*
4. *Indian Historical Review*
5. *Indica*
6. *Islamic Culture*
7. *Journal of the Rajasthan Institute of Historical Research*
8. *Journal of Uttar Pradesh Historical Society*
9. *Juni Khyat*
10. *Parampara*
11. *Proceedings of Indian History Congress*
12. *Proceedings of Rajasthan History Congress*
13. *Shodh Patrika*
14. *Shodh Sadhana*
15. *Social Scientist*

(d) *Dictionary*

1. Amba Prasad Suman, *Krishak Jeevan Sambandhi Braj Bhasha Shabd Kosh*, Allahabad, 1960.
2. Badri Prasad Sakariya, *Rajasthan Hindi Sabad Kosh*, vol. I, 1977, vol. II, 1982, vol. III, 1984, Jaipur.
3. F. Steingass, *Comprehensive Persian-English Dictionary*, Oriental Books, New Delhi, 1981; Lowe and Brydone Printers, London, 1892, 1930.
4. G. Watt, *The Dictionary of the Economic Products of India*, 6 vols., London, (1st pub. 1889, rpt. edn. 1996).
5. H.H. Wilson, *A Glossary of Judicial and Revenues Terms, Compiled and Published under the Court of Directors of the East India Company*, 2nd edn., 1968, Munshiram Manoharlal, Delhi (1st pub. 1855 by WMH Allen and Co., London).
6. Sitaram Lalas, ed., *Rajasthan Sabad Kosh*, Chaupasani Shiksha Samiti, Jodhpur, 1972.
7. S.V. Apte, *Sanskrit-English Dictionary*, Motilal Banarasidass, Delhi, 1959.

Index

For Product Safety Concerns and Information please contact our EU representative GPSR@taylorandfrancis.com
Taylor & Francis Verlag GmbH, Kaufingerstraße 24, 80331 München, Germany

www.ingramcontent.com/pod-product-compliance
Ingram Content Group UK Ltd.
Pitfield, Milton Keynes, MK11 3LW, UK
UKHW022117190926
475702UK00013B/1497
* 9 7 8 1 0 3 2 6 5 3 4 1 9 *